The Ideas That Rule Us

Nathan J. Murphy

prepolitica
London

Book Cover: Very Much So
Typesetting: Perseus Design

1st Edition 2024
ISBN: 978-1-0686110-0-1

Published by:
prepolitica
www.prepolitica.com

Editors

First Draft - Structural Editor
Danielle Anderson

Fourth Draft - Editor
David Cohen PhD

Final Editor & Line Editor
Christopher Schafenacker

Special thanks to

Deimena Drąsutytė
Ann Foweraker
Clem Murphy
Thomas Rodde
Graeme Lunn

For advice and/or hands-on support

Angelica Kaufmann, PhD
Dejan Matlak, MA
Adele Braun, MSc, MPsych Psych

For much of my life, I did not realise that I was
an actor in a grand old play. I was unaware that
my words echoed a script I was conditioned
to follow, that the lights illuminated only that
which I expected to see, and that the orchestra
was merely a recording that had been playing
since long before my birth.

CONTENTS

Introduction	1

PART ONE

Chapter 1:	The Immense Power of Ideas	7

Chapter 2:	~~Who Am I?~~ Whose Ideas Am I?	19

Chapter 3:	The Abstract and The Emotional	31

Chapter 4:	How to Break with the Ideas that Break Us	39

Chapter 5:	Your Ideas Will be Replaced	51

Chapter 6:	Ideology and Morality	61

Chapter 7:	Innate Ideas	87

PART TWO

Chapter 8:	The Superficiality of Culture	119

Chapter 9:	The Ideas that Rule Us	135

Chapter 10:	When The Abstract Corrupts The Emotional	155

Chapter 11:	Where Ideas Go to Die	169

Chapter 12:	Three Ideological Fights	189

Chapter 13:	A Life Abstracted	207

Chapter 14:	Meanwhile, In Reality…	221

Chapter 15:	The Gap Between Law and Reality	243

Chapter 16:	What Can We Do?	255

Bibliography Part 1	268

Bibliography Part 2	282

INTRODUCTION

Ideas are washed and folded into us from the day we are conceived. These ideas become feelings that determine how we think about ourselves and how we relate to others. The ideas of family, friends, and community impact how our genes are expressed just as we inherit the impact of ideas held by our grandparents and their parents before them. Ideas cut the fabric of our being and determine who we are.

Unhelpful concepts can take root into the structure of our minds and generate immense difficulty. Such ideas bind themselves so completely to our person that they provoke powerful feelings that guide our behaviour. They can compel us to do things we do not want to do. No one avoids this. The extent to which our ideas rule us is only a matter of degree. Thus, we need to work to understand them.

I am a fellow traveller, and like you, I have been on a journey. This particular journey has comprised of eight years thinking about ideas and, like all the best journeys, I did not exactly know where it would end up when I set off.

It started when I was thirty. But also, in a way, long before that.

By this point in my life, I had done *stuff*. I had invented, patented, and sold a medical product and started a string of companies in big data, procurement, and travel—not all successful. I had lobbied the government for prison reform, spent a couple of years managing international product strategy for a large company, and climbed a few big-walls—all while basing myself in London. However, like so many of us, I found myself dissatisfied, of sorts, and desiring of change.

I saved, left London, and went on a climbing trip with no planned end. A few years later, I washed up in the mountains of Catalunya, where I bought and renovated a house in a spectacular valley.

During this time, apart from trying to find out how hard I could climb, and building a location-independent business, I worked on the concepts that eventually formed this book. At first, this project could fit around my other work, but by the end, I worked two-years of eight to fifteen-hour days, to the exclusion of practically everything else. It has been arduous, costly, has a low chance of success but, on a personal level, the understandings that have resulted from this work have already made it worthwhile.

The nature of our existence means that it is hard to make sense of the world, not least because we always start at the end of the story. Behind us sits a yawning history so unfathomably complicated that the best we can do is skim the highlights and try to glean something useful, as we grope toward an unknowable future that we hope to shape.

We use ideas, useful and less useful, to guide us and help us cope with the complexity of our reality. This is just as true for the president of a modern economy as it is for a subsistence farmer in a developing country. Both are guided by the ideas that they grew up with, both have feelings that contain unrealised values, and both cannot avoid letting these feelings guide their personal and political behaviour.

I am no different. I have feelings that lead to political beliefs, but the harder I look at them, the shakier these appear to be. What feels obvious, and true, is not necessarily so. For a long time, I have considered myself to be a little left-leaning, but at the same time I have a problem with much of leftist politics, especially the sanctimonious, idealistic, and distant-from-the-real-problems side of things. Such feelings have often made me wonder if I am *actually* right-leaning, but I too have a problem with the result of much rightist policy, which can be cruel, entrenching of unfairness, and too centred on the interests of wealth.

Part of the problem with this political conundrum, one which I don't think is particularly uncommon, is that, if we take a step back and look at the historical context, many modern political movements seem hamstrung by ideas developed centuries ago—by people who lived in a very different world and who had precious little science on which to base their thinking. Although their ideas can be repackaged and squeezed into a modern context—their starting points still constrain the result.

On top of that, much of this derivative political thought does not appear to consider how these ideas have *actually* played out—over and over—since they were first developed. Reasons are found for why they failed *that time* allowing adherents to justify banging the same old drum, so we end up in a state of cyclical failure. Meanwhile, significant science-based understandings, developed over the past century, remain unheeded and unincorporated into base-level political thought. In this sense, we have a problem with entrenched ideas that bind political thought into themes that become difficult to think beyond.

For years, I did not know exactly why I was undertaking this long and difficult project. When asked, the only answer that made sense, was that *I found it interesting*. But there was more to it than that, and now, at the end of this project, I can put words to what I was shooting for. I was looking for firmer ground on which to build both a personal and political philosophy, specifically one that considered humanity's accumulated understandings of reality, that acknowledges previous thinkers, while also assessing their ideas with sober eyes—*and* considers how their ideas have played out.

To do this, I have used the lens of ideas and ideology because, at the heart of everything we do, are the ideas we hold and the behaviours they provoke. If we are to begin to understand our human reality, personal or political, we must first understand *ideas* and how they work.

In this book, I take you through the whole remit of ideas: what they are, where they come from, and where they take us. We look at the ideas that we hold, consciously and subconsciously, and how they form who we are and what we become. We examine how to break down these ideas and how to free ourselves from the grip of ideas contrary to our, or our societies' interests.

By necessity, we dig into the fields of behavioural and evolutionary biology, anthropology, sociology, neuroscience, history, and philosophy. Using this aggregation of billions of hours of scientific research, we examine the building blocks of human morality and how these impact everything from our relationships to our societies. We finish with a set of practical considerations that connect everything into useful and actionable points to help us live our lives with more freedom and a greater ability to determine our own future.

I hope that the ideas presented in this book help you, as they have helped me, live a better, happier, and healthier life. Perhaps, and I recognise this is wishful thinking, it can contribute to new ways of considering our social and political environment and help us move toward systems that work better for everyone.

Thank you, and good luck.

PART ONE

CHAPTER 1

THE IMMENSE POWER OF IDEAS

Ideas are essential building blocks of our lives and so we begin by exploring the fundamental concepts behind ideas and how ideas influence our daily experiences.

Ideas are organic by nature and are, in a sense, alive. Ideas want something; they have an aim and a value system. They not only acknowledge the existence of the future but also desire to influence it. We can consider ideas *as thoughts that guide our actions.* Everything on earth, that is not a rock, a plant, or some other part of the 'natural' world, is a result of human ideas.

Ideas can be simple. For example, the idea that a future where I eat an ice cream is better than one where I do not. This value judgement, that *ice cream is better than no ice cream,* like all value judgements, hinges on a simple idea. The same is true of ideas like *it is better if we look after the poor,* that *being educated is better than being uneducated,* or that a *wall painted blue is better than one painted green.*

Ideas can also be complex. The blue paint may be preferable because it is a symbol of a political ideology—composed of hundreds of interconnecting ideas—and held in the minds of millions of people who prefer a particular vision of the future.

Ideas can possess us and drive us toward drastically different horizons. An idea can instil a motivation so great that we will endure vast suffering for it and we may even prefer to sacrifice our lives than see the idea die. Ideas are the driving force behind all civilisations, armies, and religions. They have led to the construction of vast cities in improbable places, the exploration of space, and the destruction of our environment on a global scale.

Ideas are like the proverbial butterfly but, instead of a flutter of wings that triggers a tornado (and, presumably, some mild property damage) a world away, they are a flutter of neurons that have the potential to trigger nuclear winter and destroy life on earth. The fact that ideas have such destructive capabilities means that, outside of cosmic forces, nothing compares to their power.

Structures of Ideas

Ideas work together in families of thought, creating *structures* of ideas that we call ideologies.

The word 'ideology' originated amidst the revolutionary turmoil that engulfed 18th Century Europe. The term was first used by French philosopher Antoine Destutt de Tracy to describe a science of ideas that would help society to better understand itself. Later, Karl Marx developed a theory of ideology that saw them as sets of ideas and beliefs that serve to justify the power of the ruling class in capitalist societies.

According to Marx, these ideas were not neutral but rather reflected the interests of those who held power. In the 20th Century, the study of ideology became an important field of inquiry in the social sciences. Scholars such as Max Weber, Emile Durkheim, and Georg Lukacs developed new theories about the ways in which ideas and beliefs shaped social reality. They argued that ideologies could be seen as systems of thought that served to maintain the status quo, or as means of promoting social change and transformation.

The American sociologist Martin Seliger considered ideology to be a set of action-orientated beliefs for which it is largely irrelevant if they are true or false. The Frankfurt School suggested that ideologies should be seen as 'collective rationalisations'—systems of belief that are accepted by people for reasons they cannot acknowledge. Clifford Geertz, the American social anthropologist, argued that ideology was *a symbolic system which allows individuals to orientate themselves in relation to their social world.*[1]

For those who grew up in the Cold-war aftermath of World War II, the word 'ideology' draws a direct connection to the totalitarian regimes of the 20th Century. Today, however, most modern scholars see this as a politicised and somewhat naïve interpretation of the term. In general, the idea that *other* people are 'ideological' while *we* are not—because our society is *'based on reason'*—is at best a cultural misunderstanding or, at worst, a mindset of assumed superiority in which *the others* must be corrected.

In this book, we consider an *ideology* to be a structure of ideas that work together. Under this simple definition, all humans live within ideological structures of one kind or another and these structures compel the decisions that we make to shape our lives.

By gaining a deeper understanding of these ideas and their underlying processes, we can begin to break free from their grip, make more deliberate choices, and lead a more fulfilling life. We can live as individuals who don't mindlessly conform, but as people who can make conscious decisions regarding what to value, what to live for, and possibly, what to die for.

The Abstract

Having, expressing, and acting on ideas is habitual for humans, and doing so pivots on our capability for abstract thought. Abstract thought—thinking about that which does not exist, drawing from the past, and imagining a different future—is also central to our success as a species. Compared to humans, the minds of other animals are thought to be 'episodic' and are more confined to the present. Although something may prompt an animal, reminding it of a past event, or stimulating a desire, this is fundamentally different to the detailed and broad memories that humans draw upon for thought.

Liane Gabora, a professor of psychology at the University of British Columbia describes the difference between humans and animals:

> *"If a deer encounters a grizzly bear in the wild, this might rekindle the memory of a previous grizzly encounter, and the experience might linger for a while as it gets cemented in long term memory. But we have no evidence that the deer will thereafter mull over different potential techniques for escaping a bear, perhaps comparing and contrasting this with methods for escaping other predators. It will certainly never recount the experience to other deer or write a story or a song inspired by the grizzly encounter. Similarly, it might see a potential mate and have sexual cravings, but not build an elaborate fantasy world around the object of its desire."[2]*

Although the science is not settled on whether some animals are capable of abstract thought or not, the difficulty in proving it, and the stark lack of evidence to support it, is at least a demonstration of the vast gulf between human and other animal's abstract capabilities.

It is the neocortex, a relatively late addition to our brain, that is responsible for our remarkable ability to escape the present. Without it we couldn't imagine the future, reminisce over past events, or defer gratification. Nor would we be able to have ideas, construct ideologies, or take thoughts in the present and act upon them to change the future.*

---

* Pinpointing the exact timeline of the evolution of modern human cognition remains unclear. Even in present-day circumstances, comprehending the cognitive abilities of individuals in front of us can prove challenging, let alone attempting to understand the capabilities of those who passed away thousands of years ago. According to scientists, it is believed that humans developed the

Perhaps most importantly, the evolution of human cognitive capability enabled us to achieve what no other animal has—to create and connect around things that do not physically exist—ideas like those of politics, religion, identity, and culture. The human mind and *the abstract* have become inextricably connected, and the ideas and ideologies that resulted from abstract capabilities have gone on to play an outsized role in our lives.

For humans, escaping the present is not just an exception—it is our way of being. We do it *constantly*. While we do one thing, we can be thinking about doing something else, replaying a conversation, or mentally practising a performance. Abstract capabilities have enabled the development of complex language, technology, art, science, and an existence which is radically different to that of any life that came before us.

---

capacity for symbolic thinking, or abstract thought, over the past 200,000 years. This newfound ability, when combined with an improved working memory—which allows us to hold numerous pieces of information in our minds and use them to innovate, strategize, and problem-solve—laid the foundation for modern human cognition. The existence of such working memory can be detected through the production of complex tools, such as bows and arrows or animal traps. However, due to the perishable nature of the materials used by our ancient ancestors, very few of their creations have survived to this day.

Several types of tool technologies, and symbolic and artistic artefacts seem to disappear from the archaeological record around seventy thousand years ago which, for a time, led scholars to posit a distinct cognitive leap forward in human ability around that time. Opponents of this thesis of a sudden 'cognitive revolution' cite evidence of symbolic thinking that shows up in the archaeological record tens of thousands of years earlier but then disappears, before showing up again later.[34] They suggest that a period of climate change that made Africa drier impacted and dispersed populations, leading to a prehistoric version of the Dark Ages. And to back up this view, in the past decade, archaeologists have found evidence of symbolic thinking dating back as far as 165,000 years ago suggesting a long and slow evolution of human cognitive ability.[56]

Regardless of how it came about, human cognitive ability remains one of the most remarkable evolutionary developments, and from the archaeological record it is clear that tool techniques and symbolic artefacts that represent evidence of modern cognition became a permanent, and widespread, part of the human repertoire by 40,000 years ago.

The Ideas We Live By

To illustrate the role ideas play in our lives, let's imagine a man. Tall, stocky, with a small belly born of bad posture, good hairline, jeans, no belt, non-descript job, kind smile. Call him Thomas. Thomas from Texas. Little does Thomas know, but until today, he has spent his entire life arranging himself around a collection of ideas that are based less on reason—as he would imagine—and more on historical happenstance, general ignorance, and the result of centuries-old power struggles.

Thomas works nine-to-five in a tall mirror-glass office. The continuous stream of days is broken up into seven-day blocks—with most people having two days off after five days of work—forming the weekend. Thomas *lives* for the weekend.

The idea of the week that dominates Thomas' life can be traced back to the Ancient Babylonians, a civilisation that formed nearly four thousand years ago in the location of modern-day Iraq and stuck around for a thousand years. Like most ancient people the mysteries of the night sky fascinated them; however, without the use of telescopes they were only able to identify five of the currently recognised eight (or nine) planets. Along with the sun and the moon, these comprised the 'seven heavenly bodies,' making this number very important. The Ancient Babylonians determined that a week was composed of seven days and they spread this idea around the ancient world.[7] Accordingly, the week, which has provided the rhythm of the whole of Thomas' life, is *literally* the result of an ancient astronomical error.

Thomas' eight-hour workday is similar. During Britain's industrial revolution, children toiled ten-to-fifteen hours a day, six days a week. Working hard, for long hours in poor conditions and with poor pay had serious implications for bodies and minds. It was not until the Factory Act of 1833, some sixty years after the start of the industrial era, that the length of the workday saw regulation. It ruled that those under eighteen should be limited to working twelve hours a day, those under fourteen to eight hours a day, and children under the age of nine were required to attend school.

Later in the century, labour movements campaigned for the adult working day to be limited to eight hours. In 1889, gas workers went on strike against the introduction of compulsory eighteen-hour shifts. Using the slogan *"shorten our hours to prolong our lives"* the strike spread to other gas works, eventually winning the first eight-hour working day—which is more-or-less where things wound up. By the end of the century, there was broad support for Saturday afternoon and Sunday to be marked as a 'weekend.' Indeed, the earliest mention of the word 'weekend' occurred in 1879—a mere hundred and fifty years ago. The snowflakes won, and eventually, the weekend was embraced by employers who found that a full Saturday and Sunday break improved efficiency and reduced absences.[8]

The resulting forty-hour, five-day, working week, is a hard-won schedule, dredged from the exploitation of children and adults during the Industrial Revolution. Why it *remains*, however, is as much about culture as it is about efficiency or well-being. And regardless of this, many people still work excessive and unhealthy hours, and, with smartphones taking away people's ability to disconnect, we may well be regressing.

Thomas considers himself to be a real *American* American. He's very straight, manly, not one to worry about *feelings*. He likes trucks, jeans, and beer, and for these reasons, he wouldn't be seen dead wearing a dress—not even as a joke. Or anything pink for that matter, and certainly never shoes with elevated heels. He didn't make the rules, but he sure as hell follows them.

Cultural ideas have determined how we dress, since, well, probably forever and people get quite pent-up about it.

Take Mary Walker, for instance, the American abolitionist, prisoner of war, and surgeon, the only woman to ever receive the Medal of Honor, and if there was ever one, a true American hero. She was also a committed and vocal trouser wearer who considered that women's clothing should *"protect the person, and allow freedom of motion and circulation, and not make the wearer a slave to it."* Outrageous, I know.

Walker was assaulted and arrested multiple times for the 'crime' of wearing trousers and appearing 'masculine.' Her last arrest was in 1913 when she was eighty years old.[9] Even the *seemingly* simple idea that women could wear a pair of trousers was not accepted without violent reaction and struggle.

High heels, too, are interesting. Their story starts with the Persian cavalry, who wore high heels to be able to remain in their stirrups while standing and wielding bows. This fashion spread to Europe but originally high heels were only for men, specifically, wealthy men. A fast horse was the Ferrari of its day and so horse ownership, and related accessories, signified status. Eventually, aristocrats started using high heels to denote their position in society and, in some countries, the height of heels was even regulated based on rank.

Over time, high heels entered women's fashion, though female-wearers preferred a thinner aesthetic. How we got from there to a society where women wear heels and men, generally, do not, is convoluted but the point is that the ideas have been completely flipped.

Colours are similar. Today, pink is considered feminine, but until the early 1900s colours were not gendered because children were all dressed in white. Dyes that didn't wash out hadn't been invented yet and children's clothes needed frequent washing. Pink only became feminine in the 1940s, but before this, it was a boy's colour because it was seen to be stronger and therefore more masculine than blue, which was considered delicate and dainty.[10] For these arbitrary and ridiculous reasons, I'm still unlikely to wear a lot of pink.

Thomas likes women who 'take care' of themselves. Nice hair, make up, y'know, making an effort. Despite a tough-guy aesthetic, Thomas is particularly squeamish about female body hair and feels repulsed by the sight of a woman with unshaven armpits.

Both shaving body hair, and using cosmetics, have been practiced for millennia, but today, it's big business. Cosmetics is a 500 billion dollar-a-year industry and is heavily invested in shaping our ideas of beauty. The industry spends vast sums of money on advertising which, by necessity, must persuade you that you (and your face) is better off *with* their products than without. As a result, forty-four percent of American women feel *"uncomfortable leaving the home without makeup on, no matter the destination: movies, gym, school, work, or even the beach."*[11] Makeup has become a product so essential for some that they are even unwilling to be seen by their family, or partners, without painting a *different face* on top of their actual face. On the balance, this does not seem to be a good thing.

As a bit of a clean freak, Thomas is more insecure about his body than he cares to admit. He is especially concerned about his body odour and to combat it he showers twice daily, applies aluminium salts to block his sweat pores, and, since his teens, he has doused his skin with perfumes that contain parabens, phthalates, and propylene glycol.

Perhaps thankfully, ideas of hygiene have changed over time. In England, during the middle-ages, and up until the end of the 18th Century, it was considered 'proper' to only wash the parts of the body that were on display: the face, neck, hands, and forearms. At the time they thought that washing allowed miasma (an ancient concept of bad air that caused disease) to enter the skin through the pores. This changed through the 1800s and, by 1900 a weekly bath was a common ritual. By the 1950s, the installation of domestic water supplies enabled urban middle classes to hold concepts of personal hygiene alongside other important Victorian concepts of Christianity, respectability, and social progress. Cleanliness became associated with social standing and over time gained increased importance.[12]

Thomas would never talk about his body insecurities because the ideas he holds about male identity prohibits the expression of his emotional states. Growing up with these ideas has led to the habitual suppression of his emotions. As a result, he struggles to communicate his needs, or even the basics of his interior life, to his closest friends or intimate partners—causing ongoing difficulties in his relationships. The ideas that saw Thomas close his interior world came to prominence in the 1800s. At this time, women were increasingly considered to be inferior to men—ruled by their reproductive organs and prone to irrationality—while men were seen to be rational beings who, to be manly, must be in control of themselves.[13] Two hundred years later, these factually absurd ideas, affect the minutiae of Thomas' life.

Time too is subject to ideological meddling.

Thomas is not an early riser, and he *hates* alarms, but not more than he hates being late. For Thomas, one of the best things about the weekend is waking up naturally, not to the gut-sinking b*eep beep beep* sound. He never wonders *why* this is this such a luxury, or how the ideas around time own him, or how he may have a totally different outlook had he been born in a different place or time, however.

How we tolerate lateness, for instance, varies by region and can depend on *who* is late.[14] For a start, to be late, you must know the time. For tens-of-thousands of years of human existence time was largely based on the sun and being five minutes late was *not even a possibility*. For the last thousand years English church bells have rung out the hours, but the actual time varied from city to city. It was not until the mid-1800s that a national *regulated* time was introduced to enable train timetabling throughout the UK. People did not like losing their regional time differences but, with time, it was accepted.

Sleep has cultural nuances too. Falling asleep at work is something that is generally seen as *shameful* in most of Europe and North America. In Japan, though, the practice of falling asleep when doing something can be read as a signal of how hard you have been working. *I am a hard worker in Japan.*

Today, there is a wide body of evidence showing that short naps are beneficial for tired minds, and with huge amounts of time wasted on social media, over-CC'd in emails, pointless meetings, workplace chat groups, or general inefficiency, seeing a short nap as 'shameful' is clearly nonsensical.

Likewise, every other part of Thomas' life has been impacted by older ideas.

There is nothing we like to moralise about more than personal relationships and, especially, sex. Cultural ideas related to what sort of relationship is acceptable, or not, are by no means fixed in time. In one time and place, adultery—or even ethical non-monogamy—may see you stoned to death by a baying crowd and in another, it might be seen as a perfectly reasonable way to live your life.

Food and drink are also heavily connected to culture, and this is especially true of the consumption of animal products. Carnism, a term coined by the social psychologist Melanie Joy to describe the dominant ideology that supports the eating of animals is greatly affected by culture.[15] For many of us, the idea of eating a bacon sandwich is appealing, while few of us would choose to eat a few slices of Labrador flesh.

Which animals we see as morally acceptable to eat, and which must therefore suffer the industrialised production of their flesh, is purely ideological. There is little difference in the capacity for suffering of a cow, a cat, a pig, and a dog but the ideas of carnism mean that dogs may be eaten in China but not in Canada, horses can be eaten in Italy but not in England, and cows can be eaten in America, but not in India. Clearly, it doesn't take deep thought to identify a lack of reason in our thinking. Not only that but if we were to treat a dog or a cat in the same way that we standardise and industrialise the treatment of cows, pigs, or chickens, in say Germany, the UK or the US, it would likely lead to criminal prosecution.

This section could have easily become its own book, but hopefully, you get the point. Many seemingly important ideas have arbitrary foundations or exist on ground far shakier than we may first imagine. And, in reality, the ideas we have just discussed are *small fry* compared to the ideas that shape our societies and sculpt the fabric of our minds.

A quick note on *Ideas* and *Values*

In this book, I use 'values' interchangeably with 'ideas' because a value is simply the idea that *behaviour x is better than behaviour y.* Values orientate our behaviour and can be held both consciously and subconsciously.

We may consciously *think* that we hold a particular value only to find ourselves behaving against it. Our subconsciously held values often overrule who we think we are. Because of this, it is only our behaviour that communicates the values we *actually* hold.

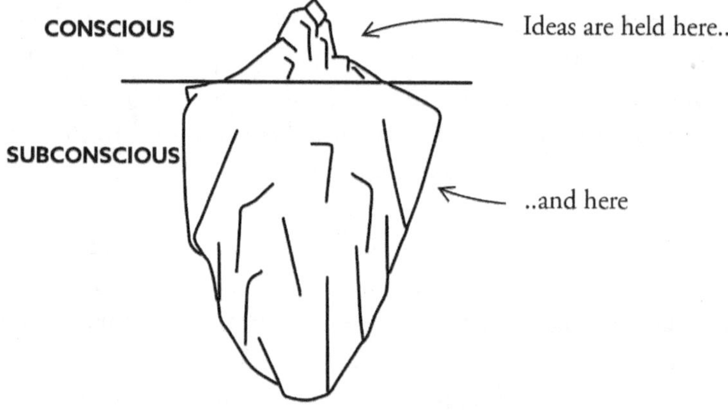

CHAPTER 2

~~WHO AM I?~~
WHOSE IDEAS AM I?

Our path in life is carved by ideas. The ideas we hold can lead us to success and happiness just as they can lead us to behave against our own interests. Ideologies can lead us toward wisdom or bind us to ignorance. They can enable our freedom or act as a prison. Because of this, it is worth understanding what ideas we hold and how they serve us.

Ideas affect us in two ways. First, our society's underlying ideas have a direct impact on the options and opportunities we have. Second, ideas play a role in shaping our vision *of ourselves*. Our self-concept, our values, and our expectations—all of which ultimately come to define our lives—are determined by the ideas we hold.

There are two ways to approach life. One is to try and achieve what we want—what we *feel* will be rewarding—and should we attain it, decide whether to change course (assuming we still can). The other is to periodically examine our motivations, desires, and goals, try and understand where they come from and if they are right for us, and use what we discover to set a more considered course.

The latter way is effortful, potentially uncomfortable, and may require us to actively make hard decisions, but it is probably not as effortful as working for twenty years to build a life that we don't actually want.

During my childhood, I wanted to be either a professional footballer, an archaeologist (Indiana Jones) or a product designer (cars and consumer products). However, above all of these, I wanted to be a millionaire. In the '80s, the decade of my birth, wealth itself was *the* aspirational path and if you were rich, you were, de facto successful.

I was not taught this explicitly—and certainly not through parental guidance—but largely from listening to conversations, through exposure to media, and the pervasive cultural narrative. The idea that *becoming rich* was a worthy goal seemed unquestionable. I did not make this calculation, nor did I question it—something difficult for a child to do in a world of all theory and no practice.

I decided against a career as a professional footballer upon realising that I was not especially good at it. Later, I discovered that being an archaeologist was more about sitting in muddy holes, brushing soil, and fastidious documentation, than exploring remote jungle tombs and cashing in on the treasure. So, a designer it was. At least with that I could invent products, take them to market (get rich), run a business (get rich), and if all that failed, land a decent job (fail comfortably).

After graduating from university, and entering the world of practice, it took several years to realise that money isn't something that I *deeply* care about. In hindsight, and seen from a third-person perspective, there I was, someone who did not care greatly about money but who had dedicated all their time to making a lot of it. The result: a late-twenties crisis of faith. *Why am I doing what I am doing? And is it really what I want?*

Satisfaction

The pursuit of satisfaction is ingrained in all animals and yet for humans, attaining satisfaction does not guarantee happiness. Our brain is moulded by evolution to ensure the survival of our genes, not our happiness, and thus tends to prioritise shortcuts and quick results. This often leads us down the path of pursuing activities that offer only temporary gratification. Whether it's money, power, or pleasure, the enjoyment derived from these quick fixes diminishes over time. When we live in societies that glorify wealth and prey on insecurity, the pursuit of lasting satisfaction becomes a path full of false turns. If we are not careful, we can end up trapped in a perpetual cycle of seeking without ever truly arriving.

The truth is that genuine satisfaction extends beyond meeting basic expectations, needs, and desires. It encompasses personal growth and the cultivation of character, ultimately leading to a deeper sense of fulfilment. In our contemporary understanding, this enduring fulfilment—or lasting satisfaction—is widely recognised as a state of happiness.

To work on my situation, I studied happiness. This seemed to be a good place to start because I figured if I was happy, whatever I was doing was probably all right. My new aim was to create a life that based on science was as conducive to happiness as possible.

To add structure to my plans, I looked to the work of Matthieu Ricard, a neuroscientist and Buddhist monk, who has written extensively on the science and philosophy of happiness. I distilled his writing down to the idea that doing *high-flow* activities (activities that totally absorb you) and doing things that *make a difference to others*, go a long way to create the conditions for happiness. Gratitude and good relationships are also important, but they are harder to measure, and I figured these would follow in the wake of my changing my actions.

To manage this, I created a simple worksheet that loosely recorded the use of my time and allowed me to visualise how my life was changing. Every couple of months, I would spend an hour estimating the amount of time I spent doing high-flow activities or things that made a difference to others and see if I was moving in the right direction.

My aim was to eliminate time spent doing low-flow activities: my job, drinking, meaningless social activities, and life admin. I replaced these with creating art, writing, rock-climbing, or doing things that helped others in some way, be it friends, colleagues, or unknown people on the internet.

To act, I made some hard decisions.

I quit a decent job and left city life behind to focus on climbing—a high-flow passion that I had not dedicated real time to. In one fell swoop, this eradicated most of the time I spent doing low-flow activities and, luckily for my bank balance, rock climbing was not polo. Living in a van, or in dilapidated beach huts, and hanging off the side of big walls was *cheap*.

Living the frugal highlife, and doing a little work as I travelled, meant that my savings could buy me *years* to figure out what I was going to do for money.

Over the next half decade, I travelled, climbed harder than I thought possible, and worked on new business ideas. And while I did, one question never left me: *Why do we live as we do, when there are so many, vastly different, options for how we can live our lives?* Or, more personally: *Why did I make the choices I made, despite having so many alternatives?*

Examining such questions forces us to scrutinise both our choices and what drove them. Thus, we need to ask two questions:

1) *Why do we do what we do?*
2) *Why do we want what we want?*

Why Do We Want What We Want?

We're all different, sure, and yet at the same time, we're rather similar. As human beings, we share a set of basic needs, but what a 'good life' looks like for one person may be very different for another. One person may feel fulfilled by fixing antique clocks, and another by dancing, or working as a nurse. Another may feel fulfilled by doing all three concurrently and, for all of them, this may change over the course of their lives. The fact that we are all unique means that there is little value in pontificating about what makes a 'good life' for everyone.

It is, however, reasonable to try to answer the question for ourselves.

To think about *why we want what we want* we must examine our socialisation. That is, the process by which we transform from a helpless baby into a capable adult. To examine our socialisation, we need to study ideas because socialisation is, in effect, the embedding of thousands of ideas into our minds to a point where adherence to them is practically automatic. Such socially held ideas and ideologies hold great power. They are, by far, the most powerful of all organic phenomena and, with such powerful forces influencing our developing minds, it is no wonder we can grow up confused.

While many animals are born ready to act, hunt, and feed without substantial learning, humans are born undeveloped and dependent on adult care for many years. In fact, our development is so slow that our brains are not fully formed until around the age of twenty-five. On the face of it, this seems like a disadvantage, but our slow development allows us to adapt to complex and changing environments, enabling vastly different behavioural outcomes. Notably, the last part of the brain to finish developing is our prefrontal cortex, responsible for regulating behaviour.[16]

Evolutionarily, the ability to be sculpted, and adapt to our environment, has been extremely beneficial. Through socialisation, we can fit into practically any social environment. In the process, we consume vast amounts of information and learn complex behaviours, customs, mannerisms, and not least, ideas of how to live, why to live, how we should behave, and *when* it is appropriate to display such behaviour.

During our childhood, socialisation is critically important.

It teaches us how to act in a way that means we will get on with people. To be generally liked is key to success. If we are poorly socialised as children, we struggle to make friends, suffer more from loneliness, are more often excluded from school, and suffer detrimental effects that can last our entire lives.

Through socialisation, we are taught what to think, value, and feel about almost everything in our lives. We are taught what success is and what it is not, what is beautiful and what is not, what a good career is and what it is not, what is good or bad, and *who* is good or bad. As we grow, our family, peers, schooling, and the media, constantly expose us to value judgements, ideas, and ideologies. Together, this forms a pervasive education, comprising millions of interactions and we are deluding ourselves if we think we can emerge unaffected.

Socialisation, Essential but Imperfect

In 1989, the fall of Romanian communist dictator Nicolae Ceauşescu exposed a grim reality that shocked the world. For decades, the regime had enforced a strict ban on both contraception and abortion while also imposing a tax on childless adults. The result was an explosion of children who were either unwanted or with parents who could not afford to raise them. To handle this, the regime built hundreds of new orphanages with signs that said *"The state can take better care of your child than you can"* and filled them with tens of thousands of children.

When foreign news organisations discovered and filmed these institutions, the conditions made global headlines. Images reminiscent of Nazi concentration camps showed skeletal children caked in faeces splashing through urine-covered floors. Children were tied to bed frames and locked in cages in dilapidated buildings where broken windows exposed them to freezing temperatures.

Babies, aside from being fed, and having their diapers changed, were left for years with nothing to do but gaze at the ceiling. Deprived of all nurturing care throughout infancy, older children were found to be in a state of minimal speech and with habituated rocking and biting behaviours.

The devastating effects of this total lack of socialisation damaged the children's ability to connect socially and function *for the rest of their lives.* Forty percent of teenagers who had spent time in these orphanages were eventually diagnosed with major psychiatric conditions and many suffered from stunted growth, stalled motor skills, and delayed language development.[17] Further studies found the orphans to have smaller brain volumes and profoundly reduced brain activity.[18]

This tragic story of childhood neglect paints a clear picture of how essential socialisation is for human development, but this alone does not mean that it is *entirely* good. Socialisation, as an evolved feature of human life, is geared toward reproductive success. While being well-socialised may help, it does not automatically lead to a happy, healthy life.

Socialisation has three interwoven layers: social integration, cultural socialisation, and economic socialisation.

Social integration is the process of learning how to behave and get along with other people. It matters because, if you are not likeable, your life will be difficult, confusing, and lonely. Such social skills are incredibly complex and packed with nuance. For example, making a joke is a subtle and situational skill. A few words said in a certain way, with the right emphasis, can elicit howls of laughter whereas the same words said differently can lead to anger and disapproval. We largely take our social skills for granted as much of it is automatic, but social aptitude can be subtle, making some people magnetically popular and others widely rejected. Even if we experience both these scenarios, it can be difficult to put our finger on exactly what differentiates the two.

Cultural socialisation, at its best, helps us operate in a society that values our freedom and respects others; at its worst, it leads us to accept, or prefer, social realities where people of certain sexualities, genders or skin tones are persecuted—or where the ideas that support corruption, slavery, or child marriage are deemed preferable.

Economic socialisation cannot really be separated from *cultural socialisation* because culture and economics are often entwined, yet money is a big enough matter to deserve separate treatment. The market has an interest in shaping our values. Vast sums of money are spent to make our preferences and desires align with the businesses that profit from them. We grow up valuing one type of work or one way of living over others and, often, this leads us to self-impose limits on our life options. Even if the things we are taught to value don't work well for us, we may still spend our lives adhering to them.

It seems obvious to say that these different forms of socialisation do not always work in our interest, even if socialisation is a cornerstone of our survival.

One of the founders of evolutionary psychology, Robert Trivers, splits socialisation into two parts: teaching, which is beneficial for the child, and moulding, which is beneficial for the parent or, as we encounter broader influences, for others. In *moulding*, socialisation shifts from being an essential education, teaching us how to cooperate successfully *with* other people, to making us valuable *for* other people. Such moulding may bend us toward supporting existing power structures or make us value only what is valuable for the economic system in which we live.

It is tempting to think that we can peel back our socialisation and find an 'authentic self' within but sadly, knowing who we might be without the influence of our environment is impossible because our socialisation profoundly shapes our brain, the expression of our genes, and ultimately helps determine *who* we become. Nevertheless, despite how deeply ideas can be driven into our developing minds, the specific ideas or values we use to guide our behaviour remain open to redefinition and change.

Ideas of The Self

Who we are, *what* we are, and *why* we are, depends on the ideas we have about ourselves in relation to others. Our *self-image*, *self-esteem*, and our *ideal-self* make up what psychologists call our 'self-concept'.

Our *self-image* is fragile because it can only be created in the context of other people. That *I am good at 'x'* depends on others being worse at *'x.'* Being tall requires others to be short. Being good-looking, fast, smart, emotional, or interesting can only be created based in reference to other people. A statistically tall person may find themselves feeling short around taller people, a smart person may feel stupid when around those who seem smarter, and people in the top 1% of the wealth bracket may feel poor when exposed to the top 0.01%.

Our *self-esteem*, too, is generally constructed of comparative elements which are closely related to the values important within our social group.

Our *ideal-self* is related to the things that we value; that is, the ideas we wish we could better embody, and these, likewise, are influenced by our social environment. As such, our ego, the self, is made up of ideas that differentiate *who* and *what* we are, and these are malleable.

Cultural ideas too, form part of our identity.

I am a Samurai, we are Samurais, our Samurai ideas make us brothers in arms, and we are willing to die for them, and for each other.

As our cultural identity forms our ideas about ourselves, we can become deeply attached to these ideas, making abstract concepts inextricable from the self.

If I am my ideas, and you challenge my ideas, then you challenge me.

Many of us have been in a situation whereby our implicit views, or lifestyle, somehow offended another person (or vice versa). It is not that we did anything wrong, merely that *our* idea of how to live is sufficiently at odds with *theirs* that it challenges their ideas, which can make them uncomfortable—even if we did nothing to create the situation. Likely, the offended party did not even understand the root cause of their irritation.

When we are insecure, or if the ideas that make up our self-concept are fragile, poorly understood, or poorly thought-through, our *self-as-a-concept* is also insecure, and we may find ourselves clinging to patchy, crumbling ideologies. It can feel deeply uncomfortable when such weak ideas are challenged because we need an understanding of ourselves, and of the world, to help us feel stable and placed. Indeed, it may feel better to react against challenges, new evidence, or different ideas, and to stick to *what we feel we know* than to face the disorientation of a world where the ideas of ourselves, or of our world, are threatened.

Whose Ideas Am I?

The reality is that we are, in general, not particularly original. We live our lives based on the ideas of those who came centuries, even millennia before us. Their effects on our values, traditions, social norms and preferences make us puppets of the dead.

While in prison, in part due to the sexual mores of the time, and in part due to a misjudged libel lawsuit, Oscar Wilde described this well. Writing about Emerson's phrase that "*nothing is more rare in any man than an act of his own*" Wilde comments:

It's quite true. Most people are other people. Their thoughts are someone else's opinions, their lives a mimicry, their passions a quotation. The idea that my passions, my emotions are a quotation suggests that so much of what I'm doing is just reiterating something that's come before and if that's right, then I might also be living an insufficiently examined life for the reason that I'm just following the footsteps of others, not coming up with anything authentic that is uniquely my own, and there's a respect in which also I'm going with the flow, running with the herd, and not examining my own existence in such a way as to ask, "Is this the one that I want to have?"

It can be difficult to accept that we are not our own. We are deeply affected by the ideas of both those who are alive and of those long dead. Hence, for most people, the question isn't "who am I?" but "who am I without other people's ideas?"

Digging into this question is a quick way to get dragged into a few thousand years of philosophy. The idea of 'knowing oneself' has been an important concept throughout history. One of the earliest references to this idea is the inscription *"Know Thyself"* etched onto the temple of Apollo at Delphi in ancient Greece. The Greeks believed that this maxim was an important reminder that individuals should strive to understand their own nature and limitations and that in doing so come to better understand the world around them.

Socrates believed that the pursuit of self-knowledge was among the most important goals of human life. He famously declared that *"an unexamined life is not worth living,"* and believed that individuals should constantly question their own beliefs and values to gain a deeper understanding of themselves and the world.

In the Middle Ages, the philosopher Thomas Aquinas also emphasised the importance of self-knowledge, arguing that individuals should strive to understand their own strengths and weaknesses to lead a virtuous life. He saw self-knowledge as necessary for moral growth and spiritual development.

In the modern era, the philosopher René Descartes is perhaps best known for his famous statement *"Cogito, ergo sum"* (I think, therefore I am), which reflects his belief that self-knowledge is the foundation of all knowledge. Descartes believed that individuals could only be certain of their own existence, and that this self-knowledge was necessary in order to gain knowledge of the external world.

Other important thinkers who have emphasised the importance of self-knowledge include Carl Jung, who believed that individuals should strive to become aware of their unconscious motivations and desires, and Friedrich Nietzsche, who argued that self-knowledge was necessary in order to overcome the limitations of one's own perspective and gain a deeper understanding of the world.

Despite the age-old nature of these questions, there is always reason to re-examine them *for our time*. This is especially true today, where we can benefit from the latest knowledge in neuroscience, evolutionary biology, and sociology—fields that barely existed just a hundred years ago. We also benefit from a greater perspective of history, access to diverse schools of thought, and unprecedented access to information.

New information informs new thinking, and with it we can build on the foundations of those who came before.

CHAPTER 3

THE ABSTRACT AND
THE EMOTIONAL

Most ideologies have something abstract in nature or in meaning at their core.

'God exists,' for example, is an idea founded on subjective experiences, wishful thinking, and fabricated artefacts. No evidence that stands up to scientific scrutiny supports the existence of a supernatural god. Try as we might—*and we have tried*—we cannot prove that God exists.

If there was verifiable evidence for the existence of a god, or any other mystical or magical phenomena for that matter, it would be the most significant discovery of all time. Research would be funded by major world religions that would stand to gain billions of newly devout followers. Although the details would be hotly contested, and highly politicised, such irrefutable evidence would usher in a religious era like nothing we have seen before—and that's saying something. However, there is no such evidence, and there are good reasons why the world's religious organisations don't use their considerable resources to fund research that could prove their cause.

What I am getting at, is that the idea that 'God exists' is about as abstract as ideas come.

Let's imagine there's someone out there who has never been exposed to the idea of god before. Call him Tim. If we tell Tim we believe in God, and if he takes us at face value, his first question might be, "so what?" For Tim, the idea that *God exists* has no emotional draw and plays no part in how he feels about himself. For believers, however, their relationship to their God (or Gods) can be deeply emotional and intimately tied to their personal and cultural identity.

So how do these abstract ideas connect at an emotional level?

Our conversation with Tim might sound something like:

You: So, Tim, about that God thing. Hear me out. *God exists!* [Abstract idea]

Tim: Um, so what?

You: Well, it's a big deal.
God is all powerful.
She created everything, including you.
She has told us what is right or wrong.
She can redeem us for the wrongs we have done.
She loves us as a mother.
She punishes us if we misbehave.
She can give us life after death.

Tim: … (awkward silence)

You: And, dude, we're her *chosen people.*

Tim: I mean, that sounds impressive, also kind of scary... [Emotional]
But count me in! We are a special people! [Personal & Cultural Identity]

Now, unless you found an exceptionally impressionable person, the journey from knowing nothing about a god to the concept forming part of their identity is likely to be a little more drawn out. What this demonstrates, however, is that for us to forge an emotional connection with *the abstract*, connecting ideas are needed. We call such ideas 'sub-ideas' and their purpose is to connect *the abstract* to *the emotional*. With some convincing storytelling and, perhaps, a little ritual, an idea like 'God exists' can become integral to our identity.

A person like Tim may eventually feel anxious when thinking about divine punishment or feel good knowing that divine justice will come to wrongdoers. The idea that God is on his side connects with Tim's cultural identity because it makes him, and his people, special and validates his ideas about how people should live. In time, Tim may even be willing to die for the abstract idea that *God exists*.

Such abstract ideas can become so embedded in our societies that they can seem like they are not of human origin but are instead an irrefutable natural order of things. Thanks to the structure of sub-ideas, when someone alludes to their *God*, others may feel emotions or bodily sensations, and may even take extreme, but seemingly justified actions. Here, sub-ideas hinge on the central abstract idea and yet without them, the central abstract idea would hold no power. Narratives built of sub-ideas weave a connection between *the abstract* and *the emotional* and build mountains out of thin air.

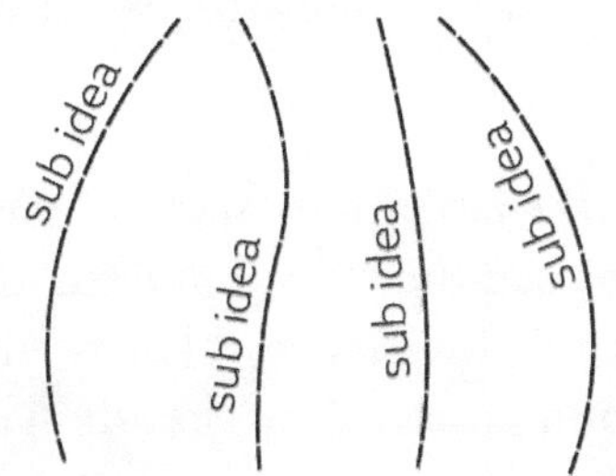

Sub ideas connect the abstract to the emotional by ascribing meaning and importance

Abstract ideas have no agency unto themselves but serve as a lynchpin binding the sub-ideas that, in turn, grip our emotions. This relationship between the emotional and the abstract is a recurring theme throughout this book and so a couple of definitions are in order

Abstract: *Existing in thought or as an idea but having no physical or concrete existence.*

Abstraction: *A distance or a disconnection.*

Impossible but Practical Realities

Our boundless imaginations gift us the capacity to suspend disbelief and enter into the realm of fantasy. Novels, films, and plays can fully absorb our attention and act not only as entertainment but as potent vehicles for learning. They can help us to empathise with others and teach us things that may be hard to learn from facts and logic alone.

Not only that, but we can enhance our skills and aptitudes in the real world merely by imagining experiences and mentally rehearsing performances.[19] Our imagination can also impact our physical and mental health and the stories we tell about ourselves can be self-fulfilling—regardless of their original relationship to reality.

Human imagination is a remarkable capability, yet it can also lead to instances where far-fetched fantasies play a central role in our societies. With persuasive sub-ideas connecting what we imagine, *the abstract*, to how we feel, *the emotional*, we can create, and structure our lives around, both constructive and destructive alternate realities.

In the 14th to 16th Centuries, in what is now modern-day Mexico, an alliance of city states formed the Aztec Empire and ruled over five to six million people. The Aztecs, bless their cotton socks, had a penchant for human sacrifice. They didn't invent the practice, but they did take it to new levels, and embedded it into everyday life. As is typical for the religions of crop-reliant cultures, the most important gods were those that affected the harvests and for the Aztecs, these gods were bloodthirsty.

Perhaps the thirstiest was the fertility goddess Tlaltecuhli, upon whose story the Aztecs based their understanding of creation. Originally a sea monster dwelling in a vast ocean created by floods, she was the embodiment of pre-creation chaos. When two other gods descended from the heavens to see what was up, they found the terrifying Tlaltecuhli sitting on top of the ocean gnashing her fangs calling for flesh to feast on. Upon deciding that the new epoch could not coexist with such terrible beast, they attacked Tlaltecuhli, and tore her in two. Her upper body became the sky and her lower body, the earth. Despite this new bodily arrangement, Tlaltecuhli didn't die and instead spent the rest of time demanding human blood as repayment for her sacrifice.[20] Why she wanted the blood of an evolved great ape is never explained but hubris is probably the answer.

Aztec art shows Tlaltecuhli as a toad like creature with long claws, a river of blood flowing from her gaping fanged mouth, and a body adorned with human skulls. This terrifying version of mother earth was responsible for the cycle of the sun and the nourishment of the earth. It was believed that if she was not fed enough, the sun's daily dance would be interrupted, crops would fail, and everyone would starve. Needless to say, not looking busy during a solar eclipse was risky business.

Likewise, the Aztec water god, Tlaloc, was responsible for everything involving rain. He was apparently less terrifying to the Aztecs, but still needed appeasing. This, too, meant human blood, but not just from anyone. Tlaloc thirsted for the blood of upset children. These poor mites were typically chosen from lower social classes and, after a night under priestly observation (sigh), they had their beating hearts pulled from their chests.

It was thought that if the children were crying on their way to their deaths, as one might imagine they would be, plentiful rain would follow. To help things along, Aztec priests were not above pulling out a few fingernails as a part of the sacrificial process. The divine servants were, if anything, hardworking, killing hundreds of thousands of people all to keep their collectively-imagined gods happy.[21]

While today it is apparent that human sacrifice is not likely to affect rainfall, for the sacrificial victims and their families, this was a reality as practical as any. If everyone collectively believes that our god desires human sacrifice, and if everyone behaves as if this is true, then it becomes what we call an *impossible but practical* reality.

As far as we know, the Aztecs *truly* did believe that human sacrifice played a role in the success of the harvest. And, as their civilisation prospered for hundreds of years, one might have argued that they were right. The evidence appeared to support their beliefs and modern meteorology was still a long way off, so who was to say otherwise?

Aztec heart sacrifice as shown in the Codex Magliabechiano—the impossible but practical realities created by our imagination are not always wonderful.

The creation of *impossible but practical* realities appears all throughout human history. If everyone believes that women are not very intelligent, emotionally unstable, and thus require the support of men, for instance, and if because of this, we deny women access to education, employment, and financial independence, we end up creating conditions that support these ideas. Women are forced into low-status positions, never attain high levels or literacy and numeracy, are precariously dependent on men, and inevitably grow frustrated. Taken all together, this provides proof of concept and what is entirely illusory appears to look *real*.

Ideas and ideologies can distort reality, creating that which does not exist and making it appear *just so*. This ability to bend and fold reality around our ideas can be as deadly as it can be liberating.

CHAPTER 4

HOW TO BREAK WITH THE IDEAS THAT BREAK US

Understanding the concept of *the abstract* and its connection to *the emotional* allows us to go one step further and look at how we can break down ideologies, understand their components, their weaknesses, and strengths, and better understand the ideological air we breathe. Doing so also helps us understand how big ideas die and how we can diminish, or nurture, ideas that matter.

Consumerism: An Antisocial Ideology

Like all of us, I grew up in a society driven by consumerism but was fortunate enough to be shielded from the full brunt of advertising as a child. I didn't watch a lot of television and lived in a fairly non-consumeristic environment. However, it'd be optimistic to claim that I haven't been impacted. I still experience the occasional urge to acquire things I don't need. I recall as a student once purchasing a watch, thinking that somehow having a 'good' watch was important. After a year, however, I realised how nonsensical this purchase was, especially since my phone had a clock, and so sold the watch. In penance, I haven't worn one since.

Consumerism and its associated sub-ideas are central in most of today's developed countries. This powerful, self-sustaining ideology remains current through constant innovation and communication. If consumer goods companies fail to keep moving, they die, and therefore massive amounts of human talent, creativity, and innovation are focused on keeping the machine alive.

The machine delivers the average city-dweller 5,000 ads per day, telling us to spend more and pushing us to internalise the values of consumer culture.[22] The result is record levels of household debt, people who spend more on jewellery and shoes than higher education, more shopping malls than high schools (in the US, at least), and a majority of teenage girls who rank shopping as their favourite pastime.[23] Consumerism affects everyone but some more than others. Our age, our social group, and our place of residence all play a role.

I'm as much a consumer as anyone. I like the idea of owning a nice car. I'd love to own a beach villa, or a penthouse apartment, or any number of other status symbols. And I probably could if I abandoned all sense of financial responsibility or was willing to enslave myself toward these goals, which, despite the downsides, remains an attractive fantasy. *To buy, and to have*, is seductive because, in doing so we anoint ourselves with the perceived status an object holds.

The big promise of consumerism centres on things we can buy and what they can do for us on an emotional, not practical, level. These benefits go further than solving a problem like *"I need a small bag to carry my things."* The right handbag does not just carry things, it makes you feel good, it may even make you a better you, it provides fulfilment, it empowers you with the idea that you can and now you *have*.

In consumerism, *new is always better than old*. Nowhere is this truer than in the world of fashion where changes in 'season' mean a dedicated fashionista (or, really, anyone who cares about looking cool) needs a new wardrobe every few months.

Here, *want supersedes need.* If we want that new top, or pair of trainers, despite having a wardrobe full of shirts or shoes, we buy it anyway. If we don't have the money, we swipe our credit card (because, after all, we deserve it, right?). No one wants to walk around in beat up shoes or drive a rusty old wreck, right? I mean, sure, if you never want to get laid… And who doesn't buy a car on credit these days? *Everyone* has debt. *Debt is an acceptable downside.*

In a consumer society, *status is marked by ownership.* If we see a woman in a sharp suit, getting out of a new Porsche with a Cartier watch, we automatically conclude that she's successful and important. This doesn't mean *she is.* She may be dissatisfied with her life, struggle under a mountain of debt, and feel deeply insecure. But who cares? In this world, appearance is more important than reality.

If you see a man in a café with worn out flipflops and a jacket mended with gaffer tape, you might write him off as a bum or someone who's failed in life or who, perhaps, has a drug problem. In reality, he might be a modest millionaire rejecting the things he once worshipped, or he might be a deeply contented family man who doesn't care what you think about his appearance. *Who* a person is doesn't really matter if they don't have *the things* because a *person without things isn't enough.*

Consumerism nurtures the feeling that if we have the right objects, people will love us. And, in a way, they do. A well-dressed person (usually) does better on a date than one with little fashion sense. Your friends coo over your new watch, and the attention makes you feel good. The admiration for the watch rubs off on you. *You* feel admired and it's almost like owning the right things might just make you happy. The dark heart of consumerism is the idea that *buying things is the path to happiness.*

Now, expectations around what you should own depend on your age and gender. At twenty, having cool trainers and the latest phone may be enough, but not at fifty. By middle age you should have a nice car, a big house, and that expensive watch. This social pressure means we aspire to own things more than *do things* because it's ownership that determines status. As consumers, we aspire toward cars, houses, fancy food, and fine hotels and it doesn't matter *how* we get there. That soul-sucking job that eats all of your time? It's acceptable so long as it pays. Working to buy things *is* our why.

Consumerism is an abstract idea and, like God, gains traction thanks to sub-ideas that play on our emotions and identity.

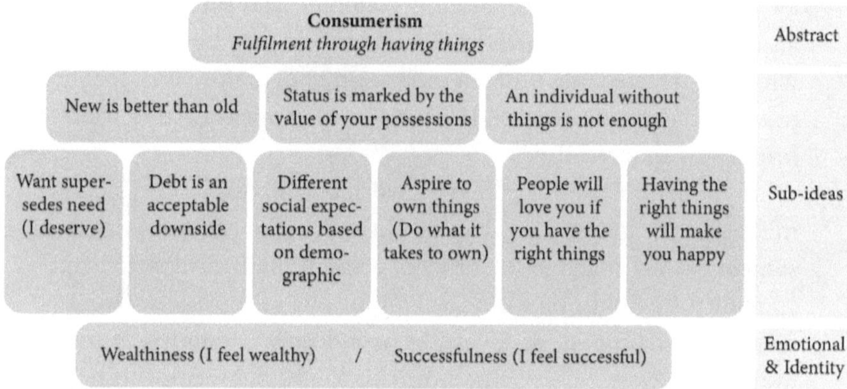

Counter-Consumerism: How Do We Buy Out?

If you want to counter an idea, it is useful to first understand its opposite; that is, the ideas that stand in opposition. Consider a thought to see how this works:

In the small social groups that characterised our evolutionary past, an individual's reputation was well understood by almost everyone. Today, in large societies unless we are a celebrity, our reputation is known only to a minute proportion of people. This creates both a problem and an opportunity.

The problem is that in our community of strangers few people know who we are so we must constantly communicate our identity, which is time-consuming and laborious. The opportunity is that we can use our material wealth to communicate certain values—but this can be done regardless of truth. We can appear rich and successful while drowning in debt; we can appear smart and professional while behaving terribly; we can appear trustworthy while committing fraud.

The fact that it is almost impossible to walk around displaying our creative, career, family, or reputational achievements, enables consumerism's greatest draw. Property, including houses, clothes, cars, watches and gadgets, provides us with an easy way to impress people we don't know and that is nearly everyone. In a culture of anonymity, displaying symbols of success *becomes* success. This is an impossible but practical reality but it's the one we live in as long as all of us continue to keep up the appearance.

Now, if consumerism promises '*fulfilment through having things*' we might oppose this with '*fulfilment through experiences*' but this is problematic. Consumer experiences have exploded in the past fifteen years as people lean toward experiential (rather than material) spending. Such experiences, by definition, are dressed for the masses, require little or no barrier to entry, and therefore also tend to be shallow, easy, and neatly packaged.

Spending our money on, say, a rafting experience, may make us feel like we aren't bowing to the god of buy, buy, buy—we didn't splurge on some tacky object, after all—but experiential consumerism is consumerism all the same.

The avid consumer can display photos of the experiences they have bought, and 'wear' them on Facebook, Instagram, or Tinder. The model consumer-of-experiences pays every time for all experiences and never develops specificity. They do not integrate in a community outside of that which has a commercial interest in them, and they do not contribute to the learning of others—or to the development of the activity—because they remain receivers of a service, not active contributors.

Of course, consumer experiences are not all bad.

They can open us up to new interests and deepen our connection to a place, but if we were to purchase *all* our experiences, we would miss out on important aspects of living. To go rafting without buying a package would mean stepping out of our comfort zones and taking risks, or better, meeting experienced rafters, building connections, and learning how to make decisions for ourselves.

The Opposite of Consumerism

So, if *doing* is not the opposite of *owning* then what is? To tackle this question, it helps to consider the opposite of each of the sub-ideas that drive consumerism, as we have done in the table below. This reveals that *contributionism* or *fulfilment through contribution* is consumerism's real opposite. Contributionism is founded in actions that positively impact your community.

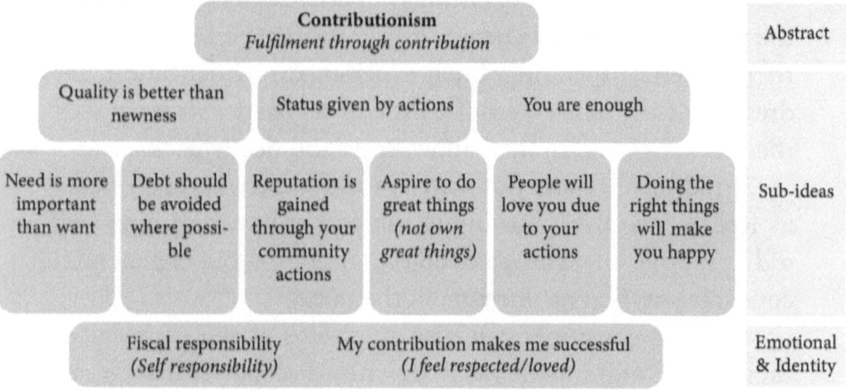

A look at the feedback cycles driven by consumerism and contributionism, respectively, reveals interesting insights. Consumerism offers immediate reward and superficial feelings of success that lead to disappointment because of their short-term nature and an inherent focus on novelty. Contributionism, on the other hand, delivers deeper feelings of satisfaction, and love, which lead to a desire to do more.

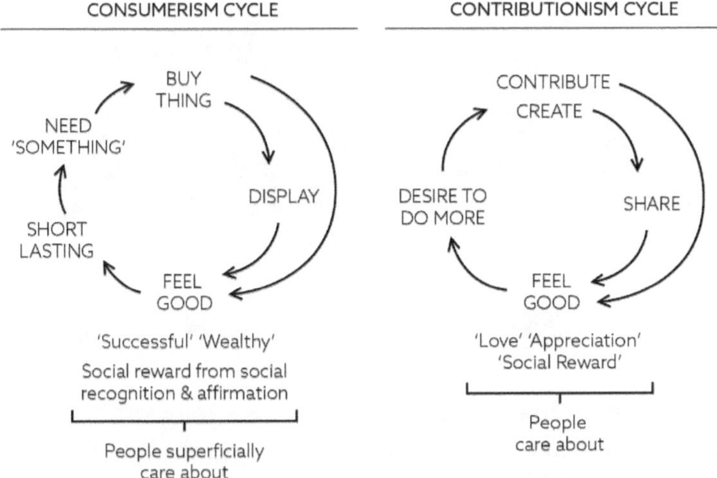

This analysis also shows that the values that make a 'good consumer' are the opposite of the values that build community, leading to the question of whether consumerism destroys community.

It is true that our basic need for community bleeds into consumer culture and people form communities around consumer products, companies, or media. There are thousands of communities built around everything from cars to software to fashion brands. This isn't inherently bad but it's shaky ground when a product that you need to purchase acts as a social lynchpin. Indeed, it's hard to see this as little more than people trying to carve out their deeper social needs through a love of things.

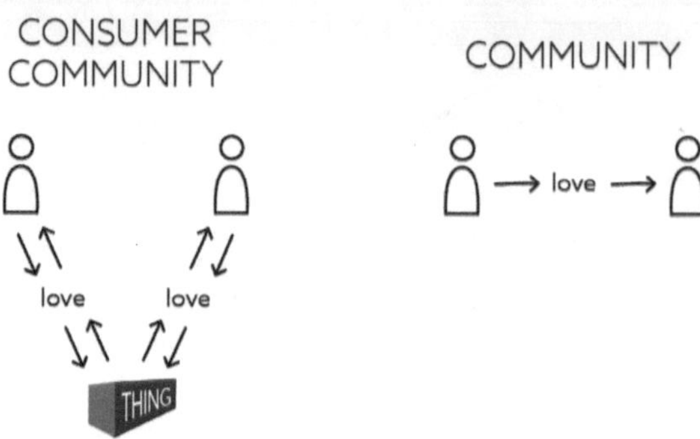

Consumer brands have been with us a long time. Roman potters branded their goods with marks, but the real explosion started in the 1800s when, during the Industrial Revolution, goods were mass-produced and sold to a wider, non-local market. Manufacturers need brands to convince the public that they could trust items made by unfamiliar companies. Over time, marketers realised that brands could be given personalities that drew association with aspirational traits like youthfulness, sex appeal, luxury, and fashion. This discovery helped usher in the modern era of marketing, and, ultimately, of consumerism.

Since then, the media and entertainment sectors have exploded and now absorb such vast amounts of human attention that they enable a constant flow of advertising revenue. The press, magazines, radio, and television grew fat on their ability to drive advertising into people's minds. Meanwhile, the internet has led rise to *social consumerism* and now delivers consumer messaging and collects personal information on a scale previous generations of marketers could have only dreamt of.

Nowadays, people consume social media on a gargantuan scale. Billions of hours are spent every day scrolling through numerous platforms and while, yes, social in nature, Instagram and their ilk are not just a poor replacement for the real thing, but antisocial in nature.[24] Social media feels hollow. If I spend a lot of time using it, I feel less, not more connected. It *is* social interaction, but somehow without the bits that matter.

Nonetheless, social media is important to consumer culture. TikTok, Snapchat, and so on enable us to 'wear' the things we do such that consumer experiences, or any experience for that matter, gain new value as commodities. At one time, you shared dinner only with those at the table; now, you share it with everyone you've ever met. Social media allows you to not only *have* the thing, but also to show you have the thing, repeatedly, to much larger numbers of people.

Product Consumerism → Media Consumerism → Social Consumerism → Reality Consumerism

What's next? What happens after social consumerism is *consumed*? If tech trends are any indication (and they always have been), the answer is *reality consumerism*. In some ways, we're already there. Gaming companies sell different versions of reality and the experiences they offer are increasingly absorbing. We can create, buy, sell, and even meet people in virtual reality. As processing power, graphics, and VR technology improves, we may hardly have to live in reality at all. We might just be able to buy the world in which we want to live (or the one we're programmed to want, at least).

Large tech companies are investing heavily in augmented realities or products that can layer digital items on top of the real world. With augmented reality glasses, you can see the current world expressed in a completely different way. This opens up endless new avenues for consumption, and for exclusion. Those without access to this new, enhanced layer, may feel left out or inadequate. The bet technology companies are making is that in the long term, bought 'realities' may even gain more value (and meaning) than reality as we know it.

The Myth of Consumer Self-Sufficiency

While working on this book I was also renovating a house in the mountains of Catalunya, Spain. My house, if the carving on the front door is to be believed, was built in 1809 and after decades of neglect, it needed significant work. I had my mind set on doing it myself. I figured that gutting the house, demolishing and replacing the roof, adding larger windows, and modernising the property would be a good challenge. In the process, I'd learn everything from major structural work to plumbing, electrics, and welding. I find there is a great feeling of self-sufficiency that comes from battling through such a project. It is also rewarding because when you complete a major phase, your *belief* that you can do something becomes *knowing* which in turn becomes confidence.

The thing is, although at the time I drafted this chapter, I had been working on my house nearly every day for eight months—mostly alone—I did not '*do it myself.*'

First, notably, a friend helped me with the major roof work in the first months, but his assistance pales in comparison to the number of people involved in the supply chains that produced every material and tool I've touched. Miners, plant workers, lumberjacks, woodworkers, machinists, distributors, shipping company employees, and delivery drivers all pitched in. And this is to say nothing of the scientists, researchers, and engineers involved in building the knowledge needed to turn raw materials into the numerous components I've used. Millions of people (living and dead) had a hand in building my house.

Regardless of this reality, the fact that I can buy all the tools and materials I need without meeting any of the people responsible for their creation means that, if I'm not careful, I can fall into the illusion of consumerist self-sufficiency.

"*I paid for it.*"

Consumerism sells a certain brand of self-sufficiency. If we can earn money, we can buy anything, and if we can buy anything, we can do anything. Why do we need to pay taxes when we pay our own way, earn our own money, and look after ourselves? Who needs a neighbour if we can buy our own milk and sugar? In a transactional society, why would we need unnecessary friendships, acquaintances, or social contact with people with whom we don't directly relate? Why would we talk to our elderly neighbour if there was no *need*?

Communities form best on a basis of need—not of niceties, but of true value exchange and of shared resources. When everything can be bought then there is less need for community, and without community, there is a greater disconnection and an increased chance of loneliness and isolation.

The American sociologist John T. Cacioppo writes:

> *In 1985, when researchers asked a cross-section of the American people, "How many confidants do you have?" the most common response to the question was three. In 2004, when researchers asked again, the most common response— made by twenty-five percent of the respondents—was none. One-quarter of these twenty-first century Americans said they had no one at all with whom to talk openly and intimately.*[25]

Consumerism creates greater distance between age groups. Where once experience and knowledge made older people a great well of information, what they used to provide is now better bought from specialists who sell information or services. The fact that anything from advice to practical knowledge can be bought negates the value of the experience older people have intrinsically gained. This means that, despite a lifetime of accumulated experience, when we stop working, the value we add to society craters. When community is built on value exchange, this inability to participate—to find a place to add value—leads to a great deal of isolation and loneliness.

If consumerism negatively impacts community, then it's in our personal interest to counteract it. We should ask our neighbour for help or advice; we should reach out to those we do not directly 'need' and work to create connections that enable some form of interdependence.

Consumerism trains us to expect an immediate exchange of benefits whereas human connection provides intangible goods which may not be seen immediately, or which may take time to understand. The rewarding feeling of living in a real community cannot be replaced by gadgets, Google searches, para-social connections, or having the ability to buy anything we want.

The ideas that dictate how we collectively behave drive society's most significant problems. If we want to drive out loneliness or uproot the sort of insecurity nurtured by relentless advertising, for instance, we need to understand the ideological structures that ground these realities.

Ideologies hold power by embedding stories and belief structures that we subconsciously refer to when making decisions—whether it is what to buy or who to vote for. If we wish to be free, we must notice these ideas, break them down, see what they are made of, and discover where they came from. Only then can we freely decide whether we subscribe.

Of course, it is possible that every idea we live by is good and well-suited to our aims, but the chances are slim and by exposing those that don't fit, we achieve the chance to live a better life.

CHAPTER 5

YOUR IDEAS WILL BE REPLACED

Things fall apart. Anything created will decay. Mountains crumble, stars fade, the chair you're sitting in will break, and your house will fall into disrepair. By the law of entropy, disorder always increases, and entropy is a fact of nature. The great scientist Arthur Eddington wrote in 1935 that *the law that entropy always increases holds, I think, the supreme position among the laws of Nature.* Later, Stephen Hawking, in *A Brief History of Time*, wrote that *the increase of disorder or entropy is what distinguishes the past from the future, giving a direction to time.*

Change is the *nature* of nature. Within our cold, entropic universe, only living things work against entropy, creating the *order* and resources they need to survive. Nevertheless, the fundamental fact is that nothing is permanent—even if we like to pretend otherwise.

A side effect of being capable of abstract thought is that we can contemplate our own death. The idea of going from *everything* now, to *nothing* for all eternity, is an uncomfortable leap and hard to accept. Even if we can cognitively accept our own demise, our subconscious, and our ego, desires to survive long afterwards and these desires are expressed in the societies we build.

19th Century Brits hoped that their Empire would last forever; Ancient Egyptians built vast pyramids to carry-over their wealth and power into an eternal afterlife; the Soviet national anthem waxed on about *"an unbreakable union of free republics"* that *"great Russia has welded forever to stand;"* Hitler proclaimed that the Reich of National Socialism would last a thousand years. It's easy to think that even if we cannot last forever, perhaps our ideas—which are arguably part of us—*can*.

It is easy to feel that some of our cultural ideas have always been, and will always be, but where change is inevitable, this cannot be the case. In our domains of direct experience, we can get a handle on the change that occurs, but it is hard to appreciate the change that is happening in the thousands of areas with which we have little direct contact. This continuous change, in every area of life, in every corner of the globe, means that it does not matter how perfectly our ideas fit the world *today*, they won't fit *quite as well* tomorrow. The social norms that created stability fifty years ago may spark a revolution today. The policy that revolutionised childcare thirty years ago may today be harmful to children. An alliance that built a successful trading relationship in the past might be a security risk in the future.

This leaves us with two choices: either we play an active role in changing the ideas of our society or we cling to old ideas until external factors change them anyway. Your ideas *will* be replaced, but with any luck, you can influence what it is that replaces them.

Adaptation

Adaptation to change is fundamental to the survival of all living organisms. Climatic changes can have far-reaching effects on an environment and its inhabitants. Such changes affect the availability of resources, shift competitive environments, and alter ecosystems. On a smaller scale, minute changes in a pathogen's genes can have devastating consequences, shifting the balance of the ecosystem it inhabits. Meanwhile, climatic changes may increase a pathogen's spread, causing predators that depend on the pathogen-affected species to seek other sources of food, or to move to different places, creating a ripple of change with unpredictable outcomes. The result of these endless ripples of cause and effect means that every species exists in a state of flux.

In essence, the constant flux of the natural world and the need to adapt to survive is what drives evolution—those who cannot adapt face extinction.

There are two main types of adaptation: reactive and evolutionary. Reactive adaptation refers to short-term adjustments that organisms make in response to changes in their environment. For example, an animal may travel further to seek food or avoid difficult conditions. Evolutionary adaptation, on the other hand, occurs over long periods of time and involves changes to an organism's genetic makeup. These adaptations improve the organism's fitness, allowing it to better survive and reproduce in its environment by, for example, evolving new reflexes, instincts, or physical capabilities.

Adaption to changing environments has led to the incredible diversity of life on Earth. Extinct organisms, found in great numbers in the fossil record, are organisms that could not adapt fast enough to the change that befell them.

Humans are highly adaptable to changes in our physical environment. Thanks to abstract thought, and the technology that has resulted from it, humans can survive in almost any conditions. We can achieve in a second what evolutionary adaption would take millions of years to produce by simply putting on a warm coat. Technology has enabled an ape from the African savanna to feel at home in the Arctic Circle, to sustain life in desolate deserts, and even live in outer space.

While humans have become adept at adapting to different physical conditions, our greatest challenge lies in our intraspecies competitive environment: the competition between different human groups. As the behaviour of our social groups is based on the ideas we hold, to succeed in a changing social environment, our ideas must also change in order to adapt.

Ideas and ideologies are subject to the same laws of natural selection as the people who hold them. If ideas lead to behaviours with poor outcomes, the social groups that hold them will eventually lose power and influence and so will the way they think. Like living organisms, ideas share common roots, cross-pollinate, and give birth to new expressions. We live less in a *"marketplace of ideas,"* as famously described by the US Justice William O'Douglas in 1919, and more in an *ecosystem of ideas* inextricably connected to the fate of those who hold them. We can see ideas as the DNA of social groups, shaping their expression and identity. Should a group be unable to adapt their ideas in response to a changing competitive environment, the long-term prognosis is poor.

For all species, death and new birth is necessary for evolutionary adaption. Only through this cycle can species adapt and survive. Likewise, if over-arching ideas are to persist, such as ideas of democracy or religion, many small deaths and new births are required.

The following examples cast this into sharp relief.

The Downfall of the Qing Dynasty

A man from a small Chinese town in 1800 was born into one of the most powerful societies on earth—a position that China had held for over a thousand years. He benefited from the fact that serfdom had been practically non-existent for nearly two millennia and that it was possible for him, a commoner, to climb the social ladder and gain status in the imperial bureaucracy should he choose to devote his life to civil service.

For centuries, Chinese technology had been ahead of its European counterpart. The Chinese developed the printing press hundreds of years before Europeans and had been producing cast iron goods almost two thousand years before westerners mastered the technology. Nevertheless, China lost its advantage when the Industrial Revolution arrived.

Failure to keep up with the times ultimately led to the foreign domination of China. The loss of technological superiority led to the fall of the Qing Dynasty, kicking off the so-called *"Century of Humiliation"* during which China was subjugated and plundered by numerous colonial powers, including Britain, France and the US. Naturally, you might ask why the Industrial and Scientific Revolution didn't occur in China when it was the most advanced culture in the world for more than a thousand years.

The answer? Technological stagnation.[26] By the time Britain clashed with China, their technology was far more advanced and the Chinese couldn't adapt quickly enough to compete. Several factors caused China's technology to stagnate while Europe's rapidly improved, including a different competitive environment, a lack of investment in technology, and a shortage of skilled workers.

Europe's many independent states created a competitive environment that drove innovation, while China had long existed as a singular empire ruled by a central bureaucratic system—achieving the opposite.

This was exacerbated by the Chinese system of inheritance in which land was divided equally among beneficiaries inhibiting the accumulation of wealth. In Europe, families could build riches and invest in arts and science—a common practice among aristocrats—while in China this was hardly possible.

Justin Lin of Peking University suggests that China's bureaucratic nature also played a role.[27] While accessible to commoners, this system diverted talent away from interests in science or technology and into the state bureaucracy, which was seen as the most honourable and worthwhile occupation at the time. Civil service examinations were arduous and difficult, required the memorising of the Confucian classic text, a feat that typically took six years, as well as the reading of many other philosophical texts. This strictly-defined and time-consuming curriculum meant that the most intelligent people had little time or incentive to explore other fields. And, once they passed their exams, they grew busy with the work of officialdom and ladder climbing.

Lin claims that the mass absorption of China's brightest people into state bureaucracy meant that *"the probability of making a transition from primitive science to modern science was reduced."* What's more, a system focused on the exact doctrine of ancient thinkers did not leave a lot of room for innovative thinking.

People from individualistic societies with less ridged hierarchies have been proven to be more inventive. Likewise, societies with greater cultural differentiation and higher levels of democracy have demonstrated advantages in scientific and technological progress.[28]

What this all demonstrates is that even if a society has been dominant for a thousand years, if it loses its ability to innovate and adapt it will eventually succumb to the changing competitive environment. Human societies are organised and operated by ideas, and thus survival depends on their ability to grow. No matter how powerful you are, too much isolation, stasis, and rigidity, will lead to decline.

Christianity in England

In 1860, while the Chinese were suffering from their failure to adapt to a changing competitive landscape, a twenty-seven-year-old English man named Charles Bradlaugh was about to speak at an event he had organised in Wigan, England.

The venue was packed and hundreds more were gathered outside. As he approached, the crowd booed and shouted obscenities. Charles fought his way inside, locked the door, and proceeded to start his lecture. Before he could get more than a few words out, a loud banging erupted. He abandoned the podium, crossed the hall, and, against his better judgement, opened the door to find a member of the clergy demanding admittance. To calm matters, he let the man in and, with great effort, again shut the door against the violence escalating outside.

He strode back to the lectern and picked up where he left off. He only managed a few more words before being interrupted by the sound of shattering glass as the angry mob began to rain fury down upon the windows. The audience jolted from their seats, their fear palpable.

As his lecture reached its conclusion, the Secretary of the local Rector found himself lodged in a partially shattered window while frenzied delinquents hurled lime and water through the ventilators. A hand suddenly jutted from a hole in the ceiling, prompting one member of the audience to leap up, gleefully proclaiming that Satan had come to collect the speaker.

Despite the turmoil, Bradlaugh persisted through his closing remarks. Afterward, as he left the venue, he was greeted with gobs of spit and a cascade of threats. Hundreds of men dogged his every step back to his hotel. This wasn't a first time, and it wasn't even the worst. Bradlaugh had previously been arrested, pelted with bricks, and even faced attempts on his life—all for simply sharing his ideas.[29]

Why? Bradlaugh was a proponent of atheism. His Wigan lecture was entitled '*What has the Bible done for England's sons and daughters?*' and while not initially well-received (to put it mildly), this changed over the years. Bradlaugh was eventually welcomed back to Wigan—and many other cities—in an impressive career that campaigned for social change and the separation of church and state.

In the mid-1800s, merely entertaining ideas that ran counter to dominant Christian beliefs was enough to incite violence. Pronouncing yourself an atheist meant courting danger. Bradlaugh had been kicked out of his house as a youth; later, his business interests imploded, and he was left struggling to find employment when customers learned of his beliefs.

More than one hundred years after his death, Bradlaugh

would be pleased at the diminished importance of religion in the UK. Although the Church retains Bishops in the House of Lords and controls many schools, their impact on government and society has greatly decreased. Unlike in Bradlaugh's time, when atheists were left without legal protection because they couldn't take an oath to give evidence in court, today's laws no longer discriminate against non-believers, who now make up the majority of the population.[30]

The importance of the Church in public has likewise been decimated. More than half the population regularly attended Church of England services in 1880. One hundred years on, this number dropped to 11% and, by 2016, less than 2% of the population reported regularly attending mass.[31] At the turn of the millennium, Government leaders were more likely to hide their faith and, like Tony Blair, claim that 'they don't do religion' than publicly announce their religiosity.

The unimaginable had happened. Within a few generations, deeply entrenched and seemingly all-powerful ideas were side-lined to a point of irrelevance.

Formal Menswear

Flip back to the picture of Charles Bradlaugh. While the black and white tones and framing of the shot give it away as something from a previous era, nothing of his dress would look wildly out of place at a formal dinner in London today.

A few years ago, I was visiting the UK capital during one of the hottest summers in decades. The heat was oppressive and inescapable. The London Underground, opened some forty years before the invention of air-conditioning, still largely remains without. During this time, a short journey in the festering subterranean heat left me dripping with sweat even when wearing a t-shirt and shorts. Nevertheless, there were *still* men in suits. Long black trousers, polished leather shoes, a collared shirt, a suit jacket, and a tie knotted tightly at their neck. Ironically, they must've all been glad for their jackets, which would be the only thing obscuring the sweat that was no doubt pouring off their bodies. Crazy? Yes. Completely normal? Also, yes.

The ideas that govern men's formal wear are so powerful that many of the wealthiest people in society prefer to be physically uncomfortable than abandon them. This is remarkable. What's the point of all that wealth and power if it can't liberate a person from such petty rules?

An alien observer would find it weird that a middle-aged man in his underpants can put on a suit and transform into a *professional*. And they may find it weirder still that without a suit this same man would lose all credibility and may even lose his job. The mores of men's formal wear are so deeply ingrained that we even have a word to express their hegemony: *suitable*.

The concept of classic menswear arrived two centuries ago as the French and American revolutions marked the decline of the aristocracy. These changes made fashion, previously defined by French aristocrats with their luxurious materials, powdered wigs, make up, cravats, and stockings, look like a distasteful display of wealth. When people were beheading thousands of ostentatious aristocrats just across the English Channel, it quickly became a bad idea to look too much like them. 'Bad optics,' as we would say today.

Ideas of social equality came to drive men's fashion and, amongst this melee of change was Beau Brummell, a British man who advocated for menswear that provided *"maximum of luxury in the service of minimal ostentation."* Supported by the patronage of the Prince of Wales, the future king, Brummell became a tastemaker and, perhaps, the first modern celebrity. He was famed for his personality, his grooming habits and most of all, his exacting style. Brummell dressed in well-fitted, full-length navy-blue trousers and a linen cravat over a linen shirt. The tailors of Savile Row turned their shops into a mecca for those wishing to see and buy into this style and they gave him free suits to market their attire. Brummell gave birth to the modern suit, and in a stroke, his attire defined the only dress suitable for a professional man.

In this chapter, we've looked at how changing ideas drove the fall of a Chinese dynasty, a national religion, and changed cultural dress codes. Only one of the subjects addressed has survived the past century intact.

Why is it that *the suit* persists when a national religion failed?

The Church of England lost relevance in the twentieth century because they failed to adapt their ideas to a quickly changing social environment. This stands in contrast to the US, where innovative and ever-adapting denominations compete aggressively to offer exactly what the people in their parishes need, and thus retain higher rates of attendance. In 2019, 45% of Americans reported regularly attending religious services and only 4% of Americans describe themselves as atheists (although more recently this has seen a notable decline).[32]

Suits, on the other hand, survived because fashion is at home with change and the suit constantly adapts to evolving ideas around men's clothing. Changes in lapels, buttonholes, shoulder pads, materials, linings, and a wide array of features enable the idea of the suit to keep pace with the times. The designs may no longer be from Beau Brummell's closet but the core idea of understated but fitted formalwear remains.

The lesson here is that whether it be democracy, etiquette, or religious tradition, when it comes to ideas, if we want them to survive, we need to allow for change. Only with little deaths and new births can our overarching ideas persist. Paradoxically, to keep an idea we love, we must constantly change it.

Although many of our ideas are constantly changing, are we *really* in a state of total ideological flux? Are there any constants that provide a basis for human ideology and society? Intuitively, we'd like to think there are and yet pinning these constants down is hard. Nevertheless, doing so is the goal of the next chapter.

CHAPTER 6

IDEOLOGY AND MORALITY

A friend of mine, we can call him Phil, landed a well-paid job running a division of an education-based company. It turned out that the company owners, based at head office several hours away, were an unscrupulous bunch. Phil told me about a time when the bosses sued an ex-employee—a low-wage, single mother of three—after she lost an employment claim for unfair dismissal. They joked about how they were going to *"take her f**king house"* but in court, the judge saw the case for what it was, threw it out, and labelled the bosses' behaviour as *"disgusting."* Later, they would boast about this as if it were some kind of victory.

These same bosses pushed Phil to stop providing tea and milk for the staff and to cut back on pens and notebooks. They ran a business worth millions and yet they were obsessed with scrimping, especially at the staff's expense. These paranoid bosses would connive against employees and find ways to discipline or fire them because they were convinced everyone was trying to swindle them out of money. They drew up contracts that disadvantaged staff or were damaging to their share options or pensions. They believed that, under the surface, everyone operated in the same way—only ever acting in their own advantage—and, as bosses, it was *their job* to stop them.

Individually, the bosses had enough to be comfortable for the rest of their lives, but they continued to claw for more, regardless of who was disadvantaged by their gain. Phil, who's not exactly an angel, was shocked by their callous treatment of others, and suggested they were sociopaths. How could people so selfish really exist? Where was their humanity?

The nature of humanity has been hotly debated for thousands of years. Some of us, like these unscrupulous bosses, believe it is right to dominate others if you can because, regardless of their suffering, they would do the same to you if they could. Conversely, there are people who believe in helping those in need because people are generally good, and life is not an endless competition.

The demoralised employees at my friend's business understood that they could not trust the management. It was not only clear that their bosses did not care about them but that they were capable of actively working against their interests. This toxic environment meant that Phil's colleagues really did work only for the money. In silent rebellion they slacked off when they could and when they had a case, they sued the company. The beliefs of the management created an environment absent of goodwill leading to behaviours that appeared to confirm their cynical beliefs. Again, we're talking about an *impossible but practical* reality.

Across all human relationships, from the romantic to the political, how we treat others depends on what we think of them. Incorrect understandings lead to undesirable outcomes, and our inherent interdependence ensures that ultimately, everyone involved is affected.

These beliefs also lead to different political outlooks and subsequently, policies. If we base policies on an accurate understanding of human nature, we can avoid creating self-fulfilling toxic environments, or systems where some people unfairly take advantage. A better understanding of human nature helps us picture and move toward creating social environments better for humans to live in.

Whatever the social realm—personal, professional, or political—the closer our environment fits the reality of our nature, the more at ease we will be. A relationship steeped in paranoid jealousy often leads to what paranoid individuals fear most; a business that does not provide adequate rest for workers suffers from lower productivity and higher staff turnover; Governments that imprison opposition candidates create an environment where everyone is afraid, including its leaders. By not heeding the reality (that romantic partners are not always going to cheat, that people need to be rested to perform, and that trampling on the rights of others puts you at risk of the same treatment) it creates an environment that delivers poorer outcomes for everyone involved.

History of Thought

For a few thousand years, most people have lived within broadly similar social structures—hierarchal systems with centralised power. As this timeframe accounts for most of our recorded history, it has been hard to figure out which came first, *civilised people* or *civilisation*. Did hierarchal systems with centralised power rein in our worst selves and enable societies to exist or did they corrupt our better nature and lead us to dominate one another? It's the all-time-classic anthropological chicken and egg dilemma.

For centuries, two narratives have shaped our discourse yet neither has any basis in fact. The foundation of the more cynical view was laid out by Thomas Hobbes in 1651 when he published *Leviathan, or The Matter, Forme and Power of a Commonwealth Ecclesiasticall and Civil*. According to Hobbes, before large societies, prehistoric humans lived in small bands and life was miserable because our innately selfish nature meant that people were locked in a constant fight of *"all against all."* The lives of 'primitive' humans was *"solitary, poor, nasty, brutish and short."* However, as we formed larger societies, by necessity, we created institutions—governments, laws, courts, prisons, and police— ultimately ruled by *"one supreme authority"* that provided the control required to repress our selfishness and stop us from ripping each other apart. According to Hobbes, as societies grew, repressive organisations became even more critical in everyday operations. In his view, moral behaviour originated with the state and without it, society would collapse into chaos and violence.

The opposing view, traditionally favoured by those on the left, was first proposed as a thought experiment on the origins of inequality by Jean-Jacques Rousseau in 1754. Rousseau also believed that humans originally lived in small bands but, instead of constantly butchering each other, they existed in a state of child-like innocence. Thanks to the scale of their societies—and, as the critique goes, that they were all poor in equal measure— these small bands were able to maintain an egalitarian structure. According to Rousseau, humans lived quite happily like this until the 'agricultural revolution' that led to the creation of property rights, and subsequently, cities, bureaucrats, patriarchy, standing armies and mass murder. This shift from the *"noble savage"* living in a state of equality to one of inequality and subservience happened due to an innocent lack of experience. For Rousseau, people did not realise that they were running *"toward their chains"* until it was too late.

These linear theories, where our societies *evolved* from simple forms of society into the complex systems of governance we have today, has been told so often by writers, historians, psychologists, and politicians that it has become a sort of received wisdom. Together, these two flavours of the same narrative, formed the 'evolution theory' of civilisation and provided an easy way to explain many things, including the seemingly inevitable presence of inequality. Hobbes' and Rousseau's ideas have shaped our political discourse for three hundred years and have had a profound political and cultural impact.

Not surprisingly, both arguments have problems. First, both imply that prehistoric humans were not sufficiently politically conscious to think critically about how their societies were run, and second, they both lead to the same conclusion. Rousseau's idea that humans could only maintain equality due to small group sizes tells us that we are stuck with the inequality that surrounds us today, while the Hobbesian story tells us that without repressive institutions we would descend into chaos. Centralised hierarchical power structures are inevitable, and inequality and repression are simply a fact of life—or, at least, so we've been led to believe.

More recent theories about the development of society have been based less on the imagination of 16th Century thinkers and more on scientific enquiry. Unsurprisingly, this has resulted in answers with more nuance.

In their 2021 book *The Dawn of Everything – A New History of Humanity*, anthropologist David Graeber and archaeologist David Wengrow, draw on ten years of examining new and old archaeological and anthropological evidence to deliver an entirely different view of prehistory. They show that prehistoric humans were not wandering around in a dream-like state but were instead intelligent, politically conscious people who actively made decisions about how their societies were organised.

The evidence suggests that there was no linear process in which humans evolved from small bands to larger groups, to towns, to cities, and eventually to states. Instead, the archaeological record shows that our ancient ancestors shifted between numerous social structures. We never lived consistently in small hunter-gatherer groups nor were we ever consistently egalitarian. Some prehistoric societies created cities with systems that prevented centralised power, others were highly centralised, perhaps for a time, before ridding themselves of their tyrants to live in different ways before changing again. People moved into and out of many different political, economic, and religious systems, in many regions of the world, in a complex and incredibly varied history—a complexity that one may expect considering the timescales involved.

Graeber and Wengrow also question the popular idea of a distinct agricultural revolution by demonstrating that the shift to agriculture happened non-linearly over 3000 years. This is a period equivalent of the time between the early Iron Age and the moon landings and is hardly something that could be described as a 'revolution.' Large towns, cities, and a wide variety of social environments centred around other forms of resource abundance existed long before anything we might call *agriculture*. Farming played a role, but was not the main source of sustenance, and some societies began using agriculture only to abandon it for a thousand years and later start again.

Wengrow and Graeber write:

> *To give just a sense of how different the emerging picture is: it is clear now that human societies before the advent of farming were not confined to small, egalitarian bands. On the contrary, the world of hunter-gatherers as it existed before the coming of agriculture was one of bold social experiments, resembling a carnival parade of political forms, far more than it does the drab abstractions of evolutionary theory. Agriculture, in turn, did not mean the inception of private property, nor did it mark an irreversible step towards inequality. In fact, many of the first farming communities were relatively free of ranks and hierarchies. And far from setting class differences in stone, a surprising number of the world's earliest cities were organized on robustly egalitarian lines, with no need for authoritarian rulers, ambitious warrior-politicians, or even bossy administrators.*[33]

The evidence suggests that we do not need the repressive institutions of the modern state to get along, even in large populations. What's more (and there's some deep irony here), it is notable that when Hobbes wrote *Leviathan*, the same institutions he credited for taming our selfish instincts were in the process of establishing the trans-Atlantic slave trade and were experiencing a busy period of torturing and hanging (or boiling or burning alive) women arbitrarily accused of witchcraft after the *"central supreme authority"* revamped the English Witchcraft Act.

If we are not selfish animals that require institutional repression in order to be good to each other, and if our moral behaviour does not originate in the state, where then, does morality come from?

How We Understand Morality

Researchers approach morality from one of two angles: either as *cultural* codes-of-conduct put forward by a group of people as the correct way to live or as a *natural* code of conduct that *"given specified conditions, would be put forward by all rational people."*[34]

The first, referred to as 'descriptive' morality, looks at the moral codes of different societies as a means of understanding their cultural values and, being culturally specific, these may not always seem reasonable to those on the outside. The second, referred to as 'normative' morality, addresses morality as a function of human nature. According to this view, morality is dependent on our biology and humans anywhere will arrive at similar conclusions for most moral dilemmas.

These two angles on morality are, of course, not wholly distinct. Moral philosophers across history have influenced the way morality is practiced and this, in turn, influences the ways it is described. To talk about how we, as a species, understand morality thus requires us to move interchangeably between these perspectives.

Immoral acts, whether normative or descriptive, require a victim. Typically, someone needs to be harmed by an action for it to be seen as immoral. To determine how bad a moral transgression is, we look at two factors: what we perceive the harm to be, and secondly, how *wrong* we perceive the behaviour to be. Together, the *harm* and the *wrongness* form a *harm judgement* that determines how we respond to the transgressor and what punishments, or preventative social controls, are required.

This too is ruled by our ideas because our perception of harm and our perception of wrongness are heavily influenced by culture. One culture may perceive sex between two men as very wrong while another may not see it as wrong at all. One culture may perceive physical punishment of children as harmful while another may see it as a form of care. In some cultures, acts that result in no material harm can be perceived to be extremely harmful. Honour killings are a good example. Still common in honour-based cultures, especially those with links to religious conservatism and fundamentalism, these killings are typically carried out against a woman who seeks divorce, refuses an arranged marriage, has forbidden male partners, or is raped.[35] Homosexual men are also often the victims of honour killings.

Despite the obvious horror of this violence, the killers feel that their victim has not only done *wrong* but that they have caused great *harm*. In particular, they feel their honour has been damaged and that by murdering the offending family member they distance themselves from the transgression and restore their honour within their community.[36] This is a clear example of how a *harm judgement* can be pushed off the charts by cultural ideas that see daughters, sons, nieces, and nephews, murdered despite not having harmed anyone in a material sense.

We see less extreme examples of this cultural amplification of harm-judgement in the harsh punishment of drug users, the social stigmatisation of divorcees, or sexual minorities, or the calls to punish those who burn flags or religious texts.

Most societies codify rules regarding moral behaviour and what counts as justice according to their cultural norms into laws. The complexity of these rules requires highly trained people to help pass judgements: lawyers, barristers, judges, or religious leaders.

To properly evaluate a moral transgression and issue a harm judgement such professionals must reconstruct scenarios, understand proximal and distal causes, and assess the consequences of the offenders' actions.

Why did they do what they did, what affected their behaviour, and what was the result? Was a killing coldly premeditated, an accident, or an act of self-defence? In each instance, the result is a dead body, but few would consider each to be equally wrong or deserving of the same punishment.

Doing What is Right

Nobody uses careful reasoning to guide each and every one of their decisions. Most of what we do is driven by intuition, impulse, or habit. This raises the question of whether we *think* or *feel* our way toward doing what is right.

Here, there are two main historical schools of thought. On the one hand there's *'empiricism,'* which asserts that morality is learned during childhood and has no innate basis; on the other, there's *'nativism,'* which asserts that some moral knowledge is built into the human brain and that anyone brought up in a reasonable environment will develop moral ideas.

In 1958, American psychologist Laurence Kohlberg, developed a third theory of moral development based on a series of simple tests that could be used to determine which of three stages of moral reasoning an individual had reached in their development. For Kohlberg, moral development was a form of cognitive development. This *'constructivist'* view suggests that we construct our abilities through self-motivated action in the world.

Kohlberg's model is built on the thinking of Jean Piaget, who in the 1930s developed theories of child development demonstrating that children think in fundamentally different ways than adults and that cognitive development is not just about acquiring knowledge. Prior to this, children were essentially seen as small adults waiting to be filled with information. Kohlberg's ideas remained dominant in the field of moral psychology until the end of the 20th Century.

In the 1990s, Jonathan Haidt introduced a *'social intuitionist'* model of morality to replace Kohlberg's, which he viewed as *"too cerebral."* After researching moral differences across different cultures, Haidt proposed that moral decision-making is based primarily on intuition and that reason serves only to convince ourselves, and everyone else, that our decisions make sense. In his view, humans *"come equipped with an intuitive ethics, an innate preparedness to feel flashes of approval or disapproval toward certain patterns of events involving other human beings."* Haidt de-emphasised reason as the primary driver of moral behaviour and asserted that moral judgement is driven primarily by intuition.

"Moral dumbfounding," or instances where people have a strong moral reaction to a given scenario that cannot be explained by rational principles plays a key role in Haidt's theories. In one example, participants are presented with a scenario where a brother and sister sleep together. They use contraceptives, no one else knows, no one is harmed, and both feel it brought them closer together, but they also decide never to do it again. Most participants strongly believe that the siblings did something wrong and continue to think this way even if they admit that, because there was no harm, there is little justification for their judgement. In Haidt's view, this is because, when people explain a moral position, they often hide, or do not understand the original reasons or processes that drive their conclusions.

Evidence in support of the social intuitive approach is plentiful. One example is a study on cheating where it was found that a certain percentage of participants would simply never cheat. When faced with a scenario in which they *could* cheat, these people's frontal cortex—a part of the brain involved in making moral decisions—remained inactive. On the other hand, other participants who cheated or would consider doing so, displayed a wildly active frontal cortex as they tried to work out the moral dilemma. For the never-cheaters, cheating was simply not an option; they did not have to make a decision because their behaviour was implicitly driven by an intuitive pathway in the brain. The moral behaviour was intuitive, so reasoning was not required.

Other studies show that people are more likely to see victimless moral transgressions (stealing from a long-dead corpse that has no heirs, for example) as having a victim when time pressure is used to force an intuitive judgment as compared to when they have time to think.[37] Haidt's achievement was showing that humans operate on an intuition first, rationalisation later, basis.

Findings in evolutionary psychology suggest that emotions play an additional part in the origins of human morality. This is especially true where kin altruism, reciprocal altruism, and revenge are concerned.[38,39] Furthermore, morality is not unique to humans. After years of studying non-human primates, Frans De Wall, the famous primatologist, came to believe that the basis of morality is not only older than human cultural institutions, but transcends our species boundaries and is perhaps older than humanity, itself.[40]

Although this debate is not entirely settled, there is a general scientific consensus that moral processes happen in two competing cognitive systems. One is intuitive, fast, and emotionally driven, the other is slow and cognitively intensive. The empiricist idea that we are taught moral behaviour falls in the face of the evidence that intuition and emotions drive morality, indicating that humans are indeed *naturally* moral—that morality has to do with our biology.

To take this further, the next question is not "what makes us moral?" but "what is the underlying shape of this *natural* human morality?" And, "is it possible to separate culture from biology?"

Behavioural Biology

In his 2017 book *Behave*, David Sapolsky, a professor of biology and neurology at Stanford University, writes *"it makes no sense to distinguish between aspects of a behaviour that are 'biological' and those that would be described as, say, 'psychological' or 'cultural' [they are] utterly intertwined."*

Behavioural biology is a complex subject because everything is interconnected, and a vast number of variables are at play. To keep things simple, we won't provide an overview of the field of behavioural biology but instead will focus only on the areas relevant to moral behaviour and how they are affected by our environment and the ideas that shape it. That is, we will examine how ideas alter and, ultimately, *rule us*.

The lay understanding of genetics goes something like, if you have a certain gene, you display a certain attribute. Brown-haired people have a brown-haired gene; tall people have a tall gene; bald people have a balding gene, and so on. The reality however, especially where behaviour is concerned, is far more complicated.

Behaviour is partially determined by our genes. It must be because our genes define the structure of proteins relevant to every neurotransmitter, hormone, and receptor. Nevertheless, *how* those genes are expressed is greatly dependent on the environment in which we develop.

Ultimately, our gene-environment interaction means that the same genes can be *expressed* in different ways. *Gene expression* is the process wherein DNA information is converted into the instructions that make molecules or proteins—a process of gene transcription and translation—that can be affected by environmental factors and lead to varying outcomes.

For example, stress in our early life, can affect our gene expression and permanently reduce our brain's ability to normalise glucocorticoid (stress hormone) secretion after a triggering event.[41,42] People who have suffered severe stress at a very young age may experience extended stress in response to upsetting experiences as adults because their brains struggle to regulate these hormones back to normal levels. Early life experiences have also been shown to adversely affect parts of the brain related to learning and memory. Furthermore, children or adolescents who experience traumatic events display increased mental and medical illness later in life.[43,44]

Violent behaviour in young men provides another example of how environmental factors impact gene expression and thus, behaviour. The story here concerns the MAO-A gene, which controls serotonin signalling. A 2002 study found that men with the *low-activity version* of the MAO-A gene were three times as likely to be convicted of a violent crime, but *only* if they had a history of severe childhood abuse.[45] In individuals who did not suffer severe childhood abuse, the gene variant predicted nothing. In other words, the presence of MAO-A gene only becomes meaningful when taken in context and this pattern of gene-environment interaction is consistent across many areas of behavioural genetics.

Gene expression can also depend on the expression of other genes which, themselves, can be affected by the environment meaning the result depends on the combination of a network of genes and how *they* all interact with the environment. In fact, a large percentage of genes work in this way, resulting in a wide variety of potential gene expressions from the same DNA. A study of 183,727 people, examining the genes that affect height, discovered that there were hundreds of genetic variants that appeared to play a part in regulating height.[46] Unsurprisingly, studies have found that behaviour is also influenced by large numbers of genes that all contribute in a small way.[47]

To further complicate things, certain sequences of DNA can, throughout our lives, jump from one location in our genome to another and, in so doing, alter our genetic expression. These *transposable elements* comprise about half of the human genome and can also be affected by environmental conditions. Environmental exposures can cause transposable element dysregulation which can lead to stress-related and neurodevelopmental illness, changes in immune response, and affect behavioural and cognitive development.[48] Transposable element activity has been shown to change with cocaine exposure, alcohol, and heat shock, and may also contribute to depression. Additionally, there is evidence that transposable elements play a role in the development of autism and schizophrenia, among other disorders, and, again, early life environmental factors can be to blame.[49-53]

The cherry on top of all this is epigenetics, which shows that our genes are also determined in part by the experience of our parents making the effects of gene-environment interactions not only lifelong but even multigenerational.

It is clear that the environment we grow up in is important for determining who and what we become. Our community, the type of parenting we receive, everything going on around us while still in the womb, our neighbourhood, diet, socioeconomic status, school environment, and even family history, can all alter our genes and thus, our very selves.

Culture and biology cannot be separated.

Ideas that Shape Us

The ideas our different cultures hold will drive our tolerance for poverty, inequality, or the prioritisation and accessibility of healthcare. Cultural ideas related to child-rearing, childcare, and gender equality will have an enormous impact on our early life experiences.

Some cultural ideas lead to a prevalence of stressed parents struggling to make ends meet while working long hours with little time for quality parenting, while other ideas prioritise fair wages that provide individuals adequate resources and sufficient time for childcare. Some cultural ideas lead to the dismantling of social safety nets, leaving vulnerable individuals in a cycle of poverty, while others prioritise systems that support those who encounter hardships. Certain cultural ideas may marginalise women and girls, excluding them from education or accepting domestic abuse as a norm, while other ideas offer women the economic and social capital to protect themselves and their children—benefiting society as a whole.*

Racism, sexism, and classism are inherent in some cultures, leading to poorer outcomes for those impacted, while in other

---

* One theory suggests that the reduction of crime between 1990 and 2000 in the USA can be traced back to the Roe v. Wade judgement that drastically reduced unwanted pregnancies and, twenty years later, led to far fewer stressed and angry young men being unleashed on society after suffering impoverished upbringings.[54]

cultures these and many other forms of discrimination, are rooted out and condemned. In some cultures, wealth generation is prioritised at the expense of health—leading to toxins in food, household products, and the air people breathe. Conversely, other cultural ideas promote regulations that reduce such environmental stressors.

In short, the ideas our societies hold lead to a wide variety of environments. The resulting gene-environment interactions can, if detrimental, cause lifelong difficulty, misery, and suffering. Depressing? Yes, a little—but now we know—and this can help inform our political choices toward creating better environments.

The Brain

While the neurobiology of morality is not well understood, there is strong evidence in support of the existence of a specific brain network that handles moral behaviour.[55]

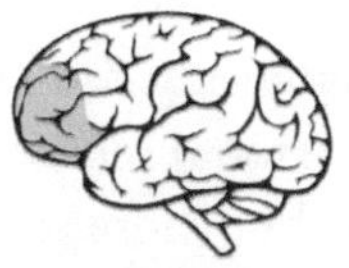

The Frontal Cortex

The frontal cortex, a large brain area that sits at the front of the skull, is important for the ways we interact with ideas and how we compute moral decisions. This part of the brain is responsible for executive function (the ability to consider information, find patterns, and act upon them), working memory (the ability to hold various thoughts and connect them together toward a goal), the ability to pursue delayed gratification, make long-term plans, regulate emotion, and rein in impulsive behaviour, among many other functions.

The prefrontal cortex, a part of the frontal cortex, further regulates activity in the brain's other emotional centres, and supports the planning and supervising of moral decisions, and the application of social codes. A damaged or impaired prefrontal cortex can lead to immoral behaviour, an unmooring from social norms, and impulsive, or sometimes aggressive, actions.

The frontal cortex is especially important for the development of appropriate behavioural responses to internal and external stimuli. It enables understanding of how, when, and why to behave in certain ways in our highly complex societies.

Reading other people's emotions and understanding how you are expected to feel—and thus respond—is nuanced and culturally specific. Aggression is celebrated in some contexts and condemned in others. Do it right when at war, while playing sports, or acting in self-defence and you might be celebrated; do it wrong and you might end up in prison. In some situations, touching someone's shoulder can be an act of compassion, in others, it can be sexual harassment. Sometimes an edgy joke breaks an uncomfortable impasse, other times it makes it worse. A look can be an invitation or a rejection and mistaking one for the other can be socially costly. Laughing too early can make you look foolish; laughing too late can do the same. The complexity of our interpersonal relationships and behaviours is mostly taken for granted but those who struggle to read social situations and respond correctly can find that it affects the entire course of their lives.

Tellingly, the frontal cortex is the last part of the brain to mature. This slow development, which finishes at around the age of twenty-five, allows decision-making to be tailored to the behavioural norms of one's social group. The result is that the brain area most important for defining who we are is also the area least constrained by our genes and the most affected by experience. This long adaption to our culturally-specific behavioural norms is another way that ideas imprint themselves on our minds.

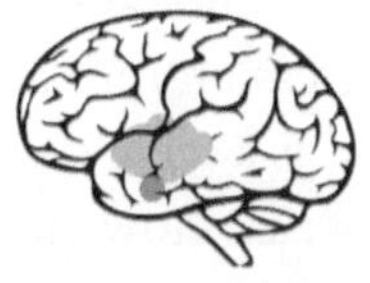

Disgust, the Insular Cortex and the Amygdala

Our sense of disgust is connected to our sense of morality and thus any conversation about moral behaviour needs to consider the insular cortex. This part of the brain activates when we bite into rotten food, smell faeces, or see rancid flesh, and drives us to retch or experience other powerful feelings of aversion. The basic nature of these reactions connects to numerous systems including those that underlie sensory, emotional, motivational, and cognitive processing.[56]

In humans, the insular cortex also reacts to abstract ideas. Thoughts alone are enough to trigger disgust, and this isn't limited to disturbing ideas such as imagining eating a spoonful of maggots or biting into a cockroach. It also activates when we think about *disgusting* behaviour—violations of social norms— or when we think of people who we consider to be 'wrong' in society. Moreover, if we imagine a group of people as cockroaches the insular cortex also drives activation of the amygdala—a brain region important to our processing of fear. This disgust of *the other*, infused with fear, has far-reaching consequences.

Studies show that a person's politics can be predicted by their sensitivity to disgust. Similarly, a study by Rachel Herz of Brown University shows that sensitivity to bitterness predicts the likelihood that a person will be grossed out by moral transgression in general.[57] When participants were asked "how angry" a transgression made them, they found no relation to their sense of taste, but when they were asked if they were "grossed-out"—the more sensitive they were to bitter tastes, and the more "grossed-out" they were by *all* transgressions. Simply by framing the question and introducing the idea that a deviation from social norms is *disgusting*, can transform something perceived as a *general* moral transgression into a *repulsive* act.[58]*

"Moral hypervigilance" is a term developed by Andrew Jones and Julie Fitness to describe how individuals who are easily disgusted by physical things are also easily disgusted by people who break moral norms.[59]

Disgust has a direct impact on our moral reasoning and plays a limiting role in our ability to empathise with others. Studies demonstrate that charitable donations drop when disgust is present, for instance, and disgust plays a role in our ability to dehumanise others.[60–62]

Animal brains have been evolving for over 520 million years. Ape brains account for only twenty to thirty million years of this; meanwhile, the Homo sapiens brain is just five million years old.[63,64] Evolutionarily, moral emotions are brand new which is why there isn't a specific part of our brain dedicated to processing moral disgust. Instead, the experience piggybacks off the same circuitry used to process physical sensations. Disgust began as an emotion aimed at protecting us from ingesting dangerous pathogens and only much later developed into a means of protecting us against moral violations or interpersonal contamination.[65]

This connection between abstract judgements and our physical sensory system is so widespread that it inevitably feeds into the way we judge other people. Sitting on a hard or a soft chair can lead us to judge another person as being less or more flexible; hunger can lead us to be less generous with money; holding a warm cup can warm our judgement of others while holding a cold cup can do the opposite.

Our brains simply have not had the time to evolve separate areas to handle the repertoire of feelings that our social complexity delivers and so the physical and the abstract often overlap and

---

* Recommend reading: Fiske's research into warmth and competence in relation to disgust and dehumanisation.[67]

create confused signals. Cultural ideas greatly determine *which* behaviours we find disgusting giving these ideas a visceral power over our emotional states and our judgement of others. Disgust, and fear of the other, combined with a reduced ability to consider theory of mind, is a potent cocktail and is implicated in some of humanity's worst collective behaviours.[66]**

Cultural Neuroscience

Cultural neuroscience is a growing field that bridges culture and biology and demonstrates how different cultural environments can profoundly impact our brain function and the sort of people we become.

In one study, participants' neural responses were shown to mirror their cultural norms.[68] People of American and Japanese origin were shown images of bodies in dominant and submissive poses. The Americans, whose culture encourages assertiveness, scepticism of authority and individual independence, exhibited larger responses in their brain reward centres when viewing figures with dominant poses. In contrast, the Japanese, whose culture leans toward deference, cooperation, and obligation to others, showed similar activity when viewing figures posing in submission.

A similar effect was demonstrated in a study where White and Latino American participants exhibited different brain reward system responses depending on whether they were earning money for themselves or for their families.[69] The latter showed greater neural responses when earning for their family, an outcome generally consistent with Latino cultural norms.[70]

Socioeconomic status has also been shown to influence how individuals think. One study, for example, showed that

---

** A study that gave participants photographs of social groups found that when the extreme outgroups were depicted, their insular cortex and amygdala activated but their prefrontal cortex did not—a pattern consistent with disgust that helps illustrate how outgroups can be perceived as less than human.[66]

working-class Americans exhibit more context-dependent thinking than their white-collar counterparts, a tendency that mirrors collectivists of other countries and likewise appears to correlate at the neural level.[70,71]

Memory function, too, has been shown to recruit different brain regions depending on a person's cultural background. Likewise, cognitive decline and other aspects related to memory appear to be culturally linked.[72]

All of this adds up to indicate that by impacting how our brain physically functions—from its reward system to the brain regions employed—our cultural norms play a significant role in determining our behaviour.

Here, ideas quietly and profoundly change who we become.

Social Morality

Before social animals there was no such thing as 'good' or 'bad' behaviour, there was just behaviour. When a female praying mantis eats a male after mating it is not immoral. The same goes for the male rabbit that kills some rabbit babies, or toads that drown a female while trying to mate. All of these are behaviours without moral relevance.

Cooperation provided humans with such a powerful advantage that we evolved to be dependent on sociality to such an extent that survival outside of a group became improbable.

As moral behaviour, and moral judgement, resulted in more cooperative social environments it became evolutionarily selective. In this, morality did not evolve to maximise our collective happiness but to increase the spread of our genes. The fact that happy people tend to cooperate better, suffer less from illness, and have better personal relationships, is merely a product of this evolutionary force rather than some kind of mythic justice.

All societies create moral conventions, and social norms, that help enable stable cooperation. Essentially, if everyone knows how to behave correctly then it is easier for everyone to avoid transgression, maintain social connections, and cooperate. In humans, as with other social animals, those who violate social codes are punished with actions that stress the transgressor and discourage antisocial behaviour. The mere existence of moral judgement makes social punishment inherent because what people think of us affects our outcomes. If everyone around you thinks that you are a loser who has done disgusting things, it will almost certainly affect your likelihood of gene replication. No matter the scale of your society, or your position in it, being the subject of salacious gossip, suffering from reputational harm, or being ostracised, is deeply uncomfortable.

Prosocial behaviour is generally perceived as morally good and antisocial behaviour as morally bad. However, what we deem to be pro- or antisocial is largely determined by the ideas or values our society holds. Despite there being common themes and even a few universals (cold-blooded murder, for instance), cultural morality takes many forms.

Meaning, Morality, and Socialisation

What a culture determines to be prosocial is linked not just to morality but to our sense of meaning. Indeed, the data suggests the two are co-dependent.

Living without meaning has been shown to be damaging to our health. Those whose lives lack meaning, but otherwise report being happy, suffer from the same gene-expressions as those who suffer from chronic adversity.[73] These gene-expressions are associated with chronic inflammation which contributes to major illnesses like heart disease or cancer. A lack of meaning has been shown to be a factor in depression and suicide and having meaning in life acts as a buffer against suicide for those with depression.[74–76] Just as having a poor diet or never exercising can ruin your health, so too can living a life lacking in meaning.

Acting for others has been found to help give our lives meaning and promote healthy states in mind and body.[77–79] If meaning in life is derived from the things we do for others, it also requires a social component of *what* we contribute and *why* it is prosocial. Thus, we return to the world of ideas and the values they inscribe.

Interestingly, Roy Baumeister, the American Social Psychologist, described one effect of social exclusion as a retreat from meaningful thought.[80] Social exclusion also appears to provoke emotional avoidance and affect our sense of future. This cognitive deconstruction is characterised by lethargy, an altered sense of time, and a failure to delay gratification.[80,81] K. D. Williams, author of *Ostracism, The Power of Silence* suggests that ostracism threatens having a meaningful existence because being ignored symbolises death.[82]

Meaning and Time

Actual time, as counted by clocks, is largely irrelevant to animal biology. Human bodies are, of course, subject to the same laws of thermodynamics as the rest of the universe but what determines our lifespan is not cosmic measurement but the mundane fact of our position on the food chain. Animals with few predators tend to have longer-lasting bodies and slower reproductive cycles than animals that face high chances of predation. *Reproduce quickly before someone eats you.*

Actual time is irrelevant to our gene replication. If it were not, our perception of time might be more accurate; instead, how we experience time—how it *feels*—varies drastically depending on what we are doing and in what circumstances. Time can fly, drag, or stand still. Ten years of routine can seem like three, three weeks of complex events can feel like a year.

In this way, we can imagine two forms of time: one belongs to the world of physics that we can measure in seconds, the other belongs to the world of genes and is measured by the frequency of reproduction. For bacteria that replicate every few minutes, gene-time moves quickly; for animals like the African forest elephant that needs twenty-plus years before achieving fertility, gene-time has a slow beat. The end of time, from a genetic perspective, has nothing to do with the collapse of stars but is simply the end of replication.

Social rejection is thus catastrophic for a species that depends on social interaction as a first step to reproduction. As such, for human genes, social rejection and isolation is catastrophic. Sociality is the continuity of gene-time—existence of sociality is the existence of a future. It makes evolutionary sense, then, that we feel terrible if we find ourselves without a group and that we feel compelled to do *anything*, including swallowing our pride, to keep this from happening.

Living outside of society is not only terrible from a gene-perspective but it is potentially damaging to the shared genes of the entire group. Ostracised people often end up living on the periphery of a community, stealing, causing disruption, wreaking havoc, or seeking revenge.[83,84] It might be that, if an ostracised individual is unable to make amends, that it is evolutionary better if they self-destruct than damage the chances of their genes being replicated by their kin.

For someone trying to survive alone in the world, decreased cognitive ability, loss of executive function, reduced ability to delay gratification, a loss of meaning, increased risk of suicide or general emotional unhinging would surely hurry their demise. Are we programmed to self-destruct in the case of total social ostracization? It would appear so.

To Summarise

Ideas that guide our behaviour have long been beneficial to our survival and such ideological structures reduce the energy required for making decisions on a day-to-day basis. Group identity tells us who to care about and who will care for us. Group thinking teaches us how to get along with others; how to cooperate, how to do business; how to organise property and communal wealth; how to have reproductive relations; and how to hunt, farm or forage.

Humanity has common problems that need to be solved to successfully coexist and these common problems always need an answer of some kind. In many areas it is not possible to have a void in terms of ideas—ideas can be shifted, changed or replaced but they cannot be eliminated. For some things we always have a *how*, the *why* is secondary.

These patterns in social morality across cultures has not gone amiss among anthropologists and cultural psychiatrists. Earlier in this chapter we addressed Jonathan Haidt's idea that human moral judgement is driven first by intuition and only later subject to rationalisation, but this wasn't his only contribution to the field. He also developed a universal moral framework he claimed to be the basis of moral order across all societies.

Haidt's Moral Foundation Theory proposes that there are *"several innate and universally available psychological systems that are the foundations of 'intuitive ethics'."*[85] These areas are: care/harm, fairness/cheating, loyalty/betrayal, authority/subversion, and sanctity/degradation. He posits that every culture worldwide constructs a set of moral principles and these principles are all based upon concerns related to these areas.

Although the structure of these innate psychological systems may be subject to academic criticism, his central theory, at a base level, the shape of cultural morality is driven by emotion is well accepted.

This chapter has covered a lot of ground so, let's try and tie up the threads discussed so far in this section.

- We know that for better or for worse, that the ideas and ideologies of our environment affect how we develop and ultimately who we become.
- Our frontal cortex has evolved to be malleable and allow us to adapt to the ideas we grow up with. These ideas shape how our brains function and this impacts numerous other aspects of who we are including our

    cognitive function, perception of stimulation, perception of disgust, visceral moral judgement, and our moral behaviour.

- From before conception, through adulthood, our environment shapes the expression of our genes and permanently affects who we are and what we become. Our environment is greatly affected by the ideas our society holds meaning their effects can be profound.

- Substantial evidence supports the theory that all of us are imprinted with a sort of base human morality. A common set of moral positions is stamped into our genes and serves to increase the likelihood of reproduction.

- Moral decision-making happens fast and is a product of emotions more than cognition—we feel first, rationalise later. Because of this, moral behaviours learned during our socialisation create visceral prejudices that can be hard to change.

As humans do not exist outside a social environment it is likely that, at their most basic, moral values are a result of *feelings expressed as ideas* which, in turn, coalesce into ideologies.

This process of rationalisation codifies the values defined by our feelings into ideas that provide the foundations of human morality. Such feelings-expressed bias philosophy, drive social reasoning and, after being filtered through power structures and cultural traditions, create the cultural morals of our time.

At their most simple, these emotionally driven moral values are simple ideas: behaviour x is better than behaviour y. This posits a value, with an acknowledgement of a future affected by the behaviour. When emotions lead to moral values, and when many emotions are innate, which *values* are innately human? Put otherwise, which emotions provide the ideas that form the foundation for human morality?

If we can answer this question, we can better understand the nature of humanity and we can make better decisions for our social environments—be they personal, professional, or societal.

CHAPTER 7

INNATE IDEAS

Not all behaviours need to be taught. Some exert themselves across cultures, throughout ages, and appear during childhood regardless of training or social interaction. These behaviours are hardwired into the human brain because they are (generally) instrumental to gene replication and thus the survival of our species. Some innate behaviours communicate values, which therefore can also be considered innate. Which behaviours are innate, and which of these lead to innate values, will be the subject of this chapter.

Questions about human nature *are really* questions about human moral nature. We all know we're bipedal, large-brained animals that communicate using language (among other basic, biological facts). What we're after when addressing the subject of our nature is not a physiological description, but an explanation of why we act the way we do.

Furthermore, any conversation about human moral nature is really about *moral leaning*. We know we are neither entirely selfish nor entirely altruistic, neither wholly cruel nor wholly kind. We're not looking for absolutes but instead for insight into how our biology biases our moral disposition. Is human nature more altruistic than selfish? Are we generally nicer than we are horrible? In which way do we lean?

Another thing to note is that moral judgement *is* value judgement. To deem a behaviour immoral is to say a different behaviour would have been better. Chapter 4 may have served to establish that morality has its origins in emotion, but this doesn't mean that there's no such thing as moral thought. The emotions that drive moral decision-making provoke value judgments that, over time, are shared, rationalised, combined with traditions, and mixed with politics to form cultural moral codes.

If we want to understand human nature, or our *moral leanings*, then, we need to understand which moral values derive from innate human emotions, behaviours, or preferences.

The argument for the existence of innate emotions and, by extension, *innate ideas* has three parts:

1. Behaviour Communicates Values

"Actions speak louder than words."
"You are what you do."
"Talk is cheap."
These and numerous other related proverbs exist because it's our behaviour, not our words, that demonstrate our values.

You can't call yourself an ardent environmentalist and take twenty long-haul flights a year. You can't claim to be a dedicated spouse while cheating on your partner. You can't say one thing, do another, and expect your words to carry value.

And yet communication requires a receiver and so *what* our behaviour communicates also depends on how it is interpreted.

If you were to watch me pick up trash every time we walked in the forest, for instance, you might think I believe that *"the forest is better without trash,"* or that *"trash is bad for the environment."* If you do not understand what trash is, however, you might think that I collect it because "trash is valuable."

Despite it being obvious for most people, without *first* understanding that certain objects are considered worthless, or being exposed to ideas of environmentalism, the ideas my trash-collecting behaviour communicates are ambiguous because the correct interpretation depends on understanding other pre-existing ideas. This is true of many behaviours—but it is not true of all behaviour.

Some behavioural tendencies are *innate*, hard-wired into our brains, and need no contextualisation to be understood. Fairness serves as an example.

If we're sitting at a table and I object to an unfair distribution of food you're not only likely to conclude that I believe "*fair food distribution is better than unfair food distribution*" or that "*fairness is better than unfairness*" but you'll probably agree. You don't need to know anything about me, or the meal, to grasp the value my behaviour communicates because a predisposition toward fairness is a biologically driven, universal human trait—and this fact tells us a lot about who we are.[86]

2. Some Values are Felt and Understood Simultaneously

The James Webb telescope required a lot of people to believe that installing a fancy scientific instrument a million miles into space was a worthwhile use of ten billion dollars. There's nothing obvious or intuitive about the values that justify this vast use of resources, so how did it happen? Why didn't people protest? Why do we collectively believe that exploring the cosmos is a worthwhile pursuit even if it costs outrageous amounts of money that could be spent relieving human suffering?

Chapter 2 was all about how if abstract ideas are to stick, they need to be supported by a structure of sub-ideas that connect the *abstract* to the *emotional*. While scientific enquiry may be anything but abstract, a similar thing is going on here. Most people are not scientists. It would take a very long time for an astrophysicist to explain to me, or any other average Joe, why it is worth spending heaps of taxpayer money to gaze upon distant galaxies when we live in a world riddled with problems.

Indeed, even if we *could* grasp the sophisticated explanation, it probably wouldn't sway us. After all, it's not scientific understanding that convinces me, you, or much of the scientific community, for that matter, of the value of science. Instead, it is a centuries-old edifice of ideas that have transformed science into a *noble pursuit*. We care about scientific discovery because it has become synonymous with human advancement, and this is a sentimental subject. This was not always the case, however.

Galileo, who was committed to house arrest for insisting that the Earth orbits the Sun, for instance, did not benefit from the *feeling* that improving scientific understanding is paramount to improving humanity. Quite the opposite, in fact. It took hundreds of years to build up the value of science to the point that spending billions on the James Webb telescope did not elicit public backlash.

For the James Webb telescope, the ideological gap between the *abstract* and the *emotional* is significant and requires a strong web of sub-ideas to support it. Some ideas require no such web at all, and it is these ideas that we refer to as *innate*.

Ideas like that of fairness are triggered, felt, and understood simultaneously. The distance between *the abstract* and *the emotional* is practically non-existent. This simultaneous *feeling and knowing*, without requiring other ideas, is a characteristic of these innate ideas.

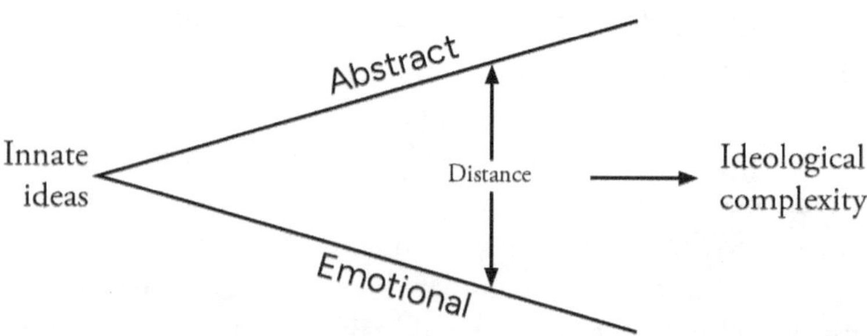

3. Not All Innate Behaviour Leads to Innate Values

Humans have many innate behaviours but not all of them communicate a specific value or simple idea. Our innate preference for fairness, for example communicates the idea that "*fairness is better than unfairness.*" The future will be better if people are treated fairly. Fairness as a human value is straightforward and stable even if what we call fair varies by culture.

This is not the case for other innate behaviours. Fear, for example, communicates no innate value. This would depend on the stimuli. Fear of sickness, fear of a grizzly bear, fearing for a character in a movie, and the fear of losing your job all communicate different values depending on the circumstance. It could be "bears are dangerous" or "sickness is bad" or "financial insecurity is scary". *What* fear communicates is dependent on the circumstances and therefore does lead to a consistent value.

Of course, we may argue that fear communicates that "*scary things are worse that non-scary things*" and, it's true, we have innate predisposition to fear certain things—like snakes and spiders—but even then, the idea that "*no snake is better than snake*" is hardly a morally relevant statement.

What we are demonstrating here is that the ideological output of many *reactive* instincts like fear, anger, or surprise, are largely dependent on the input and therefore cannot posit a stable value that can be considered innate.

To summarise, for an innate behaviour to deliver an *innate value*, the behaviour must be:
- Innate: Not acquired through learning, exhibited in normal development and, at least partially, genetically controlled.
- The values the behaviour communicates must not be ambiguous—it should communicate the same value regardless of triggering stimuli.
- The behaviour must not be a response to, or depend on, pre-existing value structures.

Which Innate Behaviours Imply Innate Values?

Some of our innate behaviours, like moving our bodies, counting, making mental maps of territory, or feeling fear when we encounter, say, a bear, derive from instinct and reflex. Others are emotionally or socially orientated, like monitoring our well-being, developing a concept of self, engaging in senses of justice and kinship, and articulating norms related to love and sex.[87]

In this work we will define 'innate' or 'instinctive' behaviours as those which are inborn and do not require learning or prior experience—taking the position of the philosopher Edouard Machery—who sees it that *"a trait must be a product of evolution rather than say social learning or enculturation."*[88,89]

Instinctive behaviours in humans are complex. They are a product of both genetic disposition and learned behaviour and can be enhanced or diminished by the ideas of our cultural environment. Because of this, human behaviour is generally a result of both innate (nature) and learned behaviour (nurture).

Beyond this broad categorisation, innate human behaviour can be characterised as either (1) Reflexive, (2) Instinctive Reactive, or (3) Instinctive Reactive *and* Proactive.

1. Reflexive

Reflexive behaviours respond to biological processes like thirst or hunger. The actions that result don't require brain activity but instead are transmitted through the body via a neural pathway known as the reflex arc. Cognitive thought isn't involved and so neither are value judgements.

2. Instinctive Reactive

Here, we're talking about behaviours driven by emotions like anger, disgust, fear, sadness, or surprise. A wide range of stimuli trigger these feelings and the actions they provoke involve emotion and cognition but that doesn't mean they deliver a stable value.

Earlier we talked about how disgust, for instance, can have a strong moral component but generally only when we hold pre-existing ideas that determine what behaviours are disgusting. Disgust in its gustatory form—felt if we smell rancid food— doesn't express a moral value any more than when we feel thirsty.

3. Instinctive Reactive and Proactive

These are the only instincts that drive innate values and there's not a lot of them.

Reactive *and* proactive instincts are reflexive in that they occur automatically and they're proactive in that they drive further action. Think sex. When we see something sexy, we don't just feel sexual desire, but we're driven to *act* (even if we resist). The same is true of empathy, fairness, cooperation, and aggression. And that's it.

These innate responses drive complex actions that, in turn, tell us volumes about the foundations of human moral behaviour. Parsing how different instinctive *reactive and proactive* behaviours contribute to our sense of right and wrong is a thorny matter, though, which means we need to take a closer look.

Cooperation

Our big human brain, to which we owe our success as a species, ended up that way thanks to our need for cooperation. We're not strong and we're not fast so our survival depended on our ability to band together which, in turn, required us to have the brain power to interpret complex social signals and communicate complex needs.

As an increasingly complex social environment led to larger and slower maturing brains, it increased the time that human infants depended on parental care. High levels of attention required for childcare meant cooperative behaviour became more selective, leading to groups with greater social support and bonding abilities. This feedback cycle of cooperative fitness meant that the selfish genes of our evolutionary history were effectively bred out because individual success depended on the ability to transcend selfishness.[25]

We need cooperation as much we need food or water, and this fact is imprinted on our genes and expressed through our body.

In fact, it has been shown by Professor Kay Tye of the Salk Institute for Biological Studies that human beings are equipped with a *social homeostasis* system that regulates internal conditions to ensure survival. This pushes social needs into a similar category as our needs for food, warmth, or water. Tye's research team found that we have neurological mechanisms that monitor the quantity and quality of our social interactions, compare these to a base-line, and motivate us to seek social contact.[90]

This preference for cooperation is displayed early in life. Michael Tomasello of the Max Planck Institute believes that we have an inborn urge to help. He makes the case that cooperation is innate in his 2009 book *Why We Cooperate* where he cites his findings that twelve-month-old babies will try to help adults find something they seem to have lost and that slightly older infants prefer helpful characters to 'bad guys' in stories.

In his book *Loneliness* (2008), social neuroscientist John Cacioppo explains that looking deeply at the invisible forces that link one human being to another helps us see something profound:

> *Our brains and bodies are designed to function in aggregates, not in isolation. That is the essence of an obligatorily gregarious species. The attempt to function in denial of our need for others, whether that need is great or small in any given individual, violates our design specifications.*[25]

Loneliness is an evolutionary gift that we carry in our bodies. We *feel* the pain of social separation because we need one another for survival. And pain, whenever present, pushes us to act—we are naturally inclined to reach out to loved ones, mend bonds, and make connections.

When we cannot remedy social pain, our health suffers. The effect of social isolation is comparable to that of high blood pressure, obesity, or smoking.[91] Loneliness predicts the progression of Alzheimers disease and has the power to alter DNA transcription in our immune system cells.[92,93]

Interestingly and importantly, simply *having* social interaction is not enough to avoid loneliness. Interactions must be *meaningful* and meaningful social interactions are *cooperative* by nature.[94]

Cacioppo talks about research conducted in the 1990s where his team quickly realised that "*it was an individual's perceptions of the social situation that mattered most.*" They found that the solution to loneliness had little to do with the *quantity* of interaction but the *quality* of it: to be beneficial, relationships must be perceived as *"meaningful and satisfying"* for those involved. Loneliness is therefore not caused by a lack of social interaction, but a lack of social interaction that we perceive as meaningful. And, this is why it is possible for people to feel lonely despite being surrounded by people.

An important study in 2020 by Eden Litt, a researcher at Meta, aimed at understanding what makes a social interaction meaningful, found that we depend on interactions that have an emotional, informational, or tangible impact on us or the people in our lives.[94]

In Litt's words, *"The single factor that most distinguished meaningful interactions from non-meaningful ones was that meaningful interactions had an impact that respondents felt went beyond the interaction itself to enhance their lives, the lives of their interaction partners, or their relationships, with emotional, informational, or tangible impact."*

The study found that *emotional impacts* were those that might lead to emotions of empathy, love, sadness or authenticity which people felt helped change their relationship or made them feel different. *Tangible impacts* were those that helped others, supporting those in need or being a recipient of help. *Informational impacts* could be based on sharing advice, teaching, advising, or instructing people, adding new information or discussing new topics. What do all these have in common?

They are cooperative in nature—meaningful social interaction is cooperative social interaction.

Non-meaningful interactions, in contrast, were demonstrated to be those lacking in impact and were described using phrases like *"no meaning," "trivial," "small talk," "nothing to offer," "not genuine," "only for time pass," and "a waste of time."* In short, beyond following social conventions, these conversations are passive—no one is adding real value.

Cooperation is also entwined with trust, which, at its most basic, is a state absent of the fear of non-cooperation. The breaking of the long-held trust of a close friend or partner is far worse than that of a stranger because the future possibility of cooperation with that person is called into doubt. It is less the event that profoundly disturbs us and more the loss of a cooperative partner—something important for our life and health.[95] Socially, a state of non-cooperation, or of uncertain cooperation, is a state of tension and this stress drives us to resolve our issues and restore the evolutionary-beneficial state of cooperation.

Non-cooperation feels less like a neutral act of *not acting with us* but something far more negative. Although non-cooperation might *technically* be neutral it feels otherwise because cooperation is the natural state and anything less gives rise to negative feelings. We are hypersensitive to non-cooperation. If someone we know walks past us without saying hello, if people refuse to help when asked, or if someone does not reply to our messages, we are likely to think negatively of them. As the ancient adage goes: "if you are not with us, you're against us."[96]

As innate a drive and as vital a need as it may be, cooperation also has a darker side. Were it not for our urge to cooperate and share resources within a social group, we would have no use for a concept of 'the other.'[97,98] We want to cooperate, yes, but we also want to know who is likely to cooperate back. Hence, we've developed myriad social markers to show one another, "Hey, I'm just like you." This includes clothes, grooming habits, routines, and an endless list of other external markers. We're drawn to those who *look* like members of our community, and out of a self-protective urge, we're compelled to be wary of those who don't. This explains our desire for visual conformity through the use of uniforms and dress codes when high levels of cooperation required. Business suits, army fatigues, religious garb, and fashion trends all say, *"you can cooperate with me; we have common values."*

To sum this section up, cooperation is a human instinct and a base-level homeostatic need that our bodies treat similarly to hunger or staying warm. We need cooperative interaction with others and when we don't, we are at risk of loneliness, which is a danger to our mental and physical health. This innate reactive and proactive impulse to cooperate nourishes the value that *"cooperation is better than non-cooperation"* and this acts as a keystone of human moral decision-making.

Many of our greatest moral accomplishments derive directly from this instinct as do many of our greatest moral failings and how we distinguish the latter from the former is not only a matter of culture but also of self-knowledge—a topic which we'll have a lot more to say about later.

Fairness

Storytellers have long understood the grip that unfairness holds on our imaginations. Cinderella was enslaved by her own family. Harry Potter was forced to live in a closet under the stairs. E.T. was abandoned on an alien planet after the rest of his species were frightened into fleeing. All of these literary protagonists have earned a perennial place in our hearts thanks to their ability to overcome the unfairness of their situation.

We are deeply moved by unfairness because, like cooperation, a preference for fair treatment is written into our genes. [99] According to Joseph Henrich, a professor of evolutionary biology at Harvard University, this is because without the principle of fairness, humans would never have made the transition from family groups to complex societies—and, as we know, we depend on society for our survival.[100]

Children as young as two demonstrate a preference for fairness and even infants show a general predisposition toward altruism.[101,102] Experiments by psychologist Katherine McAuliffe, for instance, show that young children reject disadvantageous offers and, after the age of eight, will intuitively refuse an offer that is advantageous for them such that their partner gets as much as they do. The researchers conclude that the rejection of 'advantageous inequality' is an inherently social response.

Further support for the idea that humans exhibit an inherent preference for fairness comes from a study by the psychologist Golnaz Tabibnia and her team. Their idea was to take two people and give money to one (Person A) but not the other (Person B). *Person A* could then split the money any way they wanted and all *Person B* could do was accept or decline. If accepted, great; if not, neither person would get anything. While it might make sense for Person B to be pleased by any offer—some free money is better than no free money—this was not the case. Brain scans showed that regions associated with negative feelings like moral disgust lit up in the receiving participant when presented with a stingy offer while those associated with reward were activated when an offer was fair. These responses, which were fast and automatic, show that our brains find selfish behaviour emotionally unpleasant and fair behaviour innately rewarding.[103]

To add to this, Professor Yun Wang of Beijing University conducted a 2019 study that used a version of the same game above to establish a genetic link to the exhibited brain activity. Identical twins were set to play while observed by fMRI scanners and the results suggested that genetics contribute substantially (24% to 35%) to the rejection rate of unfair proposals. This was the first time anyone had found evidence that our brain is hardwired to detect unfairness. And not only that: Wang's findings further suggest that we have an in-built desire to punish others for unfairness even if doing so comes at a personal cost. In

Wang's words: *"the neural basis underlying this fairness intuition is under genetic control."*[104]

Lixing Sun, a distinguished professor of behaviour and evolution at Central Washington University describes fairness as, *"a human instinct that underpins a large and varied spectrum of our actions. It is not, as is traditionally supposed, a purely ideological issue; it is emotion and behavior rooted in our DNA."*[105] We are hard-wired not only to detect inequity, but also to control immediate desires and appreciate the virtue of following rules. We derive emotional rewards from acting in fairness and witnessing the punishment of those who don't. [106]

The science strongly leans toward a genetic basis for fairness. This innate preference, hardwired into our brains, visible across cultures and ages, consistently communicates that *"fairness is better than unfairness."* Just as *"cooperation is better than non-cooperation,"* it too plays a pivotal role in tuning our moral compass.

Aggression

Aggression, like fairness and cooperation, belongs to the short list of innate human reactive and proactive behaviours but it operates a little differently.

There's no doubt that human beings are aggressive. Our long history of war, genocide, and slavery speaks pretty loudly. Aggression is a tricky subject, however.

The range of what counts as aggression is huge. Mean rumours are aggressive and so is murder. We can posture aggressively, be passive-aggressive, engage in purely ritual aggression, we can be contemptuous or rude, and we can use banal bureaucratic systems to inflict pain on others and claim it impersonal. Aggression can be lauded or punished. Killing people can win you a medal or land you in prison. It can be constructive—say, by driving competition or motivating self-defence—and it can be tragically and inexcusably destructive.

Heaps of science tells us that aggression is at least partially genetically determined.[107] Aggressive children are more aggressive when they are adults. Aggression can be bred into animals by mating aggressive offspring. Identical twins are more similar in their aggressive traits and criminal records than fraternal twins.[108–111]

Our taste for violence runs deep and it's been with us for a long time. According to Joshua Green, a Professor of Psychology at Harvard University, our propensity for aggression predates our development of complex reasoning:

> *Given that personal violence is evolutionarily ancient, predating our recently evolved human capacities for complex abstract reasoning, it should come as no surprise if we have innate responses to personal violence that are powerful but rather primitive. That is, we might expect humans to have negative emotional responses to certain basic forms of interpersonal violence, where these responses evolved as a means of regulating the behavior of creatures who are capable of intentionally harming one another, but whose survival depends on cooperation and individual restraint.* [112]

We know we're innately aggressive. The morally important question to ask is just how aggressive are we? Are we a highly aggressive species, or is our propensity for violence actually fairly low?

Debates have raged around human aggression (ironic, yes) for a long time. Sigmund Freud thought that aggression was an instinctive human drive; Konrad Lorenz believed that aggression was an instinct in need of an outlet; Richard Wrangham, author of *Demonic Males* (1996), argued that we're hardly better than chimpanzees—citing intragroup violence, violence against females, infanticide, and murderous raids on outside groups, as examples of mutual genetic heritage.

These speculations had wide-ranging consequences for political thought and policy but what these thinkers didn't know is that human aggression is bimodal: it can be either *proactive* or *reactive*.[113,114] Compared to other primates, human beings exhibit a relatively low propensity for reactive aggression and a high propensity for proactive aggression.[115] Neurologically, these two forms of aggression have little to do with one another—although they often overlap, they operate via different neural pathways meaning they are effectively two different behaviours.[116–119]

Reactive aggression is associated with anger, an increase in emotional arousal and a failure to regulate stress hormones.[120,121] It's the kind of aggression you might expect from a mother bear protecting her cubs or chimpanzees protecting their territory.

Proactive aggression (the kind humans excel at), on the other hand, involves planning, is not necessarily accompanied by high emotional arousal, and aims for a cost-efficient achievement of the aggressor's goals.[122–124] It's of the kind that leads to bullying, revenge, and all acts of war.

For humans, reactive aggression is ultimately costly, fractious, and harms the ability for humans to cooperate in a group and so it is rarely our first port of call. If this was not the case then, with any slight, hurt, or disagreement, we would instinctively react aggressively which would, naturally, beget more aggression and an escalation in conflict. Our society would be based on aggressive confrontation, with the biggest and strongest holding all the power—not unlike our Chimpanzee relatives—and we would look like a different animal all together. Indeed, it is considered that it was the human requirement for higher levels of social tolerance and cooperation that drove us to become a less reactively aggressive species.[125,126]

"Aggression is better than non-aggression" is not an innately held human value. Violence is only justified in a very narrow, select set of circumstances and these are determined by culture, not instinct. The likelihood of an aggressive reaction generally depends on the circumstances, but *which* circumstances trigger

reactive aggression are largely dependent on cultural ideas of permitted—or expected—aggression in a given situation.

In one culture, unknowingly flirting with someone's partner could justify a violent reaction whereas, in another, parties may find it flattering or amusing. Such variations between social groups are dependent on pre-existing ideas for what constitutes reasonable levels of reactive aggression, further diminishing the case that *reactive aggression* speaks for human moral nature.

The fact that humans have a high propensity for *proactive aggression* is not entirely surprising. Humans are extremely good at working together in acts of aggression. But does the human propensity to be proactively aggressive communicate that *"aggression is better than non-aggression"*?

Again, this cannot be the case because, to be proactively aggressive, you need to base your *calculated* aggressive actions on existing ideas. Things like: "they insulted our honour" (honour culture), "they stole our land" (ideas of property rights), "their god is wrong" (theism), "their way of life is a threat to ours" (ideas of the right way to live) and so on. Proactive aggression is *reasoned*.

Proactive aggression is far more common but no more innate. It's hard, even impossible, to think of a human group or society that doesn't participate in some form of premeditated violence but this doesn't mean we instinctually believe that *"proactive aggression is better than non-aggression."* Culture, again, drives proactive aggression.

The journey toward committing a *proactively aggressive* act, from interpretation of the stimuli to the act itself, requires a range of pre-existing ideas that do not materialise without other value-based presuppositions. Aggression is instinctual but its expression is cultural and thus it forms no part of our innate moral compass.

Sex & Death

Sexual desire is another tricky case. We're driven by sex. We see each other as sexy. We fantasise about sex. Simple shapes can trigger a sexual urge. Even smells can turn us on. The drive to reproduce is as fundamental as drives come and yet sex isn't *just* about keeping humanity going—at least not in the simple 'make more children' sense. We have sex for complex reasons and we build complex value sets around the act but this does not mean sexual desire informs basic human morality in the same ways that fairness and cooperation do.

"Reproducing is better than not reproducing" is less a value and more a basic requirement for the continuation of our (or any) species. We may build moral codes around sex but these are rooted in the prosocial as much as the procreative benefits of the act (and thus, like aggression, depend on other value-based presuppositions). Most of the sex we humans have does not result in a fertilised egg (nor is it intended to). Despite organised religion leveraging every imaginable threat (including eternal suffering) to dissuade us from doing so, we persist in having all kinds of sex because we need it not just to make babies but to reinforce social bonds, build intimacy, and maintain our physical and mental health.

The evolutionary paradox of same-sex sexual attraction is a case in point. We now know that genes influence human sexual preferences.[127,128] The influence does not come from a single 'gay gene,' however, but from lots of genes that all have a small cumulative (or polymorphic) effect that determines someone's likelihood of having same-sex sexual attraction. This genetic link is backed up by the fact that, throughout cultures, 2% to 10% of people declare having same-sex relations, regardless of how difficult or dangerous acting on those desires may be. The observation of homosexual behaviour in hundreds of different species, has made it clear that the homosexual behaviour is natural and wholly unremarkable on a biological level.

On the face of it, this implies an apparent evolutionary paradox as homosexual behaviour should have a negative effect on natural selection and therefore the trait should have been eliminated. The fact that it hasn't is strong evidence in support of the existence of non-reproductive evolutionary benefits of sexual desire.

Andrew Barron, a professor of biological sciences, argues that both homosexual and heterosexual sex favour prosocial behaviour. In his words:

> *"Same sex sexual attraction (SSSA) evolved as just one of a suite of traits responding to strong selection for ease of social integration or prosocial behavior. The prosocial benefits of SSSA would include increasing of in-group tolerance and reducing of aggression, improve social affiliation, social integration, social mobility and create and maintain same-sex social bonds – all of which could lead to greater reproductive success. A strong driver of recent human behavioral evolution has been selection for reduced reactive aggression, increased social affiliation, social communication, and ease of social integration."*[129]

The bonobo ape, our closest human relation (along with chimpanzees), evolved to use sexual behaviour as a pro-social activity leading to more sex, sex with more partners and more gay sex. In primates, homosexual behaviour has a role in appeasement, reinforcing social structures, stress reduction, improving social tolerance, play and barter. Interestingly, sex helps create and reinforce pair bonds in all studied social mammals.

Another study that examined thousands of mammalian species concluded that same-sex sexual behaviour evolved when animals started living in social groups. Although this behaviour does not produce offspring it provides other advantages such as smoothing over conflicts and helping establish and maintain positive social relationships.[130]

Humans are a hyper-social species, and our prosocial nature is part-and-parcel of the human success story. Thus, traits that enable better social integration or that provide social advantage are likely to have a selective advantage. It's always hard to build evolutionary theories that say 'this trait' is because of 'x evolutionary reason' but, where we know that sexual desire leads not only to reproduction but also to intimacy and bonding, it makes sense to understand sex between human beings as both for reproduction and social bonding.

The dual reproductive and social function of human sexual desire might imply the innate value that "*intimacy is better than no intimacy*" and yet this is more a special case of "*cooperation is better than non-cooperation*" than a distinct innate value. Sex supports cooperation, mitigates aggression, and nurtures the final reactive and proactive behaviour we'll discuss in this section: empathy. This fact points to the idea that while sexual desire clearly affects our social values, it is perhaps more of a persistent influence across the human experience than a basis for morality.

In terms of death; there is nothing like dying to throw a stick into the spokes of gene-time so humans, like most other animals, have an instinct for self-preservation—one that rides on unique brain circuits—operating non-consciously and distinct from those for feelings of fear and anxiety.[131,132] A universal preference for living clearly communicates that *life is valuable*—a value that holds a central position in human moral codes ancient and modern. This is not surprising, but it still provides a base-level presupposition for human moral leanings.

Despite our avoidance of mortal danger, when push comes to shove, evolutionary forces dictate that reproduction takes precedence. The fact that some scorpions allow themselves to be eaten by their offspring, that female octopuses starve themselves to death to care for their eggs, and that salmon take a one-way journey to their breeding grounds, all demonstrate that, although in normal circumstances, *living is better than dying*, reproduction—the extension of gene-time—comes first.

In this, humans are no different. Many parents would be willing to sacrifice themselves for the lives of their children or would certainly risk everything to protect them. Soldiers risk life and limb to fight in wars to protect their kin—or for those with whom they share the pseudo-kinship of cultural-identity.

Love trumps death.

Empathy

Empathy is our ability to sense the emotional states of others and imagine what they are feeling. Like every other *reactive and proactive* behaviour we've discussed in this section, it is hardcoded into our genes because we need it to survive. Empathy plays the essential social role of allowing us to understand and thus better connect with other people.[133]

When we think of empathy we generally think of *empathic concern*, but empathy also includes *emotional empathy* (allowing us to catch others' feelings and feel other people's suffering), *somatic empathy* involving physical reactions (for example, we may flush red when we see another person feeling embarrassed), and *cognitive empathy* (understanding other people's mental states and what they may be thinking.)

Empathy has been found to be a genetically hardwired trait.[134] Research demonstrates that affective empathy is between 52 and 57% heritable while genetic variances of cognitive empathy are smaller and observable in only 27% of people.[135]* This tells us

---

* Heritability is a statistical measure that quantifies the extent to which genetic variation contributes to individual differences in a trait or phenotype, such as height, intelligence, or personality. Heritability is typically expressed as a percentage, ranging from 0% to 100%, which reflects the proportion of variance in a trait that can be attributed to genetic factors.

A heritability percentage of 0% indicates that the trait is entirely due to environmental factors, such as upbringing, culture, or education. A heritability percentage of 100% suggests that the trait is entirely determined by genetic factors, and environmental influences have no effect. However, in reality, most traits are influenced by both genetic and environmental factors, so heritability percentages typically fall somewhere between 0% and 100%.

It's important to note that heritability percentages apply only to the population under study and not to individual people. A heritability percentage cannot be used to predict how much of a particular trait a specific individual has inherited

that empathy is genetically controlled and that our environment has a massive impact on our capacity for empathy.

Research has shown unique brain activity in regions of the brain associated with positive emotions when mothers look at pictures of their babies, corresponding to self-reported feelings of compassionate love[136] and, in other experiments, similar brain areas were shown to activate when subjects contemplated harm being done to others.[137] Together, these studies suggest that empathy is, indeed, an innate response. Joshua Greene, an author of one of these studies, writes that the data strongly suggests that these empathetic emotional responses *"have an influence on and are not merely incidental to moral judgment."*

Empathy drives the innate human value that *"caring is better than not caring"*—which, like the values driven by cooperation and fairness, *does* inform our innate moral disposition—but what it teaches us about human behaviour extends far beyond its foundational nature.

In comparison to other primates, humans are hyperempathetic. Empathy is responsible for many of our greatest feats of caring but, likewise, is the cause of many of humanity's greatest moral failings.

Empathy is a tremendous force and is worth pausing to talk about.

Humans communicate in all kinds of ways: words, tones, body language, cries, laughter, facial expressions, etc. and we use all of these to measure other people's state of well-being and to communicate our own – what we can feel about someone's condition from these cues is driven by empathy. Empathy is a whole-body system and, in the words of Franz De Wall, *"is an*

---

from their parents. It's also worth emphasising that heritability percentages are not fixed and can vary across different populations, environments, and time periods. Additionally, heritability estimates can be influenced by various methodological and conceptual issues, and the interpretation of heritability should be done with caution.

automated response over which we have limited control." We can't help but feel for others and science shows that the experience of acting in response motivates us to more of the same.

Acting out of empathy triggers the same neural networks that are triggered by the gratification of personal desire. Helping others feels as good to us as doing something for ourselves. Neuroscientists James Rilling and Gregory Berns propose that this positively reinforces reciprocal altruism and motivates people to *"resist the temptation to selfishly accept but not reciprocate favors."*[138] Empathy is rewarding and compassionate acts have been found to create a 'helper's high,' a psychological state that has been associated with better health and longer lifetimes.[139]

We don't just intuitively believe that *"caring is better than not caring,"* we feel it. This inclines us to treat others with compassion, which is a beautiful feature of humanity, yes, but unfortunately the results aren't always positive.

Paul Bloom, a Professor of Psychology at Yale, claims that we should pay more attention to the entire spectrum of effects that empathy can have on humans and society. Bloom believes that although in general, there is nothing wrong with empathy, when it is used as a guide for moral judgment and behaviour it becomes problematic[140]. He explains that empathy is linked to the part of the brain that helps us imagine other people's pain and that the brain has a neurological response when we see other people suffer.

We need to witness another person's pain to experience the sort of neurological response that drives us to compassion. The problem with this is that it makes us concentrate on the person and not the broader picture. For instance, people will donate to individual causes that they can relate to but are less likely to do so for issues with which they can't identify.

In the words of the economist Thomas Schelling:

"Let a six-year-old girl with brown hair need thousands of dollars for an operation that will prolong her life until Christmas, and the post office will be swamped with

nickels and dimes to save her. But let it be reported that without a sales tax the hospital facilities of Massachusetts will deteriorate and cause a barely perceptible increase in preventable deaths — not many will drop a tear or reach for their checkbooks."[141]

Empathy can also push us into conflict with moral norms based in reason. We *feel* empathy more than we *think* it and so we're capable of, say, overlooking the importance of vaccines from a public health perspective because we've heard heart-breaking news about a single child who became ill due to a faulty vaccine, or a bad reaction.

Large, systemic problems didn't exist when we lived in small groups which is to say the majority of human history. We saw most of the people in our community on a daily basis. Suffering, where it existed, was always near and in these contexts, human empathy served us well. In today's sprawling, complex societies, suffering is hidden from those in a position to help. This modern reality curtails empathy as a positive force and requires us to better learn to use reason and moral principles.

That's not it, though.

Empathy is terrible at driving compassion for those outside our social group. Propaganda aimed at dehumanising and justifying cruelty to those outside of our *definition of group* works wonders on humans because we are programmed to only feel for those we see as like us.[142] And, notably, this is exacerbated if we feel unsafe—research shows that we're even less likely to feel empathy for group outsiders when we feel anxiety.[143]

War is a case in point. The immense catalogue of cultural events dedicated to victims of war demonstrates that we feel profound empathy for our own fallen and yet we observe in ourselves, and in cultural rhetoric, complete indifference (and sometimes even joy) toward the suffering of an enemy.

Imagine a course. We'll call it Genocide 101:

Identify a group of people. Make the case that they are not 'us' by focusing on, or imagining, differences. Associate them with something disgusting, or better yet, *morally* disgusting. Blame them for society's problems. Create an environment of fear with them at the centre and voilà! You have created the conditions that can mute empathic responses, opening the door for the justification, and acceptance of, extreme prejudice against the target group.

The fact that our empathetic neural system is less effective at considering outsiders has played a significant part in humanity's most shameful acts. Violence against minorities of all types occurs because we're bad at empathising with anyone who exists outside of our narrow ideas of belonging. The issue isn't with empathy itself, however, but with our ability to create the ideological conditions for its absence.

In addressing empathy's issues, the essayist Leslie Jamison argues that empathy should not be seen as an end in itself but should be seen as a catalyst to *make right* the pain that has prompted it. She writes, *"Empathy should not be confused with advocacy, but acts of witnessing and listening and feeling do carry meaning. And these efforts can lead to better care by providing not only an emotional impetus but also an understanding of what kinds of care might be useful."*[144]

Empathy is valuable because it drives a universal instinct that expresses a general preference for caring. *"Caring is better than not caring"* is an idea we all innately hold, and which directs our moral compass. This does not mean it should determine our moral principles, however—or at least not entirely. Our large, complex societies create moral problems empathy cannot be counted on to notice, much less address, which is why reasoned policy-making is, perhaps more vital now than ever.

In summary

Some of the ideas we hold are written into our biology.* Millennia of genetic coding has made certain behaviours innate to human beings and a small subclass of these behaviours drive innate values that shape our moral disposition. These ideas are simultaneously felt and understood and thus come as naturally to us as using our opposable thumbs or walking on two feet.

INSTINCT	VALUE
Fairness	*Fairness is better than unfairness*
Empathy	*Caring is better than not caring*
Cooperation	*Cooperation is better than non-cooperation*

These genetically determined values have been foundational for the success of our species and form the underlying basis for all human morality.** Due to their emotive origins, these ideas

---

* Interestingly, the idea that an idea can be innate is not necessarily easy to swallow. According to Professor Iris Berent that is not unusual. Her recent study demonstrated that although we can accept that we have many innate characteristics, for example emotions, we assume that ideas must be learned and so it seems to be counter intuitive for us to think of ideas as being innate.[145]

** This work is supportive of social intuitivist theories of Haidt's Moral Foundations Theory but considers fewer qualifying 'foundations' due to their requirement of ideological presuppositions. Some of Haidt's moral foundations fit within this framework, especially those related to care/harm, fairness/cheating. Others, such as sanctity, loyalty, and authority are not supported within this framework because they are either functional subsets of cooperation (loyalty and authority) or are driven by culture and therefore have no stable ideological output (sanctity).

Loyalty enhances your reputation as a reliable and trustworthy cooperator. Authority—deference to or subversion from—is practical—as different people have different domains of expertise; we constantly shift social hierarchies' depending on individual competencies while subversion is likely to be instinctive in the case of unfairness.[146]

If we take the view that that which is sacred is what brings people together—and enables cooperation—then sanctity too is a cooperative tool and, at the very least, requires various ideological presuppositions to determine what is

could be held in common understanding long before language sophisticated enough to rationalise or debate morality arrived. It was upon the basis of these ideas that our species—the abstract thinking, pattern making, hyperempathetic, hyper-cooperative, Homo sapiens—was founded and upon which we have found vast success.

Of course, here we're not talking about individual behaviour but about the moral bias of an entire group. Generally, we prefer to care, prefer things to be fair, and prefer to cooperate—and across history this is reflected in how we act and treat one another. Just as a casino holds a small edge over its players, our genes hold sway over our societies and so our moral bias, like the house, eventually always wins.

sacred and why. In general, this supports Oliver Scott Curry's 'Morality as Cooperation' theory but suggests that although cooperation is a cornerstone of morality, it does not explain morality in totality.[147]

As this work describes an ideological *bias*, it supports, and potentially expands on "The Modest Evolutionary Explanatory Thesis" whereby *"evolutionary forces may adequately explain certain capacities and tendencies associated with moral thinking, feeling and behavior, and may explain or partially explain some of the content of our moral thought, feeling and behavior, insofar as it is influenced (individually or via influences on cultural development) by those tendencies."*[86]

A quick note before we continue.

You can get access to more!
(For free)

Deleted Chapters
About one third of this book was removed by a well-meaning and laser-focused editor. Some of these sections are now presented as a series of short essays that expand on various aspects of the ideas presented in this book.

Free Tools & Frameworks
During the production of this book (and my life), I have developed frameworks that help me to determine my direction, and monitor the changes I make in a simple, low-tech way.

References with DOIs and/or Links
Get access to an online version of all the book's references with expanded details including DOIs, links to articles, or other information. This companion web page is a better way to engage more deeply with the research that sits behind this book.

Book recommendations
In the process of researching for this work, I read well over 100 books, some of which are excellent reading for anyone interested in developing a better understanding of reality. It is my pleasure to share them with you.

Just go to:
njmurphy.com/getmore

Submit your email address &
the goods will be sent to you.

PART TWO

This book could have ended here. Indeed, it was meant to. Naively, perhaps, I didn't expect that wading into the turbid waters of ideas and ideology would pull me so far out to sea and yet here we are. You and me both. The second half of this book is aimed at getting us back on land.

Years ago, I began this project because I was struggling with two questions: Why do we make the decisions we make (especially considering the diversity of options available)? And what role does art play in changing society (is art important and why)?

Attempting to answer these questions led to considering *the political* because it is utterly entwined with *the personal*, and the culture that shapes us. We make our societies, but our societies also make us. Like the ancient symbol of the serpent eating its tail, we are all in a cycle of self-consumption and production.

At the start of this book, I highlight a frustration that contemporary political movements remain hamstrung by ideological perspectives developed hundreds of years ago. Dead, (largely) white dudes, who lived in very different worlds, put down the thoughts that we've since repackaged and squeezed into a modern context, and the results have been mixed at best.

However revolutionary, or impactful, their thinking may have been, it was not definitive. They did their best with the available tools of their time but if these great minds had today's scientific and historical knowledge, would they have come to the same conclusions? I think this is unlikely. Nevertheless, much of our base-level understanding of human and social nature is still built upon the foundations they laid.

This should probably change.

The science of the last century has taught us volumes about ourselves, both as individuals and as a species, and in the process has wiped away many of the assumptions upon which many outdated political ideas are based. We understand ourselves better and this, I'd like to believe, provides us access to the tools we need to build more effective societies.

It is important to note, that at no stage in this project have I felt *certain* of the concepts I have developed. In many moments, I've wondered if this is just a multi-year dalliance with motivated reasoning. To manage this, I have stuck to the mantra: *What does the science say? And what does it mean?* To check my sanity, I reached out to a wide array of experts and leading academics for feedback. I hired brilliant minds to critique my work and help me bring scientific rigour to the process. I attended academic conferences and presented papers on my thinking. After all this, and with the central ideas holding their ground, I permitted myself to continue.

After years of work, where have I arrived?

I now understand that we grow up in a maelstrom of ideas that we do not control. Countless ideas rule us, and many are counterproductive to the person we want to be. As a result, we suffer.

We need to allow ourselves to change and be careful to let others do the same. There is something freeing about accepting that you've been wrong, but that you've done something about it and moved on. Not always being good is human but if change is possible, so is redemption.

We are not merely our behaviour or our beliefs. Even if we hold ideas that drive certain behaviours today, these ideas do not need to define our future.

It was a revelation when I learned that the most malleable part of our brain, the prefrontal cortex—central in decision-making and managing our behaviour—does not finish developing until the age of twenty-five. For me, this explained a lot.

My early twenties did not feel *very* well considered. Retrospectively, they felt like acting in a dream or steering a boat with a rudder I did not fully control. I feel like I didn't learn to chart a straight course until my late twenties and a big part of that was questioning the values and ideas that I used to direct my life.

The dichotomy of the abstract and the emotional has helped me to understand how ideas affect me on deep levels.

The realisation that ideas can be felt, and drive emotions, that lead to behaviour is useful. Knowing this helps me understand why I have emotional reactions that sit contrary to things I cognitively believe. This, in turn, helps me understand the nature of change and how to achieve it.

The lessons I've learned in writing this book have restored a small amount of my faith in human nature. We do horrible things, but cruelty is not inherent to us. The moral arc *does* bend toward justice, and it also bends toward care and cooperation. What slows it is poor understanding and misleading information and these can be fixed.

Culture is central to both.

CHAPTER 8

THE SUPERFICIALITY OF CULTURE

Ideas outside of our *innate ideas*, thus most of our cultural ideas, are largely superficial. It can feel counterintuitive to consider our cultural norms as superficial—after all, our minds are fashioned by the values in which we live—but the incredible diversity of human society is evidence of this fact.

All human societies must solve a set of fundamental questions concerning how to live and, although we are predisposed to a bias toward care, fairness and cooperation, the resulting answers are not uniform and do not necessarily lead to good outcomes for everyone.

Despite the bizarre reluctance of some academic circles to accept it, some cultural ideas are demonstrably worse than others. Even the most committed cultural relativist would struggle to coherently explain how, say, the ideas that see girls as less valuable than boys (ideas that lead to female infanticide at a massive scale) are equally as good as ideas that lead to fairer outcomes.[1]* When it comes to assessing cultural ideas, that's an easy one, or at least it should be.

---

* It is estimated that half a million young girls are killed every year because of these ideas that are part of a *"worldwide phenomenon of the devaluation of women."*[2] These infants are commonly killed by smothering, throat splitting, poisoning, drowning, starvation, or deliberate neglect. Although there are a number of cultural ideas that contribute toward this behaviour, it is notable that there are no cultures (that I am aware of) where the killing of male children is seen to be more apt.

Other, less extreme, cultural ideas can have broad negative effects on our well-being, while other cultural ideas increase the likelihood that we will live happy, healthy lives. Individual ideas may have small effects but, in aggregate, they form the complex ideological mesh that makes up our culture, and this can have a massive impact on how we experience our lives.

Although we know that certain social conditions lead to better human outcomes, passing judgment on cultural ideas is still extremely difficult. The biggest problem we face is an inability to escape the bias of the cultural ideas that literally shaped our minds.

Is it possible for me to criticise one political or cultural system if my mind has been sculpted by a different system—making objectivity impossible? When another person's mind has been moulded by a particular situation how can I say that a *different* situation is going to be better for them? How do we avoid a colonial mindset where we intuitively *feel* our cultural values to be the best (for us, they might be) and subsequently try to rationalise the imposition of *our* ideas onto people who have developed differently?

One solution to this is that, if we can accept that humans evolved to prefer fair, caring, and cooperative conditions, and therefore that when these are not met, to some degree, we suffer—then we can probably also accept that political systems or cultural ideas that fall short of creating such conditions are worse than those that provide them.

With such a view, even if a society seems radically different from our own, with customs, traditions, religions, and systems of governance that we can barely recognise, but the culture makes for a societal expression that is largely fair, caring, and cooperative, then we can probably consider such cultural ideas to be fit for human consumption. On such a basis, all modern societies have room for progress.

This simple framework allows us to determine the quality of social, political, and cultural ideas that rule the lives of ourselves and, with great care, others.

Human Ideological Bias

The human brain may be shaped by its environment, and neuroplasticity may be greatest when we're young, but that doesn't mean we can't enact enormous renovations of our self-concept once we're grown.

All of us know someone who has gone through significant ideological change. Maybe you've got a friend who fell down a conspiracy-theory rabbit hole and now keeps a potato on top of their Wi-Fi router (a little odd) or perhaps someone who refuses cancer treatment in favour of reiki (ill-advised). Your friend probably wasn't always so kooky; they ended up on the fringe not because of any innate programming but because myriad micro shifts in their belief structure took them down that path. The same is true for individuals who either turned to, or turned away from, extreme ideologies. Derek Black, a former white supremacist, is a case in point.

Derek is the son of a Ku Klux Klan 'Grand Wizard' (and the founder of a large white-nationalist website) and his mother was previously married to David Duke (a senior figure in the KKK). The extremely racist, homophobic, and anti-Semitic environment in which he was raised formed the basis of his belief system. Home-schooled, he was taught within the ideological confines of white nationalism and strongly believed that the US was a place only for whites with European ancestry and that anyone else should "go home." As a young adult, he would be introduced as the "*leading light of the White Nationalist Movement.*" Things changed however when he went to college to study European medieval history.[3]

Derek's story is long. When his beliefs and his participation in a radio show that promoted them, was discovered by his classmates, most of his peers ostracised him. Matthew Stevenson (one of the only Orthodox Jews on campus) instead invited him to Shabbat dinner, and in doing so changed his world.

In conversation with people he had been raised to hate, and through exposure to ideas he'd never before encountered, Derek's worldview began to shift. Over time, he started to see flaws in the white-nationalistic doctrine and understand that his deep-seated beliefs did not square up with reality. He learned about advanced cultures that preceded the rise of Europe and found that modern concepts of race were, in his words, *"basically just invented."* His views changed, he split with his family, and has worked to create distance from his past ever since.

It's not easy to change our belief system, and it takes time, but it's possible. Derek subscribed to a twisted logic that saw it as *fair* that the USA be exclusively for white people. His activism on behalf of his ideology was an act of *care* for those within his extremely constrained concept of *group*. As this group expanded, so did his tolerance and this redefined his notions of fairness and care. His innate ideas didn't change but all those built upon their foundation did.

Cultures respond to *hows* and articulate *whys*. This dialectic gives rise to *practices* that become *institutions* which inform *identities*. It's a powerful process that resists but does not disable change. How different cultures solve human problems may not be optimal and the *whys* can be highly arbitrary. These solutions can have a life of their own, be transmitted as traditions of great importance, or can be amplified and blown out of proportion (think back to honour killings).

Our values are built upon a hierarchy of ideas and those that we hold as innate biases all that follow. For instance, what we understand as *fair* may change with the cultural ideas constructed around this value, but the underlying preference for *fairness* remains stable.

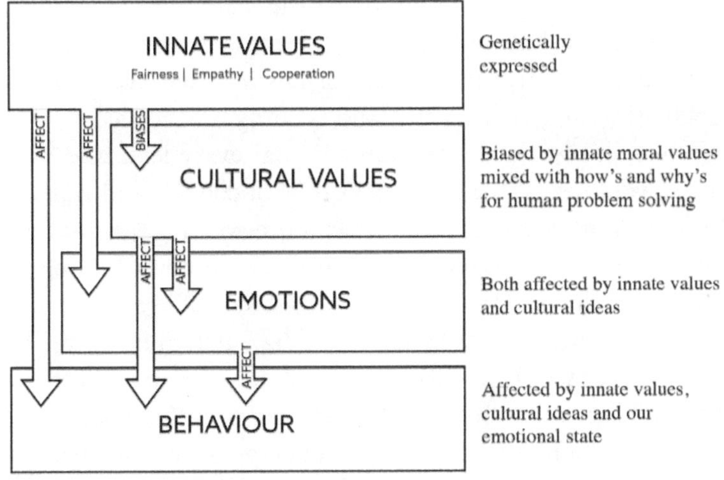

The Moral Arc

Our *innate ideas* act as a sort of ideological operating system. While these ideas may become encrusted with cultural values—ideas that are *embodied* during our socialisation—underneath it all we all carry the same basic programming.

Cultural values impact our emotional response to a wide array of social and moral situations. One person might think nothing of killing a dolphin while another might feel moral disgust. For you, punching a friend in the shoulder may be a joke, for me, it may be a great offence. A Ferrari is a signal of success for one, and a signal of misplaced values for another. You might think racism is the obvious conclusion to the differences between people while I might think the idea is laughable if it weren't so destructive. Nevertheless, as discussed in Chapter 7, we all share a common predisposition toward fairness, empathy, and cooperation.

Martin Luther King Jr. famously said, *"The arc of the moral universe is long, but it bends toward justice."* This 'bend' requires personal sacrifice, sure, but we work in its favour because we're hardwired to take care of our own. The bias of our *innate ideas* delivers a subtle but continuous force leading us toward justice—creating a collective preference for fairness that cuts through proclivities for greed, cruelty, and tyranny.

Were this not the case, humanity, at every level and at all times, would exist in a permanent state of conflict and violence. The only thing that could counteract murderous regimes would be other *more* murderous regimes. There would be no such thing as a peaceful revolution or a non-violent protest. Gandhi's actions would have been ineffective. Mandela would have gotten nowhere. The arguments of slavery abolitionists would have fallen on deaf ears. If our biology didn't reject unfairness and prioritise cooperation over competition, we'd be fine living in perpetual violence because, by reason of our nature, it would be better for us.

As far as we know, Chimpanzees, after ripping apart an out-group chimp, don't feel shame or find it hard to reconcile what they have done. Male frogs that drown a female in a pile-on while trying to mate do not suffer from remorse. A cat that tortures a mouse before killing it doesn't feel guilty. Likewise, without these biases at the centre of our nature, then it may not seem such a bad idea to eat a baby should we feel unsure of its providence, and we could watch our neighbour starve without feeling anything negative at all.

Overall, we would be *inhumane* and lacking some of the fundamental traits that granted us evolutionary success and, in doing so, defined our character. There would be no 'moral arc' toward justice, life would be about domination with no recourse, no regret, and no conscience. Humanity would be an endless festival of aggression.

Uhhhh, so, how do you explain the bloodbath that is human history, then, Nathan?

Empathy.
Empathy, and its in-group dependence, is the fly-in-the-ointment of human nature. Empathy enables a strong preference

of care for those most likely to share our genes (our kin) but allows us to be indifferent to those who don't. This enables us to switch off our empathetic response and do horrible things to those who we believe may threaten the continuation of our genes.

In modern society, our *kin* is not necessarily just who we are directly related to. The term *pseudo-kinship* describes the ideological making of kin—the feeling that unrelated people can be brothers in arms—that those who share our religion, or nation, are in a way *our family*. This capacity to make kin of anyone to whom we relate taps into the same evolutionary mechanisms that drive us to protect those who carry our genes and plays a major role in our construction of society.

The reality of empathy's out-group 'switch' is sadder than at first glance because, although we can 'turn it off' and commit acts of violence, it does not protect us from the psychological effects of our actions.

Moral Injury & Innate Values

Soldiers kill people. A willingness to do so is a basic requirement of the job and yet, despite their training, and the dehumanisation of their enemies, for many, the experience of prosecuting war is psychologically devastating. Returning combat veterans often experience nightmares, persistent negative emotions (fear, guilt, or shame), physical sensations (sweating, feeling sick), hyperarousal, irritability, angry outbursts, insomnia, depression, anxiety, and self-harm. These are all recognised symptoms of post-traumatic stress disorder (PTSD).

In the US, it is estimated that of the 700,000 Vietnam veterans, about 25% have required psychological care for delayed effects of combat exposure.[4] A study of 60,000 Afghanistan and Iraq veterans shows that 13.5% of veterans screened positive for PTSD while other studies show the rate to be closer to 20% or 30%.[5] The grim outcome of all this is that more American soldiers die by suicide than in combat. War primarily destroys minds and damaged minds not only destroy themselves but can also do profound damage to their communities, too.

Soldiers are more likely to develop PTSD in response to their own actions than to things they see, and those who inflict harm on prisoners of war, or civilians, are most at risk.[6] Now, this does not mean that a PTSD diagnosis implies you have done something morally wrong, of course, but it does raise interesting questions. Why do soldiers suffer so much after combat? And why is committing violence more psychologically destructive than witnessing it?

In *Killing from the Inside Out: Moral Injury and Just War* (2014) Professor Robert Meagher finds that 'moral injury' sits at the heart of PTSD. We suffer trauma in response to *"the transgression, the violation, of what is right, what one has long held to be sacred—a core belief or moral code"* and this inflicts a mortal wound on *"the psyche, soul, or one's humanity."*[7]

Meagher points out that the concept of moral injury is not new. He references the playwright Sophocles, born in 497 BCE and a veteran of at least two wars, and his play 'Philoctetes,' which he wrote at the age of eighty-seven. The play centres around a cosseted young soldier who is ordered to commit deeds that go against his moral code. Later, when the protagonist understands the internal consequences of his terrible actions, he tries to undo his deed, which of course is not possible. Meagher explains: *"He is wounded, but the wound in this case is self-inflicted. The malaise he suffers is that of moral injury, which he self-diagnoses and describes in these timeless words: 'All is disgust when one leaves his own nature and does things that misfit it'."*[7]

Modern iterations of this story sound eerily similar. Tim Kudy, a former US Marine Captain and author of a *Washington Post* article entitled "I Killed People in Afghanistan. Was I Right or Wrong?", tells us: *"To properly wage war, you have to recalibrate your moral compass. Once you return from the battlefield, it is difficult or impossible to repair it."* And further, he admits: *"I'm no longer the 'good' person I once thought I was. There's nothing that can change that; it's impossible to forget what happened, and the only people who can forgive me are dead."*[7]

Accounts of moral injury are plentiful throughout culture and history, and they all beg the question of what, exactly, characterises this 'core belief' or 'moral code' that has been irreparably broken.

It is not the breaking of a particular religious code, a law in a home country, or not doing as your mother told you, that causes moral injury, but the violating of ideas that characterise our species and form the basis of our morality—ideas that underly our sense of self. To lose sight of these ideas is to lose sight of our own humanity, creating a fissure in the ideological common ground that connects us to others—a disconnection forged by undoable violence.

Our tendency to extend empathy to only those who belong to our group can send us to dark places. Humans can commit atrocious violence against others, but the perpetrators suffer an internal reckoning that wreaks havoc on their self-concept because on a fundamental level, their actions are *inhuman* by nature. Our innate impulse to treat one another with empathy, and others with none, brings out both the very best and very worst in us.

The dirtiest trick of war may be that it enchants us into using our most pro-social, self-sacrificial, and altruistic nature—arguably the best of human traits—against others in acts of aggression. When the spell of perceived necessity is broken, the concept of 'the other' fades, and the fog of fear and prejudice is lifted, we must live what we have done—and we suffer.

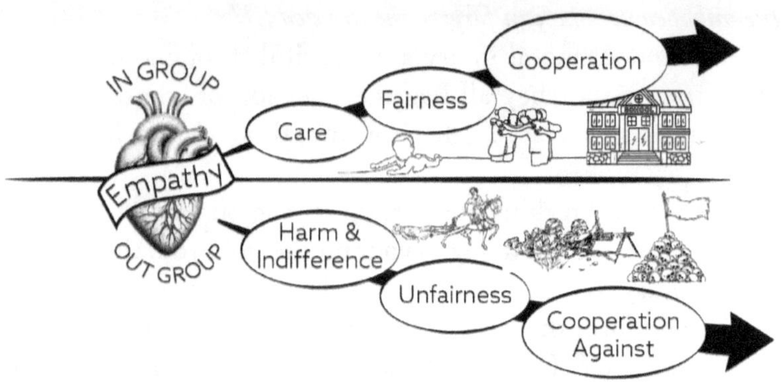

War and Religion

War is fought for many reasons, but most of all, it is fought for ideas. *All* offensive wars are ideological at heart and, if you want to prevail in a defensive war, you better have some strong ideas to fight for. Due to war's dependence on ideas, it is our most precious and culturally important ideas that lead to the longest and most intractable conflicts.

Religion comes under what anthropologists broadly call *mythological or magical thinking* and has been found to be universal in all human cultures.

Now, we may take exception to the suggestion that *our* religious beliefs are a result of magical thinking, so rest assured, I suggest that *ours* are not, but all *others* are. The *other* people get it all wrong. *They* read the wrong ancient text. *They* follow false prophets. *They* interpret things incorrectly.

Simply because of how strongly religion defines group boundaries, it can be a powerful catalyst of intergroup violence—inspiring conflicts that last for generations. Sunnis and Shias are still butchering each other fourteen centuries after a succession dispute split the faith. Catholic and Protestant differences, originating in the Middle Ages, contribute to sectarian conflict in Northern Ireland. Rohingya Muslims have been persecuted by the Buddhists in Myanmar for two generations, while the increasingly Hindu-Nationalist ideas of Narendra Modi's India are adding fuel to long-running violence between Hindus and Muslims. Sure, religion is not the only ideology that has enabled mass violence, but it certainly has bloody hands.

And, of course, religion, isn't all bad. Shared faith is a strong glue and makes groups more cooperative. From flags to gods, what we see as sacred tends to be that which brings people together. *The sacred* has social and cooperative functions.

Where we are stressed by a lack of predictability and control, religion provides ritualised behaviours that reduce anxiety. It explains why things happen to us and assures us that our existence is meaningful. If we look back to Chapter 4, and the importance of *meaning* and *cooperative social interaction*, it is no surprise that religiosity can have health benefits.

Culturally, religion is a potent educational tool and nearly all human groups have developed some version of it. What is surprising, however, is just how much global religions have in common.

Religion As an Expression of Innate Values

There is incredible variety in human religious belief. We have everything from religions with multiple animalistic gods for different occasions to those with singular, all-powerful, do-it-all gods. It is estimated that there are thousands of distinct religions, and many more gods or deities worshipped worldwide.[8–10]

Religious ideas tend to mirror the cultural-economic environments from which they originate. Agricultural societies tend to have gods that affect the weather, warrior cultures consider sacrifice in battle as the best way to a cushy afterlife, while rainforest cultures tend to have polytheistic animalistic religions that reflect the diversity of their environment.

Religions also provide explanations for *who we are* and *where we came from*—origin stories that transmit cultural ideas about identity and practice—which help to define group boundaries. Religion explains the phenomena of the natural world, and in ancient life, there was much to explain. Our environment was a mystery, we, ourselves, were little understood, and then, just as now, morality was a central concern.

It is reasonable to question, then as now, what shaped human morality. How do we share common values that aren't necessarily taught but somehow known by all? Why do we have an inner judge that knows when we have wronged? Why can we kill but be forever affected by our actions? What makes us prefer fairness? Where does the good feeling that comes from putting aside self-interest and helping others come from? Adherents will say divine intervention but if you've gotten this far, you won't be surprised that I am not convinced.

At a base level, religion codifies innately held values.

In-group care is endemic to religions. Generosity is one of Buddhism's 'perfections.' Jesus preached that it is "*more blessed to give than to receive.*" The Islamic prophet Muhammed stated that "*a man is not a believer who fills his stomach while his neighbour is hungry.*"

Fairness, too, is a central theme of all world religions. Ideas of karma, judgement day, heaven and hell, all speak to a desire to 'make life fair' regardless of what happens in the real world where life is intrinsically unfair. To feel that *justice will be served* helps things feel fair and when things feel fair, we feel good.

Lastly, religions are *highly* cooperative in nature. Everyone is subject to a shared set of rules, thus instituting conformity, and directing our energy toward a common purpose. Religion brings us together and inspires caring and charity while, at the same time, can distinguish sharp group boundaries and, perhaps, even enable us to exploit them to justify terrible treatment for those we place outside.

Why So Much Magical Thinking?

Religion is an abstract answer to emotional need. Evolutionarily, these needs arose from our increased capacity for abstract thought and the questions about life and death that followed.

As a species we crave information and desire explanations, however, for most of human existence, we have been completely unable to explain even the fundamental basics of our universe. Religion has historically provided a top-down grand theory to help us understand reality. In the modern world, we primarily use the scientific method, which was revolutionary precisely because it built an understanding from the *bottom up*—based on many small, repeatable, observations *based on reality*. Before this, many things could only be explained using the 'material' people had on hand; that is, ideas originating from imagination, stories, intuition, logic, or reason.

It is easy to forget that, until very recently, we understood very little about the natural world. The earth was considered to be the centre of the solar system until the 1500s and, only a few centuries before this, most people believed that the Earth was flat. In 1628 William Harvey figured out that new blood was not produced every day and was, in fact, circulated. Cells were first discovered in 1665, bacteria in 1670, viruses came into view in 1892, sperm was first observed in 1677, and the laws of gravity and mechanics were not understood until Isaac Newton's work in the 1600s.

Benjamin Franklin discovered that lightning was electricity, confirming basic theories of electrical charge and leading to the invention of the lightning rod. Before this, we used mystical explanations and churches would ring their bells loudly to scare away storms (making bell ringing a dangerous occupation). Until the study of strata and fossils in the early 1800s led us to understand that the earth was millions of years old, it was generally assumed, by all Christians, including scientists, that the world did not exist before the 22nd of October 4004 BCE. Later in the 1850s, Darwin published his theory of evolution. The laws of thermodynamics and many other fundamentals of physics, chemistry, and biology—essential for understanding so much about our environment—were also discovered in the same period.

Without these, and the thousands of subsequent understandings that we now take for granted, the world was largely mysterious and strange. For a species that needs explanation—a *why* for every *how*—something had to fill the void and the only explanations we could reach for were those originating in our minds—making fantasy-based understandings utterly normal.

A reliance on such a framework creates an environment where, if it *feels* right or *seems* right, it can be right. If nothing is ever *settled*, fact and truth are fluid concepts. In such an information environment, we can hardly blame our ancestors for needing some sort of big 'truth' to form a basis for their understanding. For millennia, religious ideas have provided us with *attainable* explanations with social and emotional utility.

Humans naturally seek hierarchy and categorisation of information and *categorisation* is seen as one of our most fundamental cognitive skills.

Imagine if our ancestors had found a large, beautiful, and unique crystal and, believing it to have magical properties (why not?), it became a sacred object famed for its healing properties. If later, however, someone discovered a riverbed where similar crystals, just as big, could be dug out of the mud by anyone, our magical crystal would probably quickly become *just another mud crystal*, and our ideas about its magical properties would fade. The explanation of the crystal as *"a common rock that comes out of the river"* would place it *under* other knowledge, destroying some of its mystical power.

Surviving world religions rely on that which is inherently *unknowable*—supernatural agents, impossible perfections of being, afterlives—as cornerstones of their ideologies. Concepts that remain *above* explanation maintain power; those that don't, fail.

Adding to this, our minds are destroyers of magic. We take the novel, the magical, the amazing and, via understanding, make it mundane. Although we want to *know* magic, whatever *becomes known,* loses appeal.

It is spectacular to watch an eclipse, but we don't tend to find them *mind-blowing* experiences and usually spend more time fussing about correct eyewear than considering mystical meanings. If a bright red sunset had *never* happened before it would be an incredible phenomenon but, as the entire sky regularly goes techno, we see it as *nice* but not overtly magical.

The northern lights (aurora borealis) are a beautiful phenomenon. In ancient China, they provided an origin story, inspiring the conception of an early Emperor. For Native Americans, they were caused by the spirits of their ancestors dancing in the sky (lots of light meant they were happy). For Aboriginal Australians, their southern equivalent, the aurora australis, were bushfires in the spirit world. I suspect that, for these people, witnessing the aurora would have felt like a *truly* magical experience. For us, as we know they are caused by solar wind affecting the earth's magnetosphere, it is not quite as enchanting.

The *unknown* is more interesting to humans than the *known.* By nature, we hunger for knowledge, and because of this, we find the *unknowable* tantalising. Concepts of all-powerful gods for which no evidence exists (but for which we can claim all exists as evidence), or spirits that can be glimpsed, dreamt about, or hallucinated with mind-altering rituals, feel *almost* knowable but remain forever out of reach. Religious adherents of many faiths spend their lives seeking to *know,* or to improve their relationship with their gods and, as they can never be fully *known,* their gods can retain eternal reverence.

As they say, never meet your heroes.

In this chapter, we have touched on the superficial nature of many of our cultural ideas and how it is reasonable, with care, to see some cultural ideas as being worse than others. We have discussed the interplay of innate ideas with cultural and religious values and how acting contrary to them can cause us serious psychological harm.

Overall, we can see the existence of *innate ideas* as a foundation for faith in humanity. They provide evidence of a fundamentally decent nature that can be enhanced to take care of whomever we extend our group boundaries to include. That sounds rosy, but let's now turn our gaze to the obvious reality, that most of our societies are unfair and can often be uncaring. This common reality means that societies *do not* need to be fair or caring to maintain social cooperation. So, how does that work?

In the next chapter, we will examine *force*, in its many flavours, and the ideas that *literally* rule us.

CHAPTER 9

THE IDEAS THAT RULE US

In my twenties, I lived in Hackney, North London, England. There, the local authority was notorious for handing out parking tickets and so, when a rule change arrived that meant I needed a permit to park outside my house, I was pretty dismayed. I applied for said permit but a bureaucratic blind-spot got in the way. The computer said "no." The person on the phone said "no." And the administrator with whom I booked a meeting said nothing because they didn't show up. The inflexibility of the system was maddening. With all my legal options exhausted, I resorted to carefully forging a permit and, as an act of general resistance, I made a website on which people could share complaints about the council and gain tips on how to challenge fines. This environment of petty bureaucratic control made me want to leave London and was a factor when I did.

I seem to be sensitive to social control; it inspires an anger in me that tastes of tin. I fantasise about vandalising parking meters shamefully planted into wild places, metering access to nature. Spray foam, thermite, a sledgehammer. Delicious. Like most, I have a disdain for officious types for whom saying "no" is the easy option, poorly designed or purposely obstructive bureaucratic systems, hypocritical planning authorities, busybody neighbours—in short, anyone who meddles in my affairs *without good reason.*

I often wonder where this visceral reaction comes from. Perhaps growing up with a father with a somewhat authoritarian parenting style, or maybe from the subversive ideas gently espoused by my grandfather, or possibly, from an entirely natural—and *correct*—human impulse that baulks at faceless systems of control.

Look at any aspect of your life and you'll see all kinds of ways that your freedom is limited.

Maybe you cannot afford a house but own a small plot of land and wish to erect a shelter. Good luck. Many authorities, from York to New York, would rather see you destitute, deeply indebted, or homeless than live in a property deemed *undesirable* by the law—regardless of its quality. Despite being in the middle of a housing crisis, the planning rules in England can be so petty that it can take years, and great expense, to obtain permission to turn an unused property into a home.[11] When people move into vehicles to avoid the cost of housing, authorities look to prohibit that too.

Financial organisations are no better. Credit score companies track your consumption choices and use them to estimate your ability to manage money. Consumers who do the *right sort of things* are rewarded and those who do not are punished with higher premiums, denied access to credit, face higher interest rates on loans, loss of privileges, or poorer service.[12,13] If you want to be a *good* consumer, you should take on debt as a matter of habit and if you don't, your credit score will suffer. Even doing responsible things, like shopping around for insurance, can negatively affect your ability to borrow money as higher numbers of checks are seen to be bad.

Going about your daily business is becoming more regulated too.[14] In 2014 the British Government created Public Spaces Protection Orders (PSPOs), which allows local councils to dictate and enforce any rule they feel necessary. Within a few days, and after a brief consultation with the police, a single official can ban any sort of activity in a public space. One council prohibited the use of 'foul and abusive language.' Others prohibited the gathering of two or more people, or more than four (if near a vehicle), being in possession of golf equipment, sleeping in a car or in a doorway. One council banned shouting, some banned face or head coverings, the playing of music in recreational spaces, using remote-controlled cars, or playing ball games on any street.[15-17] Other bans include drawing on the pavement with chalk, collecting for charity, preaching, revving engines, skateboarding, spitting, smoking e-cigarettes, looking after more than six dogs, and selling lucky charms.[17,18] If a single councillor sees someone poor or young doing something that annoys them, they can make it an offence and contract a private company to run around fining people for profit.

Now, of course, we need *some* common agreements, but have societies this prescriptive gone too far? Can the UK (or the US, or Canada, or Germany, or etc. etc.) really be called a 'liberal democracy' when low-level officials can make arbitrary rules that govern the minutiae of our lives? Why, even in so-called liberal democracies, are we so unfree?

Force is ubiquitous in our lives.

It is true that some force is required to help create a society where fairness, care and cooperation are protected but it can, and often does, go too far.

Force is used in many ways, the *force of law* is relatively easy to recognise, but force can be far more effective when deployed subtly.

Force can be used to make us believe that what is best for the powerful is best for us. We can be manipulated into thinking that a restrictive law is *urgently* needed despite having been quite fine without it for decades. We can be persuaded to think that it's reasonable for law enforcement to kill certain people as part of their duty, that some people within our community are our enemies, or that one man can save us all. Influencing the ideas we hold can create enormous power for those able to get away with it.

Many people have an interest in our compliance to their ideas. The less we question the more we accept, the more we accept the better we obey, and the more we obey, the more power they hold. In this chapter, we are going to examine *force* because it is present in many forms, obvious and hidden, in every social environment. From personal relationships to work environments and politics, a better understanding of *force* can be useful throughout our lives.

Why Does Force Exist?

The amount and type of *force* required to maintain social cooperation depends on how well a social system adheres to innate human values. The more a society is unfair or uncaring the more force is required to maintain cooperation.

Force is needed to make people do *what is not in their interest.* It is the exercise of power where power is defined as *"A has power over B to the extent that he can get B to do something that B would not otherwise do."*[19] Holding power does not necessarily require the use of force, however, and those who employ force may not hold power but wish they did.

Across the board, force is inextricably linked to cooperation.

The existence of a society *is* the existence of cooperation. When cooperation completely breaks down there is a state of conflict and, ultimately, the purpose of conflict is to restore a state of cooperation (in whatever form the different parties desire). Although the existence of a society is evidence of cooperation, not all cooperation is equal: cooperation can be *wilful,* or it can be *forced.*

Wilful cooperation requires a sense that things are reasonably fair and that the people we cooperate with, on a basic level, care about us and our needs. When a situation is unfair, cooperation breaks down and, if we feel that others do not have our basic interests at heart, suspicion, mistrust, and wariness take root. To maintain cooperation within unfair or uncaring societies, those in power must resort to *forced cooperation.*

Although no level of force is desirable, even in fair and caring societies the use of force is needed to control those who wish to harm others. Thus, we can speak of *just force* and *unjust force*.

Just force supports innate values and is carried out according to them. It is the minimum necessary force required to maintain fairness and care.

Unjust force exists to maintain situations contrary to innate values and is carried out in a manner that contradicts them.

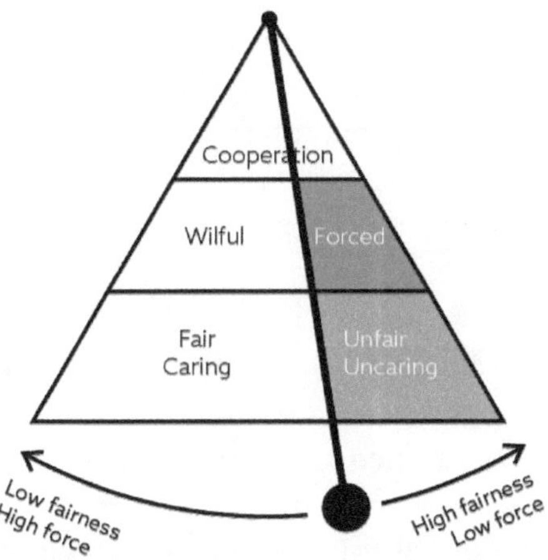

The pendulum of social cooperation.
For a society to exist there must be cooperation,
but the composition of cooperation is dependent
on the nature of the society.

The Many Faces of Force

Force comes in many guises. The spectrum ranges from the common lie—the presenting of a false reality—to disinformation, propaganda, censorship, financial penalties, property confiscation, discriminatory laws, expulsion, repression of protest, state harassment, malicious legal proceedings, imprisonment, torture, execution, mass violence, mass murder, war, and genocide. All are employed to force a state of cooperation, either by *making* people cooperate in a desired manner, or by eliminating those who will not.

In some societies, the use of force is so widespread and normalised that it even has the support of many living under it. The *level of force* that is seen to be permissible depends on the ideas a population holds—i.e. it is cultural—and can have complex justifications, but it always serves the same end.

In Saudi Arabia for example, many see it as reasonable to amputate limbs in the case of theft, to stone someone to death should they admit adultery, or to behead someone for possessing drugs. In other countries, merely advocating for such punishments would be shocking and may beckon the end of a political career.

If designing a society to live in, few of us would include stoning for adultery or beheading for drug use and it likewise proves to be true that the leaders who enforce such rules don't really want to live in such a society either (see accounts of the Saudi leader's parties with celebrities, cocaine, and prostitutes).[20] Unsurprisingly, laws of this kind are less about pious morality and more about the maintenance of power.

Saudi Arabia has a population of 34 million, of which 18 million are foreign labourers who earn less than a fifth of what an average citizen earns. It features a royal family of around fifteen thousand members, of which two thousand control the majority of the country's wealth.[21,22] At the top, the crown prince has an estimated net worth of eighteen billion dollars while it is estimated that between two and four million of the country's native Saudis live under the poverty line. The country is an absolute monarchy and there are practically no elections of any kind.

To compensate for this incredible unfairness, the House of Saud must maintain a vicious regime. A state that can execute its citizens for offences that cause little or no *actual harm*, is a state that maintains total power over its subjects. Those who dissent may end up sawn to pieces while still alive, as happened to journalist and Washington Post columnist Jamal Khashoggi, a murder authorised by the supposed "reformer," Crown Prince Mohammed bin Salman.[23,24]

In 2022, the Saudi government executed eighty-one people in one day—notably only one had murder on his charge sheet. In the same year, the government imprisoned a mother of two for 34 years merely for following and reposting dissidents and feminist activists on Twitter while studying abroad.[25] At the time of writing, one person awaiting execution is the scholar, Hassan Farhan al-Maliki, whose sentence is largely in reaction to peaceful religious ideas and the contents of his library.[20] If a citizen of Saudi Arabia wrote these words they would be at risk of arrest, decades of imprisonment, torture, and possibly, execution.

How might you protest unfairness or institute change in Saudi Arabia? At great risk. Critics of the regime can be prosecuted with a wide array of crimes including apostasy, or *"violating Islamic values and propagating liberal thought,"* or, like many, be simply held without charge.[26,27] In Saudi Arabia, *any* comment against the state can be deemed to be terrorism.[28]

The poor have no legal protection, no opportunity to improve their situation, and must endure their lot *or else*. Why does Saudi Arabia need to apply such massive, pervasive, and cruel force? Because the system they maintain is grossly unfair and cares little for those without wealth or status.

Force is not restricted to dictatorships.

The United States is a constitutional republic where supposedly *"supreme power is held by the people and their elected representatives"* but really *'the people'* that hold power in America has increasingly come to mean those with wealth. To maintain unfairness in 'free' societies, force is applied more subtly.

This may mean gerrymandering—the drawing of voter district boundaries to disadvantage certain groups of voters and ensure minority rule—or a criminal justice system with racial or class biases and corresponding outcomes. It can mean the enabling of vast financial force by allowing unlimited political donations by individuals or corporations, or it can mean an unrelenting cascade of lies delivered by news channels owned by billionaires who have little interest in the truth or, as it happens, fairness.

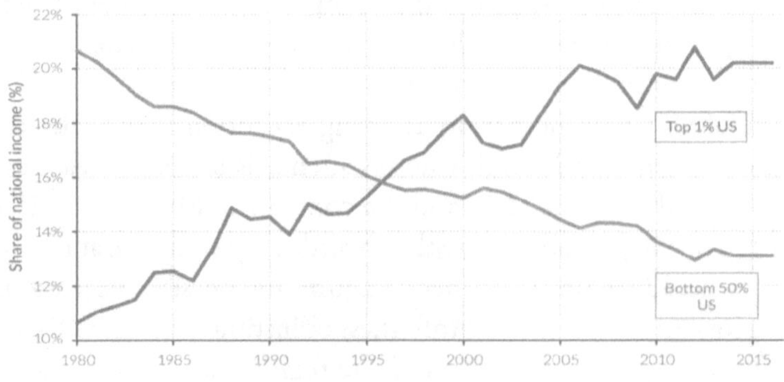

Source: WID.world (2017). See wir2018.wid.world/methodology.html for data series and notes.

In 2016, 12% of national income was received by the top 1% in Western Europe, compared to 20% in the United States. In 1980, 10% of national income was received by the top 1% in Western Europe, compared to 11% in the United States.

Over thirty years there has been a wholesale change in who gets to hold wealth in the United States.[29] This reality has inevitably affected tens of millions of people for the worse. It remains in the interest of the wealthy to maintain, or exacerbate, a system that greatly enhances their wealth.

It is hard to view America as a fair society when, despite voters choosing their representatives, it is the donor class that dictates the policy they implement, or when the primary indicator of a campaign's success is the amount of money raised—especially when 68% of political donations come from 0.26% of the population.[30] It also becomes difficult to claim that the world's wealthiest society is particularly caring when tens of thousands of Americans die annually due to a lack of health coverage, or when deductibles are so high that many cannot afford to visit a doctor.

In line with this deepening unfairness, we see an increasingly militarised police force, ever greater voter suppression, new and more powerful barriers to worker organisation, soaring household debt, and a tripling of the number of incarcerated people over a thirty-year period.[31–33]

America's degeneration into a society of *forced cooperation* is illustrated well by the election of a billionaire president who did not win the most votes, told over twenty thousand lies during four years in office, separated and caged the children of immigrants (losing track of some parents after they were deported), delivered massive tax breaks for society's richest, and, when voted out, incited a violent insurrection that aimed to overturn the result.[34] To maintain cooperation in an increasingly unfair and uncaring society an increased use of force is inevitably required.

When we look at fairer and more caring societies, we see a different picture. Norway, for example, frequently ranks at the top for happiness and equality among developed countries.[35,36] In comparison to the USA, per population, Norway has 20 times fewer police killings, imprisons 13 times fewer people, and has an electoral system that is demonstrably fairer and more representative.[37,38] Norwegians are politically engaged with voter turnouts often nearing 80%, and the country's political culture is more collaborative than adversarial.

Norway is a small country so perhaps it is an unfair comparison. Germany, however, Europe's most populous, tells a similar story. Per population, Germany has about four times less homelessness and people experiencing extreme poverty and has significantly lower levels of relative poverty.[39,40] Germany ranks 4th for the quality of its civic justice—a measure of whether access to justice is accessible, affordable, and free of discrimination or corruption—while the US ranks 38th, alongside Namibia and Barbados. The story is the same for fundamental rights.[41] When it comes to healthcare, despite having some of the best facilities in the world, the US ranks far behind Germany due to costs that prohibit many from accessing adequate care.[42]

Correspondingly, compared to the United States, per population, Germany has twenty-five times fewer killings by law enforcement, incarcerates about eight times fewer people, and far less private money is spent on lobbying and campaign finance. As an example, the campaign spending for the election of a Chancellor in 2014—the most powerful office in Germany—cost about the same as the election of *one* senator in the state of Colorado during the same year.[43]

Across the board, fairer and more caring societies can be seen to have less inequality (obviously), less relative poverty, fewer police killings, lower incarceration rates, less political corruption, fewer lies in politics, and more representative voting systems. Simply put, you do not need a lot of force to maintain a society which is caring and fair.

Increase unfairness, decrease care, and *force* will be your bed mate.

Force Against Change

Our ideas about how we run our societies must continuously adapt should we want them to remain effective. As all reform invariably results in winners and losers, if you are currently a winner, any change is generally unwelcome.

People who wish to maintain the status quo often resort to force to protect their interests and maintain yesterday's ideas—even if doing so works against their society's best interest. Using force against the changing nature of reality can reap short-term rewards but is dysfunctional in the long term.

Businesses see this all the time. In the late 2000s, the music industry tried its best to kill the MP3 file-format technology that enabled small file sizes and easy distribution over the internet. Today, almost all music is distributed this way, but it is now tech companies, not record labels that run the show.

The automotive industry likewise pushed back against reform for decades. They lobbied governments, cheated emissions tests, and spread disinformation about electric vehicles. Meanwhile, pollution and climate change didn't go away, but grew, and new players entered the market and challenged the dinosaurs that refused to pivot from combustion engines. GM, Toyota, Ford, Volkswagen and their ilk could have spent two decades investing in greener technologies, but they didn't, and now they're all stuck playing catch-up with Tesla—a company that shipped its first cars in 2009 and by 2020 had become the most valuable car company in the world. Meanwhile, China is setting itself up to dominate in an all-electric future.

Governments constantly use force against reality to protect global business interests, increase political power, and save face. In the long term, this is *always* less effective than investing in and adapting to inevitable change.

When functioning, democracy is a good system because it works without requiring significant force. Healthy democracies can adapt to change in ways that benefit their entire population, not just a few individuals whose interests lay in the past. Accordingly, well-functioning democracies have people who are happier, healthier, less impoverished, and more equal. Meanwhile, democracies that support high levels of inequality face a higher risk of sliding into dictatorship.[44–46]

Bureaucratic Force

So far in this chapter, we have talked about the relationship between force and cooperation. This has led us to address the many ways, good and bad, that force is employed to maintain cooperation in society.

Without the application of 'just force,' we would not be able to protect people from those who wish to act unfairly or cause harm, making it an inevitable by-product of our innate inclination toward fairness, care, and cooperation. The use of force can, however, get out of hand. Never is this truer than when it arrives in the guise of bureaucracy because, as we're about to see, bureaucracy drives us to depersonalise and abstract the values hardwired into our genes and when this happens, people suffer.

Birth is a risky affair, and not just for medical reasons. One place of birth can lead to a life of freedom and opportunity, while another, a mere mile over a border, can condemn us to live under a cruel, despotic regime. When we are born into a society, our consent to live under its authority is taken *as granted*. In the modern world, where it is not easy to move and acquire a different nationality, if we do not wish to obey, we must live against the force imposed on us.

It was not always this way. Land and people were not always carved up into bordered communities and people could move from one place to another without modern restrictions. The notion of sovereign states has not been with us for very long and yet it is an idea that completely rules our lives, dictating where we can live, work, and travel. This state of affairs started with ideas of sovereignty.

Sovereignty is the idea of a *supreme authority* where a person or institution has the ultimate say within a territory. The sovereign body has the 'right' to create or change laws—a right that typically depends on some form of legitimacy, be it a constitution, inheritance, divinity, or a form of natural law.

Modern ideas of sovereignty were developed in 16th Century Europe after centuries of war and power consolidation led to the creation of European states. Leading thinkers of the time, like the French theorist Jean Bodin and Thomas Hobbes, believed that sovereignty should reside in a single individual. Hobbes saw it that *the people* transferred their rights to the *sovereign* in a social contract. In this, the sovereign had to be above the law because otherwise, their authority would not be *supreme*, which would limit their ability to resolve conflicts and thus make peace impossible.

Sovereignty, in this sense, is an abstract form of *authority*. Where *authority* is usually dependant on being competent, trusted, and knowledgeable—and is earned on a personal level— *sovereign authority* is based on the idea that authority can be arbitrarily granted and those under it can be expected to defer to it without explicit consent. This hinges on the application of abstract ideas, not emotional experience.

Today, instead of a sovereign monarch, most governments rule through a sovereign body of law. Territorial sovereignty is taken for granted and the entire world is divided up into sovereign states.

The sovereign body gets millions of people to do what it wants through *bureaucracy*. Bureaucracy is essential for a sovereign state because, without it, the application of centralised decision-making is hardly possible. If the *sovereign* is the 'mind' then its *bureaucracy* is the 'body' that carries out its intentions efficiently at scale. Modern bureaucratic systems can, incredibly, enable the coordinated cooperation of billions of people but, despite obviously being necessary, we intuitively know there is something wrong with these bureaucratic systems. Even the word *bureaucracy* can raise blood pressure.

Sovereignty and bureaucracy both rely on principles of impersonal equivalency—where all are equal under the sovereign, free to do what is not forbidden, and where all get equal treatment by its bureaucracy.[47] This sounds almost reasonable, but people are *not equal*—neither in capability, nor in resources, wealth, health, circumstance, or character. Where sovereignty requires the abstraction of authority, bureaucracy requires the abstraction of fairness, and we tend to call this *equality*.

Complex individuals are turned into numbers, statistics, and principles and, because this works outside of the realms of affective empathy, the human experience behind the number is negated. One equals one, and all are the same, but equality does not necessarily mean fairness. This fact weaponises equality and enables sovereign powers to ignore individual problems.

Graber and Wengrow point out that early bureaucracies *"allowed rulers, or their henchmen, to make impersonal demands that took no consideration of their subjects' unique situations. This is of course what gives the word 'bureaucracy' such distasteful associations almost everywhere today."*[47]

Bureaucracies best serve those who fit *the mould* and the mould typically mirrors those who administer it. When bureaucrats try to account for human differences, using a system that depends on impersonal equivalence, the results are complicated, unwieldy, and become vulnerable to corruption or weaponisation.

"Death to bureaucracy" you scream from the rooftops! Slow down... Bureaucracy is not all bad. It does do many important jobs essential for living in large societies, including food standards, building codes, product and safety standards, trains that run on time, and tax collection, among many others.

Bureaucracy's strength is in the management of systems and objects; its weakness is in the management of individual lives—*the emotional*. Although trains, electricity, and building codes do involve people, people are not the *subject*. Impersonal systems of management work well when managing impersonal things.

The big problem with bureaucracy lies in matters of care.

Bureaucracies of Care

Millions rely on public assistance for support with rent, health care, food, and dignity, and with such critical needs at stake, butting up against systems that fail to account for individual circumstances can be terrifying. A bureaucrat mindlessly saying no to a house extension is frustrating; a bureaucrat deleting the roof above your head is catastrophic.

Care by nature, is personal *and personalised*; it implies the recognition and alleviation of individual suffering. To be effective, care professionals must examine patients as complex individuals with interconnected issues, and this is the opposite of bureaucratic function. The underlying function of a *bureaucracy-of-care* is in the *limiting of care*; that is, cost management, the denial of services, and the abstraction of human needs into numbers and massageable statistics.

Who among us would be willing to look into the eyes of someone who desperately needs a treatment that costs $100,000—which when shared between everyone would cost us a fraction of a cent—and say *no*? If you did, could you watch them deteriorate, suffer, and die? Could you watch their loved ones grieve, all while maintaining the line that a fraction of a cent was too much to pay? Luckily (sort of) for us, we don't have to, because bureaucracies-of-care do this on our behalf thousands of times a day and we can play along thanks to the abstraction they provide.

A big problem of bureaucracies of care is that they are often managed by those with low system dependence—those who are wealthy enough to never need social support. Inevitably, problems arise when the most secure people in society make decisions for the least secure.

Bureaucratic governance exacerbates social disconnection, enabling the powerful to cut vital services and call it *care*. When making decisions for those we do not understand, never meet, and whose suffering we do not witness, cruelty is not just easy, but it's intangible.

For those who exist far from the decision-makers, bureaucratic distance can be fatal.

Let's imagine a small community, say 150 strong, whose leader callously let an elderly woman starve, or forced her to choose between heating and eating without good reason (as if there ever was a good reason). The leader would soon find themselves on the receiving end of sharp moral judgement, and the resulting gossip would wreak havoc on their reputation.

In a large sovereign bureaucracy, however, a leader can do just that to thousands of people with the stroke of a pen and face little or no comeuppance. The fact is, we use bureaucracies-of-care *to manage* our failure, as a community, to care for the hungry, the weak, and the sick.

Bureaucratic abstraction of this kind enables politicians, like the ex-British Prime Minister David Cameron—born rich and educated at the most expensive schools—to cut welfare, cause food bank use to increase by 2600%, and see it as an *impersonal* act. For Cameron, the disconnection was so great that a few years later he volunteered at one of the food banks that his policies necessitated, photo-op included.[48]

Through the many degrees of bureaucratic separation, politicians can deny care, at scale, until they are satisfied that the numbers fit their agenda. And as they do, they can hide behind the system knowing that their bureaucratic underlings can squirm out of any bind by simply insisting that they are "just doing their job." However, the reality is, no matter how dense the subterfuge, it is *always* personal—the belief that it is not is *the* great illusion of sovereign bureaucracy. The illusion of *authority without responsibility.*

A police officer who beats a peaceful protester is not *just* following orders, he also acts of his own volition. He is both an upholder of the law *and* a violent offender. The idea that he is only the former is an illusion. And, as time passes, the regime-thug may find themselves reckoning with their behaviour in a way that their administrative bosses never will.

Front-line bureaucrats are likewise stuck in a hard place. Often, they are poorly paid, economically insecure, and fearful for their jobs. They find themselves trying to help clients in a situation where there are simply not enough resources, and they are forced to make impossible choices on behalf of the state. To cope with making such choices over the lives of desperate people, they disassociate and compartmentalise, ironically employing psychological mechanisms that mirror the role bureaucracy plays for those who govern.[49]

In recent times, front-line services are increasingly contracted to private companies—adding another level of abstraction—and, by allowing people to profit from the limiting of care, it drives a greater ruthlessness toward doing so. Private companies can be found running immigration removal centres and managing disability benefits and unemployment offices. Amazingly, or horrifyingly, in this case, those who govern have found a way to not only protect wealth through the bureaucratic limiting of care but also to profit from it.

Bureaucracies of Harm

When we look at bad governments the worst of them typically institute the most abstract systems of governance. Evil is a loaded word—steeped with historical connotations and religious excitement—but we do seem to need a word that describes the worst of human behaviour: the sort of behaviour that crosses the pale of understanding.

When we consider evil, we can imagine there being two forms: one *personal* and the other *impersonal*. The first is borne of dysfunctional emotional drivers; the second is based on the abstraction of harm.

- Personal evil could be what Luke Russel, a philosopher at Sydney University, calls *"extreme culpable wrongs,"* or what Jordan Peterson, the divisive academic, terms inflicting *"suffering for the sake of suffering."* In either case, what we mean is terrible behaviour that operates on a personal level. This variety of evil is driven by *emotion*. The perpetrator causes great suffering to another to fulfil some dark desire. Often the hardest acts to understand are done simply because a person *felt* like doing them. Emotionally driven actions can be absent of reason.

- Impersonal evil, on the other hand, refers to *the creation of* abstract systems of harm that, at their worst, can be unstoppable. These typically depend on abstract ideas taken to their extreme logical conclusions and are carried out by abstract systems of management which eliminate the value of personal or emotional experience.

The media is obsessed with psychopaths and the crimes they commit but far more terrifying are bureaucratic systems that enable normal people, who would never usually commit terrible crimes, to do so as part of their daily routine.

Hannah Arendt, the famous scholar of totalitarianism, used Nazi and Stalinist regimes as examples to highlight how bureaucracy was central to creating unstoppable systems of tyranny.

Arendt writes:

> *"The greater the bureaucratization of public life, the greater will be the attraction of violence. In a fully developed bureaucracy there is nobody left with whom one could argue, to whom one could present grievances, on whom the pressures of power could be exerted. Bureaucracy is the form of government in which everybody is deprived of political freedom, of the power to act; for the rule by Nobody is not no-rule, and where all are equally powerless we have a tyranny without a tyrant."*[50]

Bureaucracies of harm are the darkest of all human creations. Abstract systems of endless terror that apply total force with total power and that prevent even those who created them from stopping the process.

These systems carry out a single idea to its logical conclusion. Arendt writes that for the Nazis it was the belief in a 'Law of Nature' wherein distinct races with different physical and cognitive abilities competed in a Social Darwinist world where only the fittest survived. For the Bolsheviks it was a belief in a 'Law of History' wherein society was a result of a long class struggle that would only end with the end of history itself. Both fascists and communists sought to conquer the world and eradicate anyone who did not facilitate *the movement of the idea*.

Both the Nazi and the Bolshevik systems represent extreme manifestations of the human capacity for abstraction. Each elevates an abstract idea to a level of supreme importance whereby *everything* is directed toward achieving the idea's logical conclusion. Abstract systems of management—where the *idea itself* is sovereign—liberates the movement from human direction. Where human emotion and experience are irrelevant compared to the importance of the idea, violent oppression—terror—is justified. To implement totalitarian systems of terror, to enable mass cruelty, requires the complete abstraction of normal human relationships.

Arendt called this process 'atomization.' Interpersonal relationships become liabilities, not a source of strength, and the risk of guilt by association means that *"as soon as a man is accused, his former friends are transformed immediately into his bitterest enemies; in order to save their own skins, they volunteer information and rush in with denunciations to corroborate the nonexistent evidence against him; this obviously is the only way to prove their own trustworthiness."*[50]

Abstract unrealities supported by bureaucracies-of-harm invert our innate human values and, cooperation, outside of the execution of the idea, is forbidden. This is illustrated well by 'the Party' slogan in George Orwell's dystopian novel *1984*: *"War is peace, freedom is slavery, and ignorance is strength."*

Uncaring is good, fairness is bad, and unreality is best.

CHAPTER 10

WHEN THE ABSTRACT CORRUPTS THE EMOTIONAL

In the last chapter, we touched on how, through sovereignty and bureaucracy, we see complex individuals treated as uniform entities through systems of impersonal equivalence—providing *equality* but not necessarily *fairness*.

The result is that actions between people are imagined to be impersonal, that care is limited to protect wealth, and that the importance of emotional experience is degraded. To maintain unfairness and a lack of care, force is inevitably applied. Adding fuel to this fire, the wealth that *bureaucracies-of-care* aim to protect, is also somewhat abstract, and this causes other problems.

***

To avoid being enslaved to debt for thirty years for a crummy flat in North London, I bought a broken-down home in Catalunya, Spain. The three-story house, which came with a barn and some land, is nestled among ancient terraces that are typical of the region. Facing a mountain with a tidal wave of pine trees on one side and a picturesque valley, complete with a winding river, on the other, it is as beautiful as anywhere I have been on earth.

Buying the property was an interesting experience. At first, I had a thrilling thought that "*wow, all this could be mine!*" but a few months later, and with everything paid for, the house felt no more mine than it was before. *In reality*, nothing had changed.

Even after a year and a few thousand hours of hard labour later, I still feel like a visitor here and, if I *really* think about it, I am. This house is likely to be here for centuries after I'm gone, and the land itself until the sun explodes and consumes the earth. Just like the ten generations who lived here before me, I am little more than dust blowing through these rooms.

Ownership is never permanent. Things are either disposed of, destroyed or, when we die, claimed by someone else. Practically speaking, as permeance is impossible, all property is effectively rented—a rent we pay in maintenance, depreciation, insurance, or protective effort.

Ownership itself is less a fact and more a social construct. When I say, "I bought a house," what I really did was pay someone to do socially sanctioned things with pieces of paper to convince others that the property now belongs to me. It's all smoke and mirrors but it is quite effective. I *do* believe I own my home, and no one (unwelcome) has unexpectedly moved in.

Due to its abstract nature, property is a fraught concept. We require structures of ideas to make the abstract *feel* real. Rights, inheritance, taxation, an array of bureaucratic systems, and a whole range of rituals aim to socialise ownership. From marriage to housing contracts and receipts, all exist to impress upon others that a certain thing belongs to a certain person.

Types of Wealth

Property itself is based on ideas of *property rights* and these ideas underpin many forms of wealth. Not all wealth is abstract, however, and as with the common theme of this book, we can see there as being two forms of wealth: emotional and abstract.

Emotional wealth is that which tangibly impacts our lives. Health is vital. Meaningful relationships and good community standing determine our well-being. Access to knowledge reduces confusion and improves quality of life. Money and property matter but only to the extent that our needs are secure and we're able to indulge in the occasional luxury. Emotional wealth is satisfiable and has general (if hard to determine) limits. We can *be* healthy, we can have *more than enough* resources, we can have access to knowledge, and we can be cared for only so much before it becomes annoying.

Abstract wealth is that which sits above adequate means. Wealth beyond *need* tends to come with some form of unnecessary suffering: attachment, fear, additional stress, mistrust of others, or the pressures of status. Vast abstract wealth without emotional wealth is largely pointless and may even create barriers to accessing the latter. What's more, abstract wealth is inherently insecure, hard to understand, and, in keeping with the limitless nature of *the abstract*, can be accrued to no end. Our desire for abstract wealth can be unsatisfiable and, more importantly, on a deeper level, it is generally *unsatisfying*.

Money is an abstract form of value based on systems of belief. It enables the abstract equivalence of everything. Services, skills, experiences, and even life can be assigned a monetary value.[51] Organisations can be divided up into imaginary parts and sold as shares. Our time can have a price. A lifetime of labour can be described in dollar signs. Individuals can be classified as a net-cost or a net-profit to a society and thus, some can be seen as more valuable than others. Money, like bureaucracy, can transform things of emotional importance into impersonal abstractions.

Financialisaton pushes into every aspect of life, creating an illusion that everything can be bought and sold. A home becomes a speculative investment, education shifts from an act of social care to a debt-fuelled pursuit of greater earning potential, hobbies must be monetised, art becomes a place to store value, harm can be paid off, natural disasters have a cost, social connections are converted into ad-revenue, and we spend more time caring for debts than we do caring for others.[52] Aspiration gains a numerical value and conduct between people becomes "*increasingly tied to financial structures and logic.*"[53]

The more money we have the more abstract it becomes. We cannot accurately imagine a billion people any more than we can understand a billion dollars—especially as a billion dollars is not far from a billion more than we *actually* need. Holding abstract quantities of abstract wealth also enables our total abstraction from any part of society that we do not wish to be a part of, and for the ultra-rich, this tends to be most of it.

The Wealth Warp

We have not evolved to cope well with holding great wealth, and largely, we don't. Across cultures and time greed has been seen as antisocial or sinful but this has not stopped its prevalence. This is perhaps because, typically, the rich can afford to be greedy.

Humans evolved as nomadic or semi-nomadic hunter-gatherers. For hundreds of thousands of years, we lived in temporary or seasonal shelters, and this made owning a lot of stuff impractical. It was only in the last forty thousand years or so, when humans shifted toward more permanent settlements—and especially in the last few thousand years—that we experienced an explosion of *material wealth* and the different forms it can take. Considering how new this is on an evolutionary scale, it is no surprise that we struggle with its effects.

Minds that evolved largely to care about other people now do gymnastics to account for vast numbers of objects and, unsurprisingly, the result is confused. We care about our property as much as we do other people. Our cars become our babies; our outfits become our character; our material wealth becomes a measure of our person and thus, of course, we grieve its loss the same way we grieve the loss of a loved one. On a baseline, holding material wealth is an unnatural state, and deep down, we know it. Because of this, *ownership feels fragile.*

Abstract wealth exerts a subtle but pervasive pressure on

those who hold it and the more we have the more susceptible we are to its pressure. Accumulating significant wealth leads to psychological effects that cause problems for individuals as well as society.

Material wealth breeds *attachment*. Attachment is primarily driven by the merging of our external wealth and our internal identities. If we identify as being wealthy and successful, the idea of losing wealth can feel paramount to losing *who we are*. What's worse, if our social circle is also built around wealth, it's not only a blow to our identity, but to our sense of belonging.

Wealth culture sucks in the wealthy, and its aspirants, like ants to sugar and represents the pinnacle of consumerist ideology. *What you have* defines your worth, and what you spend is how you show it. Wealth culture is sexy, status-driven and highly, *highly* aspirational. It is easy to believe you'll be happier if only you could become rich despite numerous scientific studies and two millennia of philosophy and theology, saying otherwise. Money is useful, sure, but it makes a terrible goal and *more than more-than-enough*, is probably already too much.

The pursuit of abstract wealth at the expense of its emotional counterpart is not just personally damaging, but socially destructive, too. Holding excessive wealth leads to higher levels of entitlement, less empathy, and a tendency to assume hard work alone justifies one's social position.[54] The poor are accused of being lazy and talentless and the rich are esteemed as luminaries when, even in fairly egalitarian societies, this has been proven to be untrue.[55]

Despite its allure, abstract wealth is not necessarily good for those who hold it either. Typically, there are few ways to get exceptional treatment within a social group. One is to do exceptional things that lead to respect and deference, another is to be vulnerable and require exceptional care, and lastly, we can do something *awful*. Contributions that gain social respect may take a lifetime of effort but, with abstract wealth, we can find ourselves *born* into exceptionality.

Wealth can make somewhat mundane people *seem* exceptional. For these people, to lose wealth is also to open the door to the awful truth that they are not as special as they have been led to believe—a door that must be kept shut, even if at the expense of emotional wealth or others in their community.

Those born into abstract wealth grow up in a world where wealth is the ultimate marker of success. This leads children to have a relentless drive to turn themselves into highly marketable commodities—causing young people to choose hobbies, not based on what they enjoy, but based on what will look good on their resumes. Due to this pressure cooker of achievement—and other related factors—wealthy children tend to be more distressed than low-income children and have a similarly high risk of psychological disturbance, anxiety, or drug or alcohol use to self-medicate.[56,57]

Sam Roddick, the daughter of the Body Shop founder Anita Roddick, observed that for the extremely wealthy *"relationships become transactional, and that is something that is extraordinarily emotionally damaging. A lot of very wealthy people are not accountable to their community, they're not accountable to the people they love, they show their power and control through transaction, and they are unhappy, from what I can tell."*[58]

The (Actual) Problem with Capitalism

Inequality is the bedfellow of extreme wealth. With inequality driving so many problems and with capitalism driving so much inequality, it's easy to characterise capitalism itself as a social evil, but to do so misunderstands the problem.

Numerous large-scale experiments have aimed to abolish capitalism, and not only have they failed, but they have brought about problems far worse than inequality.

The Soviet Union violated nearly all concepts of human rights, was responsible for tens of millions of deaths, and was plagued with corruption. The Communist Party of China starved or killed upward of thirty million people during Mao's "great leap forward," while its recent economic success has depended on remodelling itself into an authoritarian-capitalist state. China continues to oppress all forms of dissent and is actively involved in a genocidal campaign against the Uyghur people.[59] In the 1970s, the Khmer Rouge aimed to purge Cambodia of capitalist ideas and, in the process, murdered and starved millions of people, killing one in four Cambodians. Cuban communism resulted in a corrupt one-party state that allows no freedom of expression, holds elections with no opposition, and features state-enforced poverty wherein antibiotics, soap, toilet paper, and other essentials, are often in short supply. Capitalism has proven itself capable of provoking significant suffering but attempts at its eradication have proven to be far worse.

Primarily, capitalism is not an ideology. It is a system of economic cooperation ruled by the economic laws of supply and demand in which individuals control property for personal gain. Of course, one might argue that the concept of private property is itself ideological but if it is, the idea goes back a long way. According to Graeber and Wengrow, *"If private property has an 'origin', it is as old as the idea of the sacred, which is likely as old as humanity itself".*[47]

This is not to say that many ideologies have not been formed to support or justify capitalism's inevitable downsides.

Chief among these is the thinking of Adam Smith, widely considered to be the father of capitalism. Smith believed that increasing private profit would increase collective wealth and this would benefit society as a whole. Self-interest, according to Smith, was morally justifiable and this could be interpreted to mean that *greed is good*. Unsurprisingly, this idea was quickly adopted in certain circles.

"Cynthia!! It turns out that ah' mills filled with 'alf-starved workers and thee 'uge profits they generate—it's God's moral work aft'r all!"

Meanwhile, Smith's ideas that expressed greater scepticism about the benefits of unmitigated self-interest were (unsurprisingly) not taken up with such glee.

Capitalism remains the most effective system of economic cooperation the world has ever seen, and it is unlikely to be surpassed. It has proven itself effective at driving innovation, productivity, and economic growth, and has increased global living standards in a way never seen before. It does, however, have fundamental flaws.

The problem with capitalism is that, when it does not exist in a strong regulatory environment, it leads to gross unfairness, environmental catastrophe, and the corruption of the state.

Unconstrained, capitalism corrupts democracy by remodelling it in its own image—*that you need capital to play the game*. When successful capitalists gain significant influence over the government, coming at the expense of the electorate, then it naturally results in policies that provide a greater advantage to Capital—leading to the accrual of greater wealth and influence. The result is the shift from Democracy into Corporatism (the control of the state by corporate interests) and as inequality is exacerbated, Oligarchy (rule by few). As force is an inevitable by-product of unfairness, an increasingly authoritarianism regime is likely to follow.

Without government intervention, capitalism devours itself and turns into something far less useful, corrupting not only institutions but also itself. Ultimately, unconstrained capitalism is inherently unstable, and regulation and taxation are the bitter medicine that maintains its usefulness.[60]

Stripped of its political and ideological crust, capitalism is simply a system of economic cooperation. It's neither inherently good nor bad, as a system—it is simply amoral.

Capitalism is not *fair* or *caring* because it does not intrinsically 'balance the scales' for those born without capital or for those whose health means they cannot participate. Unconstrained capitalism is *inhuman* because it lacks fairness and empathy. Capitalism needs governance as much as today's governments need capitalism, and the government's role is to add *fairness* and *care* to the capitalist system of *cooperation*.

Take It From Anyone but Me

When taxation is fair and a government is trustworthy, people are generally willing to pay their share—unless that is, they happen to be very wealthy. A 2021 estimate of US tax evasion estimated that *"the top 1% of earners accounted for more than a third of all unpaid federal taxes,"* and another study discovered that tax evasion increases through the income distribution.[61,62] Off-shore tax-haven leaks, like the Panama Papers, demonstrated the immense scale of the tax evasion industry that caters to the wealthy.

Attachment to wealth, and a compulsion to get more, naturally leads to a desire for money to be a) easier to accrue, and b) harder to lose. A greater advantage to Capital and a lower taxation on wealth therefore becomes a predictable political goal. Reaching this goal may involve hampering unionisation, suppressing wages, cutting corporation or wealth tax, and creating legal paths for massive tax avoidance—which is not exactly in the interests of the other 99% of people in your society.

For the wicked to achieve these aims, they must mount a powerful PR campaign that convinces the poor to support their agenda. There are three basic ways this is achieved:

1. Make Them Believe There is Not a Problem

Gaslight the poor by persuading them that they are not *actually* poor and, in fact, *they have never had it so good!* If they *were* poor, they would not be able to afford phones or televisions. Gross unfairness, according to their manipulative logic, is better because success should be rewarded and 'wealth creators' are required for the creation of jobs. Also, when the rich get richer so does everyone else because of a 'trickle-down effect' so everyone benefits in the long run. (Although as it happens, when the rich get richer the rich just get richer.)[63]

If this isn't convincing, then it must be explained that the less well-off struggle, not because the system is unfair, but because they lack the talent and work ethic of the wealthy. Anyone can 'make it' if they just put in the time and there are no problems you can't fix yourself with a little gumption.*

2. Shift the Focus of Their Anger Downward or Outward

It is important that when people feel angry, they don't gaze *upwards*. Luckily, despite the wealthy hoovering up more money than ever, blaming external powers or foreigners for people's worsening economic situation is as easy as ever.

While the wealthy enjoy the benefits of foreign workers—lower labour costs and cheaper domestic staff—it is those with lower incomes that suffer all the downsides. Aside from competition for lower-wage jobs (serving Capital perfectly), they also compete for schooling, housing, and healthcare services. This makes immigrants the ideal scapegoat for all the problems in society. Telling the poor that the reason they have less is because of *other poor people* is a fantastic lie.

Don't have an immigrant community? Don't worry, a foreign power will do. China, for example, is easy to paint as an evil empire that took all our manufacturing jobs—but only if you gloss over the fact that it was capitalists who moved production overseas, to cut costs and increase profits, in the first place.

---

* It has been shown that it is better to be born wealthy in America than it is to be intelligent. Success in life is greatly affected by the wealth of your parents.[64] Although hard work is part of success, our ability to work hard and succeed is also dependent on our brain which is, in no small part, a product of our environment. Poverty largely has a detrimental effect on developing minds, and worse, the more adversity we have faced as a foetus, child, or adolescent, the harder it becomes to claw our way out. Bad luck compounds.[65]

3. Make Them Fear Other Options

Lastly, if people can't be disabused of the idea that the rich are taking an ever-greater share of the pie, they need to be made to fear the alternatives. Tell them stuff like: *they* will take away your freedom, enact Sharia law, remake Venezuela in Virginia, or worse, they will tax you more.

To sum it all up my dear, *poor* friend: "It is actually fine, it's not *that* unequal and *if,* just *if,* there is a problem, it's probably *your* fault. And, actually, unfairness is good for you and society, and the super-rich do a lot of good (look at the Sackler museum thingy). The real problem is the immigrants taking your jobs, changing the things you love, and, of course, that country that stole our factories. If you think that *someone else* will help you, think again. What *they* want is to take everything you have, tax you more, take away the things you love, bring in more immigrants and, in the end, destroy society. Now, kindly cooperate, we need your vote."

Tyranny: Innately Corrupt Systems of Power

Societies depend on a structure of ideas to provide stability and, the bigger the idea, often, the more abstract it is. Ideas of nation, origin, history, purpose, and traits, alongside ideas that aid cooperation, like property rights or justice, all enable societies to function at scale.

Some ideas are integral to our society, and without these ideas holding sufficient power, our societies face instability. Such ideas include those that define our nation, its borders, and ideas of how we share power. If considerable parts of our society do not share these ideas, then we face the risk of conflict and instability.

Even dictators provide stability compared to the chaos of a civil war and for such regimes 'it could be worse' is both a threat and a reality. This reality means that poor ideas are far more preferable to the risk of *no ideas*—setting a low bar for the ideological structures required for social stability. Like the air we breathe, we can get used to a stink.

Dictators and autocrats are often brought into power with some form of popular consent. As they ascend, to-be dictators are often very popular with those who bring them to power. Perhaps the people were sick of poor economic conditions, political stagnation, or of corruption and scandal. The 'strong man' (they are almost always men) who is not afraid to 'say it like it is' excites people into believing that only he can turn things around. Even if the maverick has questionable ideas, *anything* that makes things change is better than an endless status quo.

In the following years, the new leader gets rid of laws that limit his power, corrupts the judiciary, decimates the free press and extends the length of his term. The to-be dictator has a very fixed idea of how the country's government should change: it shouldn't. The strong man is not without problems, though. He must also pay off those who keep him in power and, as time brings inevitable change, he must silence the growing chorus of voices that speak out against him.

Those who *take* power are always afraid. The dictator knows that his position is a social construct that relies on the same ideas and bits of paper he trashed on his path to power. As people start to realise how corrupt the regime is, people start to demand more say on how the country is run, and the opposition gathers support. The dictator and his cronies are prepared for this. They arrest opposition leaders and put them in jail. They use the police to identify those who support them—clamping down on journalists, bloggers, academics, or activists.

Despite his hard power, what the dictator fights against, is not so much people, but ideas. The idea that he can be wrested from power, the idea that his truths are lies, the idea that his rule is failing, the idea that something else can be better. When the people become more forceful in asking for change the dictator is left with two options: he can either surrender power or apply more force. However, to change things based on people's demands abets the idea that the people have power—a slippery slope. Meanwhile, the longer he clings to office, the more force is required, leading to political arrests, torture, killings, and other atrocities.

When you destroy ideas of reasonable treatment, you cannot expect to receive it yourself. Muammar Gaddafi, the Libyan dictator of forty years, was dragged out of a drainpipe and jubilantly murdered by his own people. Saddam Hussain was pulled out of a hole in the ground by American forces and later hung by an Iraqi court for the mass killings of civilians. What more could either Gaddhafi or Hussein expect? For decades both had treated their people with arbitrary detention, disappearances, torture, and extra-judicial killings.

The autocrat that strips their enemies of their wealth fears the same treatment and goes to great lengths to hide wealth in safe places. The dictator that poisons their opposition lives in fear of every meal. The tyrant that executes his opponents fears the same fate should they lose grip on power.

Saddam Hussain was so afraid he hired surgically altered body doubles and used to have several meals prepared in different locations so no one would know where he ate. Vladimir Putin, who has poisoned many of his enemies, has been reported to have hired several tasters to allay his fears of being poisoned. Kim Jong-il was too afraid to travel by air and would only travel in his armoured train when conducting international visits. Likewise, his equally paranoid son purged and executed members of his own family. Pick a despot and you will find a life lived in fear, paranoia, and distrust.

This is true all the way down the chain of power. When a policeman brutally beats a political dissident at the behest of his commander, he reinforces fears of what might happen if he were to defect or if *his people* lost power. The businessman who screws over business partners spends a career afraid that others will do the same to him.

Our behaviour communicates values and establishes the norms that we can expect to live by. To the old saying "*do unto others as you would have them do to you"* we might add *"as you do unto to others, you do unto yourself."*

Compounding the moral hole that authoritarian leaders climb into is the fact that their regimes do not rely on strength but on weakness. Initially, they prey on human frailties to gain power; our tendency to believe that which we *feel* to be true, and the fundamental weakness in empathy that, when exploited, opens the door to fear and hatred of others.

Once in power, they rely on the avarice and cowardice of those who trot along to their tune. Those who take the payment, enjoy the corrupt distribution of power, look away from the injustice done to others, or who will commit cruelty in the name of the regime.

Authoritarians build towers of power out of human weakness. Their regimes exist as literal expressions of human frailty and of our worst capacities for moral failure, in such regimes, *weakness is strength.* For the dictator, being surrounded by corrupt, weak, malevolent people serves only as fuel for their worries.

Aristotle believed tyranny to be an unnatural human condition and, two thousand years later, evolutionary biology has proven him right. Tyranny—being unfair, uncaring, and steeped with unjust force—is contrary to innate morality and such regimes must fight constantly against the fact that they are at odds with nature itself.

CHAPTER 11

WHERE IDEAS GO TO DIE

In the last chapter, we talked about abstract and emotional wealth and how the obsessive pursuit of the former inhibits the cultivation of the latter. We've looked at how accruing vast amounts of property is an unnatural human behaviour and how prioritising money and other forms of abstract wealth over our physical, relational, and emotional well-being not only hurts us as individuals but also damages our societies. Greed is personally and socially destructive and the inequality it drives inevitably leads to social dysfunction. Modern capitalism is a case in point and the only solution is through regulation and appropriate taxation. As force is often used to create or maintain unfair or uncaring situations, change, as vital as it may be, doesn't come easy—but it does come. Ideas of all stripes die and are replaced by new (hopefully better) ideas and, understanding how this occurs, is the first step to making it happen.

***

Not everything that dies is killed and this is especially true of ideas. The death of an idea often looks more like a slow march into oblivion than a cataclysmic bang. Even ideas that are systematically hunted rarely succumb but rather retreat underground only to reappear years, decades, or even centuries later.

A striking example of this is the atomist and secular ideas of the Ancient Greek philosopher Lucretius. Lucretius believed the world was made of minuscule particles that move perpetually and randomly through a void. He saw the origins of life as the result of these atoms knocking against each other and assembling in novel forms, and death as the process of our atoms breaking free and continuing in their movement through the void. This remarkably astute philosophy concluded that there was no afterlife, no punishment or reward after death, that death should not be feared, and that it was the basic forces of the universe that created life—not a god. Although atomist ideas thrived in Ancient Rome, the rise of Christianity and the subsequent suppression of heretic (nonconforming) ideas, meant that Lucretius's ideas were almost completely lost. A thousand years after writing, a monk saved the last manuscript containing Lucretius' ideas from rotting away in a remote monastery cellar and passed them to his wealthy patron in Florence. Years later, after being copied and shared, Lucretius' writing went on to inspire enlightenment thinkers whose scientific descendants went on to prove him right.

Because of the infinite paths ideas can take on their path to success, if we want to know *how* ideas succeed, it is more useful to understand how they die. Ideas of any importance are rarely killed but are instead replaced piecemeal, to the point that their original form becomes unrecognisable, or falls so far from relevance that there is no place left for them to persist.

The Two Ways Ideas Die

Death by Stagnation & Irrelevance	Where ideas are not (or cannot be) adapted to fit a changing reality and lose relevance over time.
Death by Subversion, Debasement, and Replacement	Sub-ideas are replaced with other ideas, subverting the meaning of the core idea. Connecting sub-ideas are debased until the core idea becomes weakened and vulnerable to replacement.

Countless cultural norms have gradually grown irrelevant and all but disappeared. "Britching," for instance, was common in the 1800s. At a britching event, boys signalled their transition to manhood by losing their shorts and donning britches, or long trousers, for the first time. It was a celebrated rite of passage that, today, has all but disappeared. Where did this tradition go? In the main part, cheaper clothing production and changing fashions simply made britching irrelevant. Did anyone fight to keep it going? Not really. Britching lingers on in limited social environments but, for the masses, it's dead and nobody really cares.

The death of ideas by *subversion, debasement, and replacement* is messier. Ideas are often caught in extended ideological struggles. Competing ideas subvert existing beliefs and shift their meaning away from their original intent. Sub-ideas are debased and replaced; the *abstract* is divorced from the *emotional* and, eventually, switched out for something new. All our most important ideas are always under threat, and it is hard to intervene in their subversion unless we tune into the process.

Take the United Kingdom's exit from the European Union, for instance.

The EU is an ambitious project whose original intent was to bind European countries together in mutual dependence and create "lasting peace in Europe." Ideas of imperialism, nationalism, and racism combined with new forms of mass media and industrialised economies triggered a world war that engulfed the world in mechanised destruction. From the ashes rose support for formalised ideas of human rights, respect for territorial sovereignty, and, in Europe, a desire to stop endless war on the continent.

Ideas of European integration long preceded World War II, however. Widespread talk of uniting the continent emerged in the 1800s after the fall of Napoleon's Empire and was bolstered by the liberal ideas of the French and American Revolutions. These ideas grew in popularity after the First World War, and in 1920, John Maynard Keynes, alongside other leading economists and academics of the day, called for a free-trade union of European states.

Before the Second World War had ended, Winston Churchill was already thinking about the creation of a 'Council of Europe' and in 1949 the idea took root. Initially, the 'Council of Europe' was more focused on human rights issues but over time turned its attention to trade agreements, starting with the formation of the 'European Coal and Steel Community.' As leaders believed that coal and steel were the most critical industries for war, they hoped that tying them together would reduce the risk of conflict.

In 1992 the Maastricht Treaty was signed, officially creating the European Union and presently 28 countries and half a billion people, enjoy free movement and hundreds of thousands of businesses benefit from low friction trade.

Not everyone favoured European integration though, and some, especially certain very vocal Brits, were steadfastly opposed. The Daily Mail, The Daily Express, The Telegraph and The Sun, all owned by wealthy Eurosceptics, engaged in a targeted campaign to denounce the European Union. They bombarded the British public with hundreds of falsehoods, now known as 'EU Myths.' The idea of 'freedom of movement' became about immigrants taking over local communities, claiming benefits, and taking jobs.[66] 'Human rights' were subverted into *really* being the EU preventing the deportation of convicted terrorists and foreign criminals. Common standards, food, labour, and environmental protections became about red tape and bendy bananas. Regulations to prevent accidents at work became 'health and safety gone mad.'

After 47 years of storytelling, combined with the failure of the European Union to properly address the downsides of integration, the Union's virtuous founding ideas were debased so much so that, in 2016, the British people voted to leave. The 'Vote Leave' campaign succeeded for many reasons. The depreciation of facts, populist oversimplification, fearmongering about Turkish immigrants, and the promise to give £350m a week to the NHS—were all effective—but these messages only landed because people were ready to believe them. The ideological landscape had been prepared; the European Union had already long meant something different to Brits than to those in Brussels.

The idea of the European Union had no hope of surviving in the minds of those who little understood its purpose and were subjected to decades of lies and political scapegoating. The European Union's biggest failure was, perhaps, to not effectively communicate its benefits to its citizens on an ongoing basis.

On the day of the vote, leave voters did not *feel* that the EU was good for them and voted accordingly.

How Ideas Survive

While there are two main ways in which ideas die, there is only one way that they survive, and that is through continuous adaptation.

The Political Scientist Michael Freeden has *adaptation* in mind when he explains that *"ambiguity as well as certainty are two necessary features of any ideology. They extend its life expectancy, and are vital to the (imagined) harmony and stability normally sought through the political process."*[67] Rigid ideologies become irrelevant over time. Only those that are flexible endure.

Force can, of course, keep an idea alive but only through its continued application. When force wanes, so too does the idea's vitality. And, as the distance between *reality* and the *forced reality* grows, the force required increases and with it, the risk of failure. Persistent ideologies supported by force must either exist in a state of *extreme coercion* or undergo *managed change* to allow a level of adaption that makes the level of required force sustainable.

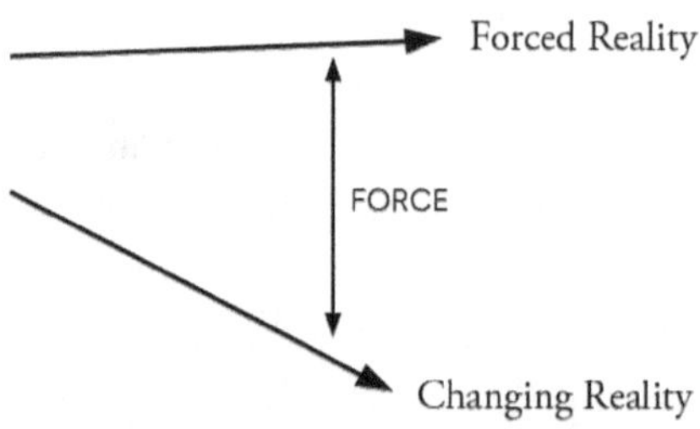

The Birth and Re-birth of Ideas

Where do new ideas come from?

Like wondering what happens when we die, some ideas are present by the nature of thought. Other ideas are expressed innately, or to fulfil the *hows* and *whys* of common human problems. Other ideas still are a result of innovation, be it technological, scientific, or social, but few ideas come out of a vacuum.

Even when breakthrough thinkers communicate ideas that change the world, their ideas have typically been developed by many people working in the same field. The breakthrough individual just happens to be the one who finds convincing language and proof enough to make their ideas relevant.

Ideas that species changed over time preceded Charles Darwin by thousands of years, for instance, and he wasn't the only one working on a theory of evolution at the time that he published *On the Origin of Species* (1859). Ancient Greek astronomers promoted the idea of a heliocentric solar system (one where the earth and other planets orbit the sun) influencing thinkers, including Copernicus, whose model eventually gained broad acceptance nearly two thousand years later. In a 1675 letter to Robert Hooke, Isaac Newton famously stated, *"If I have seen further it is by standing on the shoulders of Giants,"* acknowledging his dependence on those that came before him.

As the rise of the scientific method decoupled thought from the limitations of philosophy or religious dogma, it enabled the imagining of bold new futures. At its heart, science is the pursuit of facts but, without the supporting architecture of ideas, facts serve little purpose. Scientific discoveries lead to technologies and understandings that change the world, but the nature of the resulting change depends both on the quality of the science and the ideas in which it gets wrapped up.

Scientific discovery has led to vaccines, antibiotics, and contraception, eradicating horrible diseases, preventing countless deaths by infection, and enabling family planning. It has also led to the development of nuclear weapons, capable of destroying life as we know it. Discovering the fact that we can create bombs that use fission to vaporise cities is one thing, the idea that we should, is another.

It is not uncommon for certain 'serious' professions to look down on 'the arts,' and see them as a kind of silly, unserious activity, but without art, in the broadest sense, discoveries would struggle to be realised. To change the world requires not just discovery, but the cultivation of the belief that a discovery means something.

As it happens, facts are notoriously bad at affecting behaviour and many studies demonstrate that we are not the reasoned, fact-abiding creatures that we often imagine ourselves to be. For the human brain, *feelings* matter more than *facts*.

Research shows that we are also particularly good at ignoring information that makes us feel bad, obliges us to do something we don't want to do, or threatens our identity, values or worldview.[68]

Sure, but me and you, we are smart, so it won't affect us?

Unfortunately, motivated reasoning and intelligence can go hand-in-hand.*

The political scientist Milton Lodge writes: *"People who have a dislike of some policy—for example, abortion—if they're unsophisticated they can just reject it out of hand"* but, *"if they're sophisticated, they can go one step further and start coming up with counterarguments."* That is, experts are just as susceptible to emotional bias as anyone else, they're just better at constructing a convincing argument to support their case.

Likewise, evidence suggests that smart people are more likely to believe fake news when it fits their worldview and that established experts are more likely to dismiss new information that debunks their existing beliefs, it can even make them more certain of them.[69,70] No matter how smart we are, what we *feel to be true* can be more powerful than a heap of facts, and this causes problems when it comes to changing the ideas we live by.

Storytelling is central to the establishment of ideas, and this is as true of the stories we tell ourselves as of those we are told. Take, for instance, the fact that the climate has warmed 0.08 °C every decade since 1880 and ocean acidity has increased from pH 8.2 to pH 8.1 since the start of the industrial revolution. Dry as a bone, dull as dishwater.

Now, consider that in this same time frame, hundreds of millions of people have been displaced and many have died preventable deaths. The world is *literally* burning, the ice caps are melting, and the sea is rising. In the last century, 543 animal species have gone extinct and that's only the ones we know about—the natural world is disappearing and very little is being done to slow the decline. This description reports on the same issue cited in the last paragraph but with more emotional meaning.

We believe what we *feel.* And this has everything to do with

---

* Motivated Reasoning is when emotional biases lead to justifications or decisions based on desirability rather than an accurate reflection of the evidence.

the important role narrative plays in fostering cooperation and building society. Creativity can give birth to new ideas and support the growth of those that already exist.

The Role of Art in Ideological Change

Thinkers, writers, poets, painters, comedians, journalists, and filmmakers—broadly, artists of all stripes—transmit information in ways that capture attention, enabling facts to be felt and allowing them to be incorporated into belief.[71]

Storytelling is a deeply human activity. It is linked to increased cooperation within social groups, making it a socially important and highly influential art form.[72]

Stories can enable audiences to 'connect the dots' without being *told* what to think, and better, without being explicitly told that *they are wrong*. Stories can allow us to understand the experiences of others and allow us to create an emotional connection with those who are otherwise abstracted from our lives. Captivating stories aid the physical changing of our minds by helping us create new connections and causing us to think about them long after we experience them.[73] Effective art can lay the groundwork for broader change by making our positions feel less *absolute*, thus opening the door to the validity of other ideas and easing the enactment of social change.[74]

It is hard to pinpoint where art 'changes the world' not because it doesn't but because we require many *conversations* to change our beliefs. Shifting beliefs takes time, and different forms of communication work for different people, in different ways, for different issues, and at different moments. A single piece of art, perhaps a film, may crystallise a decade of gently accrued knowledge—making the experience feel transformative—while watching the same film ten years prior may have had no such effect.

Adding to this complexity, *effective art* tends to communicate one point very well, meaning that many conversations, across a range of related sub-ideas, at different times, in different forms, with different people, are required to challenge strongly held ideologies.

In essence, good art allows us to *feel* values. Artists, therefore, encode facts into an emotionally relevant format, and this makes art central to ideological change.

On this basis, artists, thinkers, writers, filmmakers, and activists, have three important roles in society. 1) To keep desirable ideas relevant through the iteration of sub-ideas, protecting them from irrelevance or from being subverted to other, less desirable ends, while pushing against conservative forces that would see them never change. 2) To challenge undesirable ideas, new or resurgent, and to debase their sub-ideas, disconnecting them from the cultural identities that form around them. And 3) to conceptualise new ideas that better interact with our ever-changing environment.

Ideological Decay

For a period, I spent time in South Africa and dated a white woman born in the mid-1990s. Hers was the first generation to grow up without first-hand experience of the Apartheid and while her friend group was diverse and she supported the 'Rhodes Must Fall' movement, her parents were stuck in the past. Like so many of their generation, they held the view that *"you can date anyone, just don't bring a black boy home."* They were racist and all the changes in legislation notwithstanding, their ideas didn't seem to be going anywhere.

Laws can institute change, but they can't transform ideas.

How long will it take for these opinions to change? How long will it be until young white people in South Africa can introduce a black partner to their parents without worrying about what they will think?

Disapproval of interracial relationships is a good indication of racist sentiment. Whites might accept black people going to the same school as their children, or a black person leading their country, but they may still feel uncomfortable about a black person entering their family. Desegregation does not become any more personal than when a member of the former *out-group* becomes part of your ultimate *in-group*.

In America, this has been studied. In 1958, six years before the Civil Rights Act legally ended segregation, approximately 4% of US adults "approved of interracial marriage." By 2010, this number had leapt to 87%.[75] Here, significant change took fifty years to arrive, and, in 2010, the work was far from done.

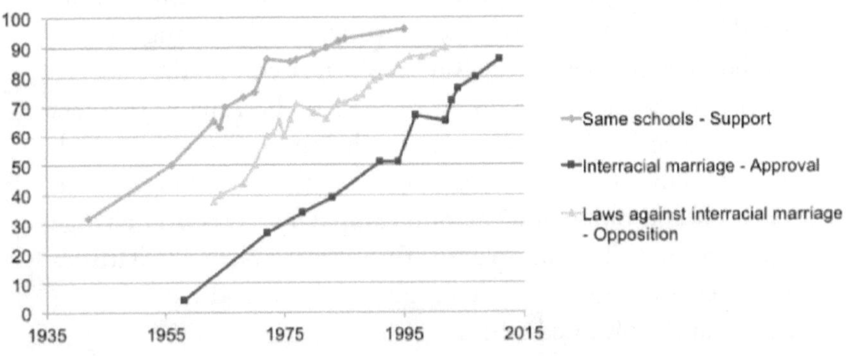

Fig. 1 (W): Principles of Equality - Schools and Interracial Marriage
(White respondents)

Same Schools: "Do you think white students and black students should go to the same schools or to separate schools?"
Interracial marriage: "Do you approve or disapprove of marriage between blacks and whites?"
Laws Against Interracial marriage: "Do you think there should be laws against marriages between blacks and whites?"

Chart showing the compiled results of several national surveys that have been tracking white Americans' racial attitudes from as early as the 1940s up until 2010.[75]

That substantial ideological change takes *at least* a half-century to arrive turns out to be a fairly consistent rule of thumb.

In 1979, research carried out in the UK showed that drink

driving was seen as mostly acceptable and nearly two-thirds of young male drivers drank-drove on a *weekly* basis. The Road Safety Act that introduced the first legal blood alcohol limit had been passed in 1967 and yet attitudes remained relaxed, to say the least. Since the first public information film about drink driving in 1964, the British government has spent tens of millions of pounds on advertising and awareness campaigns, and the widespread use of breathalyser tests led to hundreds of thousands of prosecutions. In 2015, a survey by the campaign group THINK! found that 91% of people felt drink driving was unacceptable, and 92% would be ashamed if they were caught doing so. Again, the shift was nearly 50 years in the making.

Ideas around smoking show a similar trend. In 1962 seventy percent of British men smoked.[76] In the same year the Royal College of Physicians produced a ground-breaking report on the effects of smoking, cementing its link to lung cancer, cardiovascular disease, and COPD. When faced with the evidence of the harm they were doing to their bodies, many smokers interviewed at the time were nonchalant and unconcerned. What followed was fifty years of smoking legislation, tobacco taxation and public information campaigns to try and change opinion and behaviour. In 2019, The Office of National Statistics recorded that 15.9% of British men smoked, and half of these said that they wanted to quit.[77]

Likewise, research on attitudes toward homosexuality in the UK shows that in 1987, 84% of people considered same-sex sexual relations to be either, always (64%), or mostly (11%), wrong. By 2012 this view was reported held by under 30% of the population. By 2017, this had declined further to just 17%.[78,79] If acceptance of homosexuality continues to increase at a rate of 1.9% per year, it won't be until 2027, or exactly 50 years after the 1987 study, that this phase of homophobia bites the dust.

Studies into the intergenerational change of religious beliefs in immigrant families likewise demonstrate how deep-seated cultural ideas can change. When people with strong ethno-religious identities move to a country that has a different dominant religion or is largely secular, it takes just three generations for their descendants to come to express the same beliefs of the local population—regardless of how strong the initial immigrant's faith.[80] Religious beliefs, carried through families, perhaps for millennia, *gone* in sixty years.

A final example arrives in the form of the Nazi weaponization of antisemitism. The Nazis used a wide range of pseudo-science, stereotypes, and conspiracy theories, to justify their crimes against Jewish people. After World War II, and the shocking facts of the Holocaust were uncovered, Germans were put through a program of "de-Nazification." In 1945 antisemitism was an integral part of German society; by 2006 only 5% of Germans held anti-Semitic views. Despite the devastation of the war, the national guilt, the brutal atrocity of the Holocaust, the war crime trials, and the criminalisation of antisemitism, it still took 70 years to go from mostly anti-Semitic to mostly-not-anti-Semitic. Interestingly, the regions where anti-Semitic ideas are most popular today are the same regions where the Nazis were most popular, and studies show how these regional antisemitic ideas may be traced as far back as the Middle Ages.[78]

This quick look at six different areas of ideological decline indicates that wholesale ideological change takes around fifty to sixty years, and sometimes a little more, to occur. What this tells us is that changing people's minds takes significant work, and that change will be slower if not supported by laws, enforcement, and broad social pressure.

It is also clear that natural life cycles—older people dying, and new people being born—play a significant role. In fifty years, over half the people alive today will be dead. Their ideas may live on, but regardless of how strongly they felt, their children may care significantly less about the things they held dear, and their grandchildren might not care at all.

This understanding also raises the concept of ideological

security, where, for any idea our society holds important, it is possible to imagine that its destruction is only fifty years away.

The Death of God

Let's look closer at the debasement and replacement of a pervasive and powerful idea. In Chapter 3 we mentioned Charles Bradlaugh, the atheist who dedicated his life to challenging religious ideas in the 1800s. He was a man before his time, leading a fight that arguably, in Britain, was eventually won. Once central to national identity, Christianity is now largely irrelevant for the majority of British people.

This process of secularisation had been gaining momentum since the Enlightenment and accelerated in the 20th Century. Since the census of 1851, when the Church of England enjoyed a weekly attendance of sixty percent of the population, attendance has dwindled to less than 1.5 percent today.[81] It did not have to be this way. Other countries maintained high levels of religiosity despite their modernisation, so what happened to Christian ideas in England?

The following table shows how the Church of England was seen in the 1800s: a highly respected institution that anchored the 'moral values' of the mighty British Empire. It held its ground against science when it came to questions of ethics and the Church's views on sexuality, marriage and divorce were enshrined in law. Christianity was widely seen to be the one *true* religion and Britain had a strong Christian-Nationalist identity.

Prevalent Ideological Structure (Turn of 20th Century)[82]

Christian God Exists *Anglican doctrine is correct expression of faith*	Abstract
Highest moral authority[82] — Other religions are wrong — The Bible is truth	
Sexuality, family planning, and gender roles dictated by religious code* — The church should influence laws, policy and international affairs — Protestant interpretation is the most accurate expression of Christian faith** — One should condemn other religious beliefs, or avoid them — All answers and guidance you need can be found within the bible — Science should not interfere with questions of morality, they are in the domain of religion	Sub-ideas
Conservative moral values / Christian-Nationalism	Emotional & Identity

To discuss the decline of Christianity in England, we will look at each of the sub-ideas and examine the factors that caused them to be debased and replaced by other ideas.

The Highest Moral Authority

It has largely been the Church's own behaviour that has discredited the idea that the church should lead on questions of morality. The Church of England fought long and hard against non-religious marriage, pushing to maintain organised religion's

---

* Bradlaugh, C., Besant, A. W., & Britain, G. (1877). The Queen V. Charles Bradlaugh and Annie Besant. The book is a transcript of their trial with the addition of an introduction where they explain what they did and why they were put on trial.

** Nickolas G. Conrad, of Washington State University, explains that the couple lived in separate lodgings when they were in a relationship.[83] Bradlaugh thought that this was a good way to protect his girlfriend's dignity and social reputation. Furthermore, at the time, sex was forbidden by the church unless it was done between a married man and women. So, even though the law did not explicitly forbid them to live under the same roof or to have sex outside of wedlock, the religious character of the social norms and society in general led people to ostracise those that chose to live a different life.

monopoly on *coupling*. Likewise, it fought against gay marriage, and almost every aspect of gay rights. It recently fought against no-fault divorce—to uphold laws that force people to stay in unhappy relationships unless proof of a narrow set of moral transgressions could be found.

While non-heterosexual people were imprisoned and treated terribly at the turn of the 20th Century, and today 92% of Britons are comfortable with gay people forming a part of their community, the Church of England still condemns homosexual behaviour. [84,85]

Hypocrisy also undermines moral authority. While the Church fought against providing equal employment rights for women within its organisation, it was battered by a seemingly endless string of paedophile scandals and revelations of cover-ups. While the organisation postured a progressive stance campaigning against zero-hour contracts and corporate tax avoidance, it used the zero-hour contracts for its own staff and invested in the companies they railed against.[86] After decades of scandal and being out of step with the times, the Church itself has firmly debased the idea that it is the *highest moral authority* for most British people.

Other Religions are Wrong

The act of passing judgment on other faiths is practically a part of religious tradition and infidels have long been the subject of discrimination. Nevertheless, the idea that "other religions are wrong" has lost ground as the world has gone global and people have gained awareness of cultural diversity.

The revulsion provoked by the Holocaust drove a new era of religious tolerance that saw the right to practice religion into a universal human right. Such ideas make asserting that other religions are *'wrong'* a difficult position to hold, and religious leaders have had to make peace and respect each other's mutual validity.

Improved religious education, better representation of minorities, increased immigration, and societies that actively work to make room for, and respect, other religious beliefs, have diminished the idea that a single religion can be considered as the only truth. As such, this entire sub-idea—that the only valid religion is Christian Protestantism—has been replaced by other ideas that became dominant inside and outside of the Church.

The Bible is Truth

Christians believe that the Bible is 'God's word' and is the source of ultimate truth. Ever since the Enlightenment, this idea has been going out of style and other metrics for assessing veracity have gained traction.

The rise of science has led to the marginalisation and exclusion of Christianity from the public sphere.[87] Where for centuries the bible was seen as the be-all and end-all, and nothing was worth knowing outside of the church's teaching, the scientific method opened the doors to acknowledging ignorance, which is a stance toward knowledge completely at odds with Christian religious doctrine.

The Enlightenment was the beginning of the end of the belief that the Bible was a reliable tool for understanding reality. The scientific method led to thousands of new understandings that challenged religious doctrine, whether it was the age of the earth, our place in the solar system, or Darwin's theories of evolution. Progressively, ancient ideas have become less relevant and harder to defend.

With the sub-ideas of British Christianity debased and replaced, the prevailing ideas at the end of the 20th Century looked something more like the following:

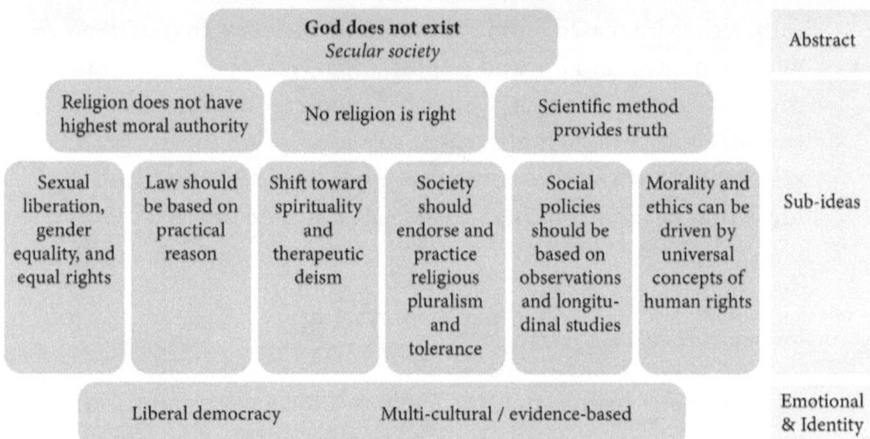

This shift away from organised religion did not happen in all countries, however. Many, including the US, still maintain their religious grounding despite driving rapid economic and scientific advances. The question thus becomes: Why did the Church of England do so badly? What went wrong?

The Church of England's notable failure lies in its inability to address declining membership. Ultimately, it did not adapt to meet the changing needs of its congregation, and it could only do that because it *doesn't need* members to survive.

Thanks to a combination of ancient endowments, including huge tracts of land and property, and an investment fund worth over £10bn ($12.5bn) the Church of England's leaders can afford to put off the hard decisions required to institute change. Thus, churchgoers are largely irrelevant to the organisation's income, and thus survival.

This is very different from the United States, for instance, where religion is a more decentralised affair, and churches compete for membership. If an American church doesn't have enough members, it dies. American churches must keep pace with the changing times and must engage in real efforts to keep Christianity relevant to Americans.

In the 1800s, the Church of England was a leader of social change in word and deed and, especially thanks to its efforts in educating the poor, it held a central place in the public sphere. Over the 20th Century, education shifted away from the church and into the hands of the state, diminishing the role the Church had in society.[88] It became politicians, not priests, who publicly championed the poor and it was the state that did something about it.

Today, the Church continues to seek involvement in public decision-making, yet it lacks cultural relevance and fails to make the kind of contribution that warrants influence. Any change that would allow the Church to regain relevance is likely more change than its remaining members are willing to accept, and so the institution continues its hapless slide toward oblivion.

In short, the Church of England has blown it. They stand with their moral authority in tatters, pontificating over a population that cares little for their doctrine and that considers their influence to drive conflict, not peace.[89] No wonder, then, that few are willing to defer to them on important matters.

Change or Be Replaced

People are often bemused by company rebrands. A logo change that costs millions of dollars might seem absurd, but imagine a brand that hasn't changed since the 1950s. Would you trust it? Would you even look? Businesses cannot afford to be replaced so they engage in constant change.

Likewise, pop stars live at the bleeding edge of change and must create novelty for consumers in order to stay relevant. When Justin Bieber or Miley Cyrus went from *innocent* to *adult*, people (older people, I guess) were outraged, but this rebranding allowed them to retain their connection to their audience as they too changed. If pop stars stay still, they are quickly replaced.

Political ideologies also need to change if they are to hold sway. In 1780, Britain considered itself a democracy even though less than 3% of the population could vote.[90] In 1832, The Great Reform Act extended the vote to men who owned property and had an annual income of £10 or more. Universal suffrage allowing women (over the age of 30) to vote did not arrive until 1918. In 1969, the voting age was brought from 21 down to 18 and, finally, all legal adults could vote. Throughout all these periods British society was seen as a 'Democracy' but the variation of between 3% and almost 100% of adults being eligible to vote suggests that the sub-ideas of democracy changed significantly over time. Democracy today is the product of a continual process of adaptation and is vulnerable just as any other idea.

Now, let's look at a few ideas that are important today.

CHAPTER 12

THREE IDEOLOGICAL FIGHTS

After a period of relative ideological stability, where between the end of the Second World War and the end of the century the ideas of democracy, human rights, and territorial sovereignty were generally enhanced, we in the West, are living through a new period of ideological tension.

As the last wave of European authoritarianism slides from living memory, those who desire uninhibited power, and the destruction of democratic institutions that block their path to it, are regaining the ideological space required to develop their ideas. This space, once blackened by the horrors of the Holocaust and the butchery of war, has once again become fertile ground for populist and far-right leaders. The political processes of fascism are creeping back in modern guises, exploiting the same human weaknesses: the proclivity to make decisions based on fear, to imagine that all problems are caused by *the other*, and to believe simple stories that speak to our anxieties.

Globalisation did not work as Western thinkers thought it would. One-party states like China did not slide inevitably toward democratic openness and dictators did not yield to their dependencies on external trade. Instead, they used their newfound wealth, and the dependence that democratic states had on their resources, to pursue violent campaigns, ethnic cleansing, and increased regime control. Simultaneously, they worked to undermine democratic ideas, funded extremist political parties, and used unparalleled access to Western citizens to feed them disinformation and conspiracy theories to disrupt our politics—helping to create a constituency ripe for the populist and authoritarian candidates they favour.

In Europe, it threatens the entire European project. In America, we see the resurgence of far-right white nationalism imbued with conspiracy theories seeping into mainstream politics.

The failure of the European project, or an authoritarian America, would result in a seismic shift in global power and politics. An authoritarian America would be an ugly place, especially considering its capabilities for surveillance, a ready-to-go militarised police force, its vast prison capacity, and unparalleled military power.

The dissolution of European cooperation would make European states far easier to bully, subdue and corrupt, which would be of great value to both Putin's Russia and Xi's China. Countries like Hungary, whose populist and authoritarian-leaning leaders are already openly opposed to democratic institutions and actively working to undermine the rule of law, would quickly side with authoritarian states, creating serious security vulnerabilities. Larger European economies would lose the bargaining power they once had and would compromise on ethics even more than they do so now. The days of Europe as a beacon of liberal democracy would be numbered.

To gain power, authoritarians, fascists, and extremists of their ilk, depend on the widespread belief of myths that tell of a threat from 'the other' that only they can resolve, and of an idealised past that only they can revive. The idealised past signifies a lost greatness which may be religiously, racially, or culturally pure (or a combination of all three) and is usually patriarchal.[91]* The

---

* Many extreme fantasy-based political ideologies tend to idealise patriarchal structures and stereotypical masculine identities. The resulting reality, however, is that the so-called 'real man' is merely one slavish to the ideas of his masters. Rather than being strong, independent, or brave, the *true* ideal man does, and is, exactly as he is told.

fear and aggrievance that results, justifies having otherwise unsavoury people in office.

For Hitler it was the Jews and a mythical Aryan agrarian past; for Mussolini, it was any 'non-Italians' and the myth of Rome; for Putin, it is 'the West' and the greatness of the Soviet Union; for Trump it is immigrants and, ambiguously, making America great again. These ideas are reliant on both fiction and theories of conspiracy like that "the Jews are trying to destroy Germany," that "the West is conspiring to destroy Russia" or that "Americans are being replaced."

Who believes in the myths of these would-be tyrants? Clearly, many people do, this is evidenced by history, but it can be hard to imagine that you and I, with all our well-read smarts, could be taken in by these would-be masters. We should, however, not be so quick to imagine ourselves immune.

When we look at ideas that have dominated popular political opinion or that deeply affect our lives, they may not always be as logical or based on truth as we might hope. What we believe—belief being a feeling of confidence that something is correct or true—often relies less on evidence, and more on the fact that the people we are close to also hold the same beliefs.

This social component of how we understand reality warps our thinking in ways that are hard to see. Beliefs and social norms can have unquestioned foundations and as a result, many popular conceptions cause real harm while having little basis in reality.

To explore this, we look at the ideas behind the housing crisis, drug prohibition, and climate change denialism. Although these ideas are not fascist myths, their underlying structures carry some of the hallmarks. Where drug prohibition creates a 'disgusting' underclass and justifies cruelty toward them, housing prices enrich a small minority at the expense of almost everyone else, and climate change denialists use disinformation and conspiracy theories to sow confusion and foster inertia.

The following three topics give a snapshot of how ideologies can creep into norms and carry us to undesirable places.

An Idea Yet to Peak: High House Prices

What's life for? An uncontroversial view is that life is not for paying off a huge debt for overpriced housing. This seems obvious, but it is what most of us do for most of our adult lives. Today, if our twenties are for saving a deposit, and we buy at thirty—which would be comparatively young—then our thirties, forties, fifties, and early sixties, are for paying off the debt and the interest it accrues.[92,93] With the rise of forty-year mortgage products, many will not clear their debt until well into their seventies. The story of the modern housing crisis is a story of accepting ideas that have led to a worse outcome for practically everyone.

Some years ago, when I was thirty, I had saved the princely sum of £60,000 ($80,000) for a deposit. Had I bought in London, however, where I lived at the time, and borrowed the maximum possible, all I could buy was a cramped, run-down, two-bed in a deprived area with poor transport links. I could not bring myself to invest so much of my life into something that represented such bad value for money and that, ultimately, I did not even *want*.

While industrialised food production and manufacturing have enabled the cost of essential goods to fall dramatically compared to income, housing has done the opposite. Since 1965, home prices in the US have increased seven times faster than income, and in the UK, house prices have doubled compared to wages since 1970.[94–96]

The price of housing does not sound like an issue with an *ideological* basis, but when we take a closer look at the causes of high house prices, an ideological picture emerges. "It's just supply and demand" you cry, and that may be so, but what determines housing supply? And for that matter, what affects demand?

We are back to ideas.

The Dominant Ideology of House Prices

High prices are justified	Abstract

House prices (should) always go up	There is not enough land to build houses	To pay a lot for housing is part of life	
Houses are a safe long-term investment / House prices going down is a disaster	The country is crowded with too many people / It is driven by simple supply and demand	The housing ladder has long been part of life / Young people are just complaining – it was no easier before	Sub-ideas
Home ownership is a sacrifice but it's worth it / Young people are snowflakes			Emotional & Identity

Few ideas impact our lives so materially, and obviously, than the ideas that squat beneath the housing crisis.

The steady rise of house prices over the past thirty years has given rise to the idea that house prices always go up. Thus, housing is a safe investment, and it is worth being mortgaged to the hilt. However, house prices rising faster than both wages and inflation is not only unsustainable, it also doesn't make sense. Houses get older and as they do, they need costly and disruptive renovations, thus *they should* depreciate in value accordingly.

We might see high prices as inevitable because there's not enough land, or there are too many people, but there are holes in this logic too. Yes, in some urban areas, there is little available land for development, but even there, obtaining permission is arduous, and many investors simply buy-and-hold land because handsome returns can be made without building. In the UK, it has been calculated that the area of land taken up by England's 2,000 or so golf courses is enough to build eight million new homes, increasing the housing stock by 35%.[97] This is not to say we should build over golf courses but more that there is no lack of space.

The cost of land is not driven merely by demand. *Permission to build* also contributes significantly to its price, and this is tightly controlled by local governments. Here, the stroke of a pen can multiply land values, and notably, it is an area of government long famed for corruption.[98] This restriction on supply, means that in the UK, the land-value part of a house price is 67%. In the US it is 41%—although this varies from 15% in Huntington WV, to 62% in Los Angeles. Thanks to this, the *land-value* part of the UK's housing stock amounts to £6.1tn, almost three times the value of all household financial wealth.

Population growth is of course a factor, but price has little to do with it and the building of housing stock to match it would have been achievable had it been considered important. It is also true that cities that become increasingly centres of economic activity see higher prices, but this isn't the whole story because real estate is getting more expensive everywhere, not just in urban areas.

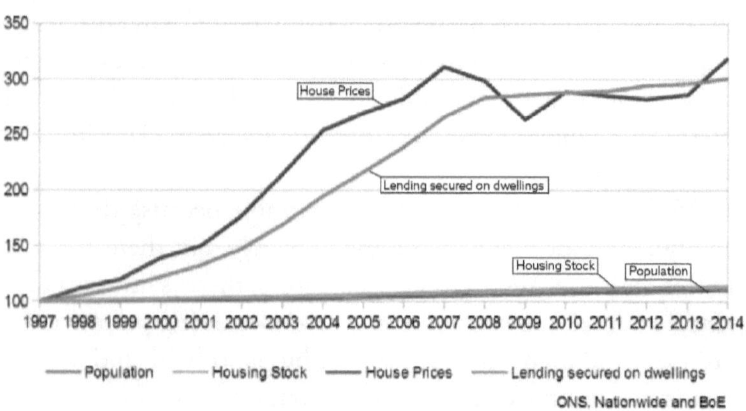

*House prices in the UK from 1997 to 2014
compared to population and housing stock.*

Other factors have an impact on house prices.

There has been enormous growth in foreign buyers who wish to store their wealth in countries with good legal systems. This movement of wealth tripled in the decade following 2010, especially coming from Asia and the Middle East. Chinese foreign property investment alone grew from $5bn in 2010, to $120bn in 2017.[99,100]

Adding to the pressure of foreign buyers are property investors, who buy multiple properties to rent out. Due to the tax relief on mortgage interest, British buy-to-let landlords were able to outbid residential buyers, increasing price pressure. This created a cycle where buying became less affordable, increasing demand for rentals, and making buy-to-let more attractive to property investors.

Interest rates, which sat at record lows after the 2008 recession, have also played a significant role by making borrowing larger amounts more affordable. And, when buyers get very little space for their money, by necessity, they tend to gravitate to the maximum they can borrow out of necessity, further adding pressure to price.

Should something be done about it? Many people think not. For some, buying a house is a cultural rite of passage which has never been easy, and those who complain are merely entitled. The fact is, those buying their first house today, *do* have a much harder time. In 1997 the average house cost 3.6 times the average annual salary, by 2021 it was 9.1 times.[101] Young people have not eaten too many avocados, housing has become significantly harder to buy, and higher rents make it harder to save for large deposits.

Is it *really* a problem though? Is this not something that can be fixed by pulling up boot-straps and leaning in?

The human and economic costs of the housing crisis are not insignificant.

For those who do not own a home, the high cost of housing is parasitical. It drains people of resources, choices, and quality of life. Long mortgages mean that some will pay for their house twice over, and money spent on interest is money that does not go into a pension, early retirement, or to support their children. This black hole of wealth equates to billions of lost consumer spending as people forego luxuries out of necessity.[102]

Record numbers of young people live with their parents to avoid high rents or to save for a deposit. Thanks to housing costs, it is estimated that sixty percent of adults under forty-five will put off, or put on hold, major life decisions such as changing careers, getting married, or starting a family (in America by 3-4 years).[103,104]

Businesses must also deal with increased property costs, and by necessity, pass these on to consumers. When viewed across the economy, in both private and public sectors, high property prices are essentially a pointless tax on everyone and everything.

The sad truth is that, if everyone in the UK was given a pay rise of £1000 a month, almost immediately, house prices would shoot up to 'accommodate' this new wealth as larger mortgages would become affordable to everyone. It is a kind of madness, where most of our excess wealth, all the gains from automation, information technology, increased productivity, industrial farming, and manufacturing—all the extra money that could have made a material difference to our quality of life—has simply gone into the inflated value of land.

Central to all of this, is a central idea of *what we believe housing is for*. Is the purpose of housing to enable the enrichment of landlords? Or to provide wealthy individuals from iffy regimes a safe place to park their cash? The housing crisis rests upon ideas, and these can be changed.

The Oppositional View

The oppositional view would be to see housing as primarily serving the purpose of providing shelter, security, and enabling family life. This view would be critical of the overwhelming control that government—local and central—has over planning permission, and that prevents people from building houses, or even living in non-traditional or non-permanent structures. It would argue that people should not be forced to pay most of their pay-packet simply to have a roof over their heads.

The oppositional view sees unaffordable housing as a moral wrong.

Housing should be affordable — Abstract

House prices are too high & increases unsustainable | There is enough land to build on | High house prices cause social harm — Sub-ideas

Primarily, houses should be homes not investment products | House prices are sustained by government policies | Planning restrictions create artificially high land value | With good policy lots of land could be built on in a sustainable way | High property prices are a transfer of wealth from the poor to the rich | Life stages delayed, diminishes risk taking

Progressive - action can be taken | Unaffordable shelter is oppressive — Emotional & Identity

In some countries, it is possible to buy land, and on that land, you have the freedom to build a structure to live in. There may be regulations to do with safety or dealing with waste—and it might be difficult to connect to services—but this does not in itself restrict people from building a home. If we see access to housing as a right, not a luxury, then we should be able to build something to live in when shelter is otherwise unaffordable.

People indeed tend to desire aesthetic control over their local area. This has partly to do with a desire to avoid change, and partly to do with how house values may be affected. Is it justified for these concerns to take precedence over people's right to shelter?

If building standards simply dictated that any structure must be environmentally friendly and built to safety standards, then off-grid houses, tiny homes, or eco-homes, would be viable options and people could access good living conditions for a fraction of current prices. However, in the UK, and many other places, restrictions remain extremely prohibitive.

An Endless Unwinnable War

Some drugs are bad, others are good. Using one costs you your job, and using another gets you a promotion. One gets you locked up, another gets you a lock-in. One addiction is excused, and another is stigmatised.

In many societies how drug users are seen is far more dependent on a drug's legal status than the harm it causes. In Ireland, for example—where over eight percent of the population struggles with alcohol-use disorders, and eighty percent of people consume alcohol—a 2017 survey reported that fifty percent of people said that drug users *really scared them*," and forty-four percent perceived people addicted to drugs as "*more as criminals than victims.*"[105,106]

Why consuming alcohol in Ireland—a drug that kills hundreds every year and costs their society billions—is not considered 'drug use,' while taking other drugs is, has a lot to do with the ideas of prohibition.[107,108]

Ideas around drugs, and their prohibition, have an illustrious history.

The prohibition of alcohol in Sharia law dates to the 7th Century and although the smoking of hashish has existed throughout the history of Islam (during the medieval period, it was accepted for therapeutic uses only) today it is considered haram—forbidden. In the Ottoman Empire, coffee was deemed to be an intoxicant, and prohibited by Sultan Murad IV, but after his death, the prohibition was quickly overturned. As coffee found its way into Europe it was banned as "the Devil's work" but this too was overturned by Pope Clement VIII, who thought coffee too delicious to leave to the infidels. In the 1600s coffee houses were seen as hotbeds of seditious political activity in England and were banned.* It was opium, however, due to its addictive and incapacitating properties, that kickstarted the modern history of drug prohibition.

In the early 1800s, British traders in China had a problem: to satisfy the growing European demand for silk, porcelain, and tea, large amounts of silver were required. As the Europeans had little to sell the Chinese, this one-way trade created a large trade deficit and a regional currency shortage. The entrepreneurial Brits figured out that if they imported opium from their colonies in India, they could sell it to the Chinese and earn back the silver required for buying goods.

It became a popular racket and imports of opium to China skyrocketed, as did opium addiction. The Chinese reacted by seizing and destroying opium stocks and banning further imports. The opium traders were furious and well-connected. They lobbied the British government, who in response, launched the first Opium War, which they won, forcing the Chinese to sign a treaty that ceded Hong Kong but stopped short of expressly legalising the opium trade.

Sensing vast opportunity and with support from France, the British attacked again and defeated the Chinese in the Second Opium War. The victors forced the opening of ten more ports to British trade, permission for foreigners to travel into central China, and the legalisation of opium. By 1850, opium imports to China generated up to twenty percent of the British Empire's revenue and one tenth of the Chinese population was addicted to the drug.[109]

The dire social problems that the opium trade caused were noticed by Protestant missionaries who had travelled to the newly opened country. They created the 'Anti-Opium League in China' and in 1899, published a report called *"Opinions of Over 100 Physicians on the Use of Opium in China,"* [110] the first anti-drug campaign which had a significant effect on British opinion.

---

* Some scholars think that switching from ale, a depressant, to coffee, a stimulant, helped accelerate enlightenment thought and in this case, the establishment was right to fear it.[116]

Over in America, a by-product of the Civil War was an opiate epidemic. The Union Army alone had issued millions of opium pills to its soldiers and a great number of soldiers returned home addicted or using opium to deal with injuries. The introduction of the hypodermic syringe played a role too, with both doctors and patients overusing the drug.[111] By 1880, it was estimated hundreds of thousands of Americans were addicted to opium. Laws passed in 1895 and 1915 restricted opiate sales and stopped over-the-counter sales.

The American government also had a missionary problem. Like their British counterparts in China, American missionaries were outraged by the opium trade in the Philippines (at the time an American territory) and campaigned for its abolition. The government succumbed and proposed a law that punished the import and possession of opium. In America, as opium was seen to be connected to Chinese people, prostitution, and gambling, the bill faced little opposition and passed in 1909. Almost immediately, opium prices shot up and pushed addicts toward opiates with more potency.

Internationally, attitudes were changing. In 1912, thirteen nations attended the International Opium Convention, resulting in the first international drug control treaty. Later, this treaty was incorporated into the Treaty of Versailles, signed at the end of the First World War—becoming international law—with the notable change that it prohibited not just the trade, but also the *use* of narcotic drugs. In criminalising possession, they set the stage for the dehumanisation and cruel treatment of addicts the world over.[112]

In America, the religionists were on a roll, and the Temperance Movement led to the federal prohibition of alcohol from 1920 until 1933, a period that saw a tremendous rise in organised crime that exploited the demand for black-market alcohol. The aggressive policing tactics of this era, and the hard-line attitudes toward drugs, set the stage for the next round of prohibition.

The association of drug use with the counterculture and civil rights movements in the 1960s and 70s presented a political opportunity. The 'war on drugs' was launched by President Nixon in 1971 and enabled government agencies to demonise and attack groups that opposed the Vietnam War, and the racism of Jim Crow-era America. Decades of punitive enforcement and mass incarceration followed.

The journalist Dan Baum wrote that John Ehrlichman, Nixon's aide on domestic affairs, told him that:

> *"The Nixon campaign in 1968, and the Nixon White House after that, had two enemies: the antiwar left and black people. You understand what I'm saying? We knew we couldn't make it illegal to be either against the war or black, but by getting the public to associate the hippies with marijuana and blacks with heroin, and then criminalizing both heavily, we could disrupt those communities. We could arrest their leaders, raid their homes, break up their meetings, and vilify them night after night on the evening news. Did we know we were lying about the drugs? Of course we did."* [113]

History has demonstrated that, whether a drug is seen to be *bad* largely depends on who is doing it and who is selling it, which has a lot to do with the ideas of *group*. Those further from the centre lack access to fairness and care, while those who are closer to power are immune to punishment. The executives who drove the recent opioid epidemic in America, and made billions from abject suffering, have not found themselves in prison while other, poorer Americans, are serving life sentences for selling small amounts of non-addictive drugs. [114,115]

Whether we see addicts as victims or criminals, suffering health issues or immoral degenerates—human or *less-thans*—greatly depends on the cultural ideas we hold.

The Ideological Structure of Drug Prohibition[117]

			Abstract
Illegal drugs should remain illegal			
Illegal drugs are harmful for health and society	Illegal drugs should continue to be forbidden	People using illegal drugs should be punished	
Illegal drugs have no positive effects and are solely harmful	Illegal drugs finance organised crime and terrorism	All illegal drugs are harmful and use is immoral	The only way to stop the harm of illegal drug use is prohibition and enforcement	Drug addicts are prone to violence, theft and other crime	Dealers must be severely punished Drugs use deviates from majority values[118]	Sub-ideas
Prohibitionist / Conservative		Moral panic / Righteousness				Emotional & Identity

The war on drugs—drug policy over the past fifty years—has been an unmitigated disaster. UN member states have labelled the campaign a "complete failure." Today, all kinds of drugs are readily available, and in cities, drugs can be ordered to your door, any time of day or night.

Correspondingly, the use of drugs, and deaths caused by them, have increased steadily over time. The human cost of policies that turn health issues into criminal issues has profoundly damaged the lives of millions of people.

Mark Kleiman, one of the leading drug policy experts in America, once opposed to decriminalisation, eventually concludes that *"nobody's got any empirical evidence that shows criminalization reduces consumption noticeably."*[118]

The basic economic reality is that higher levels of prohibition enforcement merely leads to higher prices, increasing the incentive for the trade of drugs.

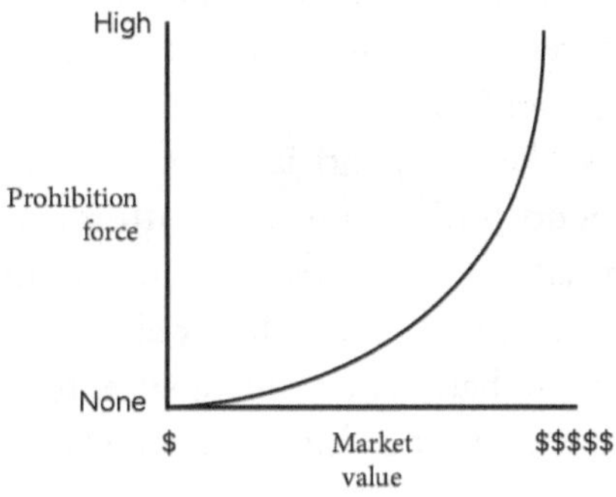

The self-defeating nature of drug prohibition.

An opposing ideological structure would look something like this:

Drug use should not be criminalised						Abstract
Drug use is not always harmful		Drugs should be regulated		Addiction is driven by health issues		
Some illegal drugs can be beneficial for mental health or pain relief	Some illegal drugs are not harmful when used responsibly	Legalised drugs can be regulated and taxed	Prohibition and its enforcement has caused more harm than good	Addicts need help—criminalisation and incarceration does not help	Poverty or social issues drive people to drug production and distribution	Sub-ideas
Evidence based			Empathy / Care			Emotional & Identity

Some countries have taken the evidence on board and have seen reductions of drug taking, addiction, deaths, and crime and have seen increased tax revenues. The Netherlands, which has one of the most progressive drug policies in the world, controls drug sales through licensing. Here, drugs are of known quality and purity and have appropriate labelling, drastically reducing the harms of drug use. Cannabis alone brings in hundreds of millions of dollars of tax revenue every year. This money is not only used to address social problems but is kept out of the hands of criminal organisations.[119]

In the US and the UK, politicians continue to pursue harmful policies and spend billions on drug enforcement, needlessly enriching criminal organisations and causing entirely avoidable suffering at home and abroad. Most politicians know what is wrong but choose to habituate an ideological reality of their own making and do their best to hide from the facts.[120]

Climate Denial
Oil Against Reality

Climate change is an extremely complex problem that requires both global cooperation and changes contrary to many corporate and national interests. It is arguably the biggest challenge that humanity has ever faced, and the stakes are high. Scientists predict massive ecosystem damage, the extinction of hundreds of thousands of species, and a significant increase in extreme weather events. Floods, droughts, storms and wildfires are all set to become worse and more frequent. Entire regions of the world are predicted to become uninhabitable, and societies will need to deal with the effects of mass migration, increased conflict over resources, and sea level rises which may threaten the homes of up to four hundred million people.[121] At the current pace of change, by 2090, hundreds of cities, from Miami to Bangkok, will no longer be habitable.

Are we taking appropriate action? Not really.

It is not like we haven't been warned. First identified by Guy Callendar in the 1930s, by 1990, the link between climate change and human activity had gained broad scientific consensus. Still, most of us do not *fully believe* the gravity of the situation, even as scientific predictions come to pass, and we see record temperatures, summer-long wildfires, and violent flooding year after year.

According to a 2022 poll, *"the environment, pollution and climate change"* only ranked as the most important problem facing the country for *two percent* of Americans. In 2021, it was found that although forty percent of Americans considered climate change to be a *"very big problem,"* thirty-four percent considered it to be a small problem or not a problem at all.[122,123]

The ideas of *climate change denial* probably form the biggest barrier to effective climate change action. Using the tobacco playbook of the previous decades, climate deniers backed by the fossil fuel industry pushed climate denialist ideas and, despite being in opposition to scientific consensus, these ideas have found their way into mainstream political conversation.[124]

The ideological structure of climate change denial is as follows:

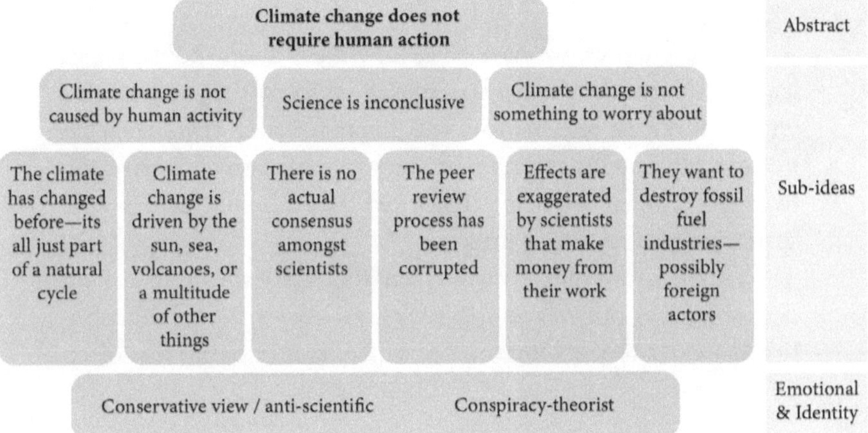

As taking climate action not only involves diminishing the fossil-fuel industry but also making personal changes to how we travel, what we buy, and how we eat—it has naturally met resistance from conservatives.[125]

A 2013 study of climate change denial literature found that ninety percent of denialist books had no peer review from relevant academic institutions and most books were published by Republican think tanks.[126] Over the last twenty years, as the evidence of the effect of fossil fuels became hard to counter, vested interests adapted their strategy, shifting from outright denial of facts toward economic arguments—claiming that climate action will cost jobs or cause global economic instability.[127]

Disinformation, conspiracy theories, manipulated statistics, and pseudoscience, drive a strategic ambiguity that prevents change by disrupting the very process of *making up our minds*. As the connection between *the abstract* to *the emotional* becomes harder to forge, it becomes harder to connect with the ideas of climate action, and thus change our behaviour.

Climate change denialism is a huge barrier to initiating the urgent action climate change requires. The end result? A relatively small number of people may end up with an extra twenty years of easier shareholder returns, at an incalculable cost to global society and life on earth.

In this chapter, we have seen how ideas about housing can lead entire generations to struggle, how ideas that are at odds with reality can lead us to wage a war for fifty years with no perceivable benefit, and how the very mechanism of connecting to important facts can be disrupted by malicious actors who sprinkle doubt into our minds.

We will now move away from specific issues and take a deeper look at our relationship with *the abstract:* a relationship fundamental to the human experience, and one that can often be fraught.

CHAPTER 13

A LIFE ABSTRACTED

The Latin *Homo sapiens* means 'wise man' but when we consider the cyclical nature of our collective mistakes, this may be an overstatement. Our capacity for abstract thought, more than wisdom, is the defining feature of our species and this is just as likely to bind us to ignorance as it is to lead us to wisdom. *Homo abstractus* might have been a better name for us as *the abstract* permeates every aspect of our lives.

Even compared to other large-brained social animals, the abstract properties of the human brain operate in a class of their own. A mind untethered from the present, or to only that which *exists*, allows humans to imagine and create different futures and different ways of living. Biologically speaking, this is a superpower and we have used it to escape the biological determinism that limits all other forms of life.

No matter what animal we compare humans to, this bizarre cognitive ability and the diversity of behaviour it drives, make us by far the weirdest species on earth. We are the true freaks of the animal kingdom.

Human Beings, Nature's Weirdest Animal

The Duckbill Platypus—an egg-laying mammal with venomous spurs that uses electro-location to hunt for prey.

The Portuguese Man-o-war—a floating colony of different zoonoids functioning as an individual jellyfish

A Tardigrade—a miniature creature that can survive almost any conditions, including exposure to outer space.

The Human – a psychologically complicated ape with the power of abstract thought. Spends more time orientated in what does not exist, than what does. Bizarre behaviours include putting Tardigrades into outer space.

Possessing a mind with vast capacity is not plain sailing, however, because every aspect of human experience is, in some way, shaped by *the abstract*. Like all animals, our experience of reality is determined by how our minds process information but, in our case, this includes the past, present, and future plus all the related ideas we carry. Sensory information is filtered through a melee of ideological intuitions, deep catalogues of memories, related thoughts, expectations, and feelings, before prompting an emotional output.

Unlike other animals (as far as we know), we spend about fifty per cent of our lives *outside* of the present moment. Our wandering minds imagine future events, past actions, imagined scenarios, worries, to-do lists, things we said, or might say, or how we will achieve goals that also exist in an imaginary future.[128,129]

Our brains took a long time to evolve but our capacity for abstract thought is relatively new in the making.

Five hundred million years went into laying the circuitry we share with other animals and just ten million of those went into sculpting the ape brain. The early *Homo erectus* brain appeared only two million years ago and a further 1.5 million years was needed before this grew into the brain we share today. In effect, our minds have undergone an explosion of increased capability in a hot minute.

This rapid melding of a new abstract mind on top of our ancient emotionally-focused brain has meant that our abstract capabilities do not perfectly interface with what came before. It's a bit like bolting a rocket engine on the back of a wooden cart: it *will* go a lot faster, but we also cannot be too surprised if it occasionally catches fire, the wheels fall off, or it doesn't quite end up where we intended.

The brain took five hundred million years to evolve, the Hominini brain (the brain of great apes) occurred within the last ten million years, and the brains of Homo erectus (the brain of Homo sapiens, Neanderthals and Denisovans) within the last two million years.

Like all animals, we are *emotional,* and our emotions drive our behaviour, but for humans *the abstract* complicates everything.

Yes, we can imagine and create things that do not yet exist, but we are also able to think ourselves into such distress that we kill ourselves. Although we can create intricate philosophies and live our lives to the ideas they promote, we can also imagine people, who merely have *different* abstract thoughts, to be so disagreeable that we run around killing them.

In short, *the abstract mind* is far from perfect. It is a messy adaptation that happened to be extremely selective and, as a result, a significant part of *the work of being human* is untangling the messy nature of an unlimited mind.

The Perception Problem

This messy nature starts with how we perceive reality.

Dr Lisa Feldman Barrett, Distinguished Professor of Psychology and Director of the Interdisciplinary Affective Science Laboratory (IASLab) at Northeastern University describes perception as *"an everyday kind of hallucination that creates all of your experiences and guides all your actions. It's the normal way that your brain gives meaning to the sensory inputs from your body and from the world (called 'sense data'), and you're almost always unaware that it's happening."*

Take seeing and recognising an object as an example. Visual sensory information works in association with top-down and bottom-up signals that drive perception. Bottom-up signals come from our sensory organs and include our sight, touch, smell, hearing, and internal body conditions. Top-down signals refer to mental representations that draw from a deep catalogue of memories of objects from previous representations.[130]

All these signals involve emotional components, be they aesthetic-driven emotions linked to representations, or cognitive dissonances that feed our perception.* In this way, perceptions are *concepts of objects* or mental models. These mental models are developed over time through learning, forming new models that

---

** Leon Festinger conducted the initial study on cognitive dissonance by examining a cult that believed in an impending flood that would destroy the earth. When the predicted flood failed to materialise, Festinger observed how the cult members responded. He was particularly interested in those who had made significant sacrifices to join the group. While less devoted members were more willing to acknowledge their error and move on, those who had invested heavily in the cult were more likely to reinterpret the situation in a way that affirmed their beliefs. They saw the lack of flood as a sign that their dedication had spared the earth, rather than accepting that their beliefs had been incorrect.*

According to the theory of cognitive dissonance, when people take actions that contradict one or more of their beliefs, they often experience psychological stress. This discomfort arises from the inconsistency between their actions or ideas, and they may attempt to resolve this dissonance by changing their beliefs or actions to make them more consistent. This internal conflict is triggered by new information that clashes with existing beliefs, and individuals may feel compelled to resolve the contradiction in order to reduce their discomfort.

aid future perception. Because an object can never be experienced in *exactly* the same way twice—even in a controlled setting—perception and cognition are ongoing processes.[130]

Though it might be a sort of hallucination, and while it is true that how we experience something alters our perception, our minds *do* create relatively accurate representations. We make errors and omissions but, in general, it has been advantageous for us to perceive reality relatively accurately and, in our interactions with the physical world, our minds work reasonably well.

Abstract information is another story, however. When our mind is untethered from the material world, things get messy. And at a time when more and more of our information is not based on direct experience but on ideas, news, stories, gossip, facts and "facts," this becomes increasingly important.

The *abstract mind* is made up of the past, the future, and the values we hold. Memories of past events can be cognitively recalled or, they can be lost to cognition but remain *felt*—and thus still affect our perception. The ideas we hold about the future create expectations that influence perception and the ideas of our socialisation affect how we feel about new information by driving intuitive bias. All go to affect our day-to-day emotional experience.

Think about a dog.

The dog is about to get a treat. It's excited. It's wagging its tail. Maybe the crinkling sound of the packet creates anticipatory excitement. The dog can smell the treat and salivates. The dog eats the snack. The snack is gone. The dog may hang around, hopeful for more—and the mental model of the snack giver might gain some positive sentiment—but as far as we can tell, that is about it for the story of the dog and the snack.

Now think about being offered a treat, yourself.

Should you say yes? Is it an appropriate moment? Would it be impolite to refuse? How's it going to make you feel? Should you offer to share? And if you accept: Was it worth it? How does it compare to other treats? Maybe the flavour reminds you of something or someone. Maybe it tastes different than expected, making it less pleasant. Maybe deeply embedded ideas about food and self-control lead you to feel guilty about indulging—affecting your feelings of self-worth. Maybe you might *really* want another one, but feel too uncomfortable to ask, creating an internal tension as you fantasise about *just one more*. Maybe you'll think about it tomorrow, next week, or next year, re-experiencing the event with associated good or bad feelings. The abstract mind can make even simple things wildly complicated.

Now, I am not suggesting that the dog and the human necessarily differ in how intensely they *feel*, it is just that the variables that lead to emotion are far more complex for humans than for other animals.

I always understand things better through pictures and diagrams and so I've included a few in this chapter. What follows is a simplified illustration of the mind and the way it interacts with reality.

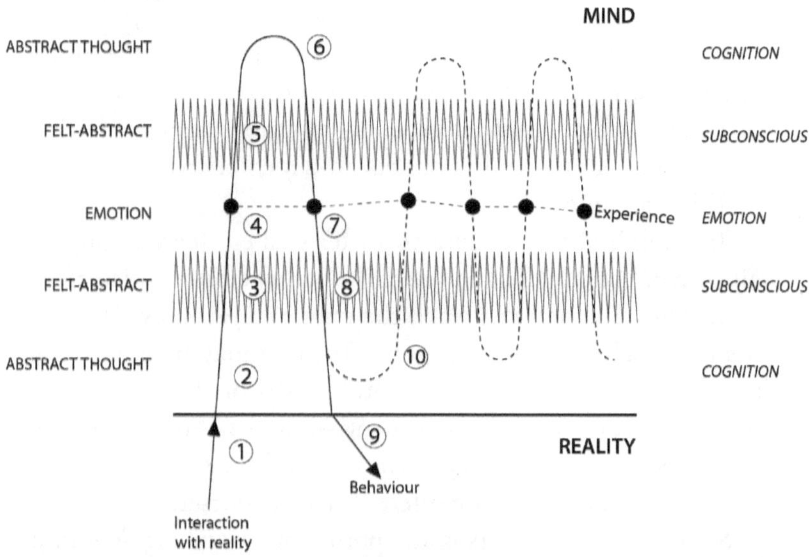

The processes represented in this diagram are not linear (as depicted) but rather a mix of simultaneous top-down (conscious/unconscious cognition) and bottom-up (sensory) signals resulting in what mathematicians, who try to model cognition, call *incomputable combinatorial complexity.* The abstract mind is incredibly complex but it's worth trying to understand it.

(1) We encounter a stimulus, tangible or not. For example, we see an object (2) Pattern recognition and abstract cognition create meaning and initial judgement. (3) This judgement is simultaneously affected by ideas-felt, flash-judgements, and memory. (4) These give rise to emotions that are affected by our current emotional state. (5) This mix of emotions can trigger the *abstract felt*, deeply held ideas, and memories of past experiences. (6) These feelings can be processed, compared, considered, enhanced, or diminished by cognitive thought. (7) Which then again passes through the *abstract felt*, memories, feelings and biases. (8) All of this shapes our emotional state. (9) Which influences our decisions and our outward behaviour.

(10) It's not over, though. We continue to experience *the experience* in the abstract. We can relive the event through our memory, we can pour over the details, analysing every part of it—extending a single glance into a lifelong experience. These experiences, even if long forgotten, can reside in the *abstract felt*, sitting in the subconscious, and impacting future interactions when triggered.

In this, an *Experience* is the sum of a series of emotional states provoked by sensory information passing through conscious and subconscious processing.

The complex amalgamation of the *abstract felt* influences how we perceive and react to our environment. Sometimes, unrelated events can become coloured by the emotions associated with the abstract felt. Fireworks may trigger emotional distress in veterans, while survivors of abuse may be overwhelmed by sensations like touch, smell, or sound, associated with their past traumatic experiences. Outside of extreme examples, the *abstract felt* and the associations it generates can shape our perceptions, experiences, and behaviours in ways that we are not consciously aware of.

It is this dichotomy of *the abstract* and *the emotional* that creates the difference between *knowing* and *understanding*.

For example; I may *cognitively* hold the idea that killing animals is bad (knowing) but still have a habit of eating them. Until the idea is held emotionally (understanding), leading to intuitive behavioural choices, conscious effort and willpower are required to ensure that my behaviour matches the ideas I hold to be true.

This connects back to our discussion in Chapter 4, where *felt* ideas and ideologies were shown to lead to fast, intuitive, moral judgements—*this* is wrong, *that* is right, *this* is disgusting—with cognition coming later to justify, or rationalise the way we feel.

A Life Abstracted

An abstract mind bolted onto an ancient, emotional brain leads to a dualistic existence; whatever exists in an *emotional* form, has an *abstract* counterpart. In this, *the emotional* is important for our personal well-being and *the abstract* is important for achieving goals, organising large-scale cooperation, and optimising efficiency.

All of us spend tremendous amounts of time abstracted from the present moment.

If I'm walking home, I'll have my key at the ready hundreds of meters before reaching the door. Sometimes I'll plan what I'm going to do when I get inside. Sometimes I'll be lost in a thought about something I'd heard or done earlier in the day. I don't experience the walk because I'm absorbed in *the abstract*.

If I'm not careful, my mind wanders from the present moment during most of my waking hours and instead dwells on future plans, the past, that unresolved issue, the news, and everything except *the experience of now*. When *I am* careful, I spend my day away from my phone, I meditate, I focus on my food as I eat, and I consciously spend time in the magnificent natural environment in which I live.

It's hard not to slip into abstract thought and yet doing so is bad for us. In the words of Harvard Psychologists Matthew Killingsworth and Daniel Gilbert: *"A human mind is a wandering mind, and a wandering mind is an unhappy mind. […] The ability to think about what is not happening is a cognitive achievement that comes at an emotional cost."*[131]

Happiness is a tricky subject.

Dr Andrew Steptoe, Professor of Psychology and Epidemiology and Head of the Research Department of Behavioural Science and Health at University College London, explains that happiness is composed of *"several constructs, including affective well-being (feelings of joy and pleasure), eudaimonic well-being (sense of meaning and purpose in life), and evaluative well-being (life satisfaction)."*[132] The Dutch sociologist and pioneer in the scientific study of happiness Ruut Veenhoven offers a more succinct definition: happiness is *"the overall appreciation of one's life-as-a-whole."*[133]

It's hard to appreciate your life if you're never present to experience it. Living in the abstract distances us from the emotional states that satisfy our biologically determined psychological needs. If we consistently experience unsatisfying emotional experiences, our lives too will be unsatisfying.

The Covid-19 pandemic illustrated just how true this is. We no longer met people face-to-face but instead through blurry video calls. When we did meet in person, social distancing and masked faces meant emotionally driven aspects of communication like facial expression, and touch, were lost. The way we experienced the world narrowed, our lives were limited, and we became more dependent on abstract forms of information and stimulation. The result? A 25% increase in anxiety and depression worldwide, an explosion in conspiracy theory thinking and, in some quarters, a deepening mistrust of authority.[134–136] The pandemic exacerbated the alienation created by so many modern living trends and the outcome was increased suffering.

Here, *alienation* refers to a sense of disconnection or separation from oneself, others, and the world. The forces of modernisation, which values efficiency and productivity over emotional experience and well-being, exacerbates this abstraction of life.

It is clear that an abstracted life is not good for us, but it also tends to be convenient, efficient, and scalable, and because of this, it also tends to be extremely profitable—making change difficult. Our smartphones are essentially machines of *the abstract*. They encourage abstract communication (messaging) and abstract social relations (social media), and they allow us to avoid the *present moment* by ensuring we're always entertained.

Social, media and gaming companies aim to monetise every aspect of life, be it reading the news in bed, scrolling while on the toilet, or gathering pictures for Instagram while on vacation. Our attention is shifted from the present to the abstract. Today, many of us type more words than we speak, and studies show that teenagers spend more time texting than interacting face-to-face—and that they prefer it that way.[137]

Much work has become abstracted from its result, and the result for many jobs is of little emotional value. We sell stocks, create 'content,' and collect clicks. We live in the era of "bullshit" jobs first described by David Graeber and later illustrated by a YouGov poll wherein 37% of Britons reported believing that their jobs *did not* contribute "meaningfully" to the world. A lack of meaning is a lack of *emotional* value and is indicative of work that leans toward the abstract.

Worse, most of us also live entirely abstracted from our food and its production. Food grown in one place is consumed by people a thousand miles away. Animals are abstracted from their personal and emotional value and raised on vast farms where they become numerical values in a global supply chain. Cruelty, pollution, and waste are hidden from view and marketing departments keep us tuned into the stories we want—or are cultured to want—to hear.

Sex can be replaced with pornography and for many, it is the primary source of sexual pleasure and excitement. Even those in relationships may rely on abstract fantasies to help things along, often using ideas produced by companies. Pornography teaches objectification—the abstraction of emotional value—and it does so on a vast scale. Dating apps provide an abstract version of dating, a shallower emotional experience that provides the ability to swipe left or right while assessing bodies without minds.

Childhood, too, is increasingly abstracted from the reality of the world and the inherent risks that lurk within it, leading to children who struggle in life.[138] Children are heavily surveilled, reducing a sense of agency, while simultaneously being cajoled toward abstract goals that shift their focus away from the present and toward future expectations.

The abstraction of life leads to the hollowing out or limiting of our emotional experience. When we try and fix it, our efforts can be stymied by the same process. Although an urge for social connection can be sated by abstract relationships, they are unlikely to satisfy us in the way *personal* relationships do. Just like when eating junk food—the poor nutritional value does not satisfy, so we seek to consume more.[139]

Like consumerism, the system can be perpetuated *because of its dissatisfying nature*. The cultural values that lie behind abstract systems can lead us to seek answers from within its confines. And, as with all the ideas that truly rule our lives, it can be hard to think, and live, outside of them.

The Calcification of *The Abstract*

In my late twenties, after five years of running a technology business, I could *feel* myself becoming boring. I spent most of my time writing business emails and doing work-orientated things. I was all numbers and salutations. To push back, I decided to get creative. I drew, I painted, and I wrote a children's book. I didn't expect success in any of these areas, I just wanted to stop my brain from restructuring itself into a boring shape.

As I write this book, I can feel the same thing happening. I'm reluctant to go on adventures that I would've once craved because *I've done that before* and *I know what it'll be like.* I don't want the hassle of planning, booking, and learning my way around a new terrain when I know familiar places are fine. I have a counter-intuitive desire to shrink my world because, somehow, too much has become *known* and the more time I spend in what I know, the more *known* everything feels to be. *In reality,* when I do travel, what I discover is interesting and enjoyable, but even sitting here, at my laptop, I feel a resistance to doing so.

I've been too *functional* for too long. This current and intense work phase is now four years and counting. Over this time, my projects have taken me over and there's no off-ramp in sight. *I feel like I must work.* This creeping *functionalism* combined with a *knowing*, a sort of 'boringness of experiences,' is something that happens to a lot of people as they age but we should not buy into this delusion. Nothing is knowable, and no place or experience is the ever same, things change, and we do too. Forgetting this is dangerous but it's also normal, even natural.

When we do the same thing over and over the neurological pathways used to execute the action go through a process of *myelination.* Their myelin coating thickens, and the pathway grows faster, perhaps hundreds of times faster, forming efficient pathways that essentially create habits of thought. The brain will always tend to do the easiest thing and heavily myelinated pathways are just that. The more they are used the more they become part of our way of being. Repeating the action becomes easier and easier (or harder not to do), creating habit, and the more we fall into a routine, the harder it becomes to change.

Dr Loretta G. Breuning, a professor at California State University, explains:

A habit is a real physical pathway in the brain. Electricity flows effortlessly down a well-developed pathway, which is why the behavior comes easily. A child who builds good habits will find it easy to take self-care steps, and a child who builds bad habits will find it easy to do things that damage their long-run well-being.[140]

This does not just apply to children, of course. Our brains are continuously adapting. We can build new neural pathways, or we can let those that are already established dictate our behaviour and determine our well-being.

In the words of Frank Outlaw, an American supermarket founder (but often attributed to Ralph Waldo Emerson, Lao Tzu, and others):

Watch your thoughts, they become words; watch your words, they become actions; watch your actions, they become habits; watch your habits, they become character; watch your character, for it becomes your destiny..

If we let this *boringness* develop, *the abstract,* starts to form the predominant aspects of our neural circuitry, narrowing our openness to the true nature of reality and dulling and diminishing our emotional experience. Heavily myelinated pathways of expectations and imagined realities, close our minds to potentially rich emotional experiences. This leads to a loss of wonder, surprise, joy, and a reduced desire to experience *the new* because it is felt to be *known*. When all has been said and done, what is the point in saying or doing?

If we spend large amounts of time worrying about money, mortgages, function, profit, loss, ownership, and attainment, and very little time on fun, play, creative expression, and emotionally valuable relations, we can expect to experience a neurological change, a structural shift, away from one and toward the other.

As functionalism, expectation, socialisation, and *knowing,* shape our circuitry, *the abstract* slowly calcifies, ossifying our minds into a sort of dullness so ubiquitous that we consider it a key characteristic of *adulthood.* This calcification becomes a metaphorical and neurological weight that we carry, making us heavy, less flexible, less adaptable, and increasing resistance to our life's very movement.

Unchecked, it leads to stagnancy, pessimism, and a joylessness that erodes the possibility for happiness.

CHAPTER 14

MEANWHILE, IN REALITY...

In general, we like to think that our behaviours are based *on reality,* but as we discussed in the last chapter, if we consider the complexity of perception and cognition, this is not as straightforward as it seems. Unfortunately, as our behaviours interact *with reality,* if we want our actions to succeed, we need to learn to distinguish *the truer nature of reality* from misleading perceptions caused by inaccurate information or subconscious feelings.

Our ability to understand, and act on, reality is probably the greatest defining factor in how successful we will be across every sphere of our lives.* Thus, building an accurate understanding of ourselves, our relationships, and our social and economic environments is critical to our relative success within them.

We may develop a deep understanding of economic and financial realities, and this will help us gain success in these fields, but we can still wind up deeply dissatisfied if we do not also take the time to understand our personal and emotional realities and act accordingly. Likewise, we may understand

---

* When I say *"our ability to understand reality is probably the greatest defining factor in how successful we will be across every sphere of our lives,"* this does not therefore suggest that the wealthy understand reality better than anyone else. This is more in terms of comparative likelihoods. For example, if you are born in poverty, and suffer challenging circumstances, or health issues, then holding a more accurate understanding of reality will lead to greater success compared to others with similar life experiences who have a poorer understanding of reality.

ourselves well, and be emotionally fulfilled in our younger years, but suffer later in life because we did not put sufficient effort into understanding and acting upon the harsh economic realities of long-term financial planning.

Understanding the broad aspects of reality that are important for our lives is *not easy* and the constant change that occurs within our environments, and in ourselves, means that building, and learning to act on these understandings is the work of our lives.

Our direct experience of reality is limited. We are only able to sense a tiny portion of what's out there. We can only be in one place at a time, we can only experience a limited range of a few spectrums, and the vast majority of what we understand about our social reality is based on second-hand information, stories, or imagination.*

Like all animals, *exactly what* we are able to experience is largely limited to the information important for extending gene-time. Evolution means different aspects of reality are important for different animals; thus, we perceive only what we need to thrive. Some animals have a powerful sense of smell, others can sense minute subaquatic vibrations, and others still can pick up on variations in the planet's magnetosphere—all aspects of reality that humans are practically blind to.

Until we invented scientific equipment (or co-opted animals), entire realms of information sat out of the reach of our understanding. This limited range of our sensory information allows us to feel that reality is *understandable* and simpler than it is. Put simply, we have not evolved to understand reality in all its complexity.

---

* Humans are able to only sense a tiny portion of the electromagnetic spectrum—namely what we call visible light—meaning we are blind to the other 99.997%. Likewise, we are deaf to all sound frequencies outside of the 20 Hz to 20 kHz range. Our sense of smell, although sensitive to sulphur odours (short-chain thiols) emitted by rotten foods, when compared to other animals, is remarkably poor.

As scientists peel back the layers of our physical reality the complexity they discover is staggering. From the trillions of galaxies that make up the universe to the bizarre behaviour of subatomic particles, the more we look, the more complexity we find. Life adds to this complexity. The human brain is unfathomably complex. Social realities, composed of millions of brains are so complicated they are literally impossible to understand. All social scientists can do is discover broad truths, generalisations, or likelihoods, and even that is difficult.

Drill down into any area of reality, from the molecular complexity of a starfish sucker to the gravitational waves of deep space, and you'll discover so much complexity that it's hard to comprehend just *how* complex the world is.

Reality and Perception

What we desire as an outcome of our behaviour can be driven both cognitively and subconsciously. Cognitively, we may desire one outcome but our behaviour, in no small part driven by the subconscious, can conflict with our rational goals. We may *rationally* want a relationship to work, but we subconsciously desire the confirmation of a *felt* belief that people cannot be trusted, and as a result, we sabotage without even quite knowing why.

Likewise, how we experience the world tends to mirror our beliefs.

If we imagine everyone to be hostile, we generally find hostility, and if we imagine others to be kind, we often find kindness. The subconscious seeking of confirmatory information means that we exist in a cognitive system of self-perpetuating bias which causes us to behave in ways that both reflect our feelings and perpetuate them. This process can generate seemingly *overwhelming evidence* making changing our minds difficult and leading to a closing down of possibilities.

Such *felt understandings* can easily supersede rational knowledge and, when *felt ideas* become deeply connected to our identity, we can become defensive and prone to motivated reasoning when such ideas are challenged.

The result can be an unconscious resistance to new information—that could help us improve our understanding of reality—and thus, this tendency ultimately prevents us from living better lives. When these biases are mixed with poor or confirmatory information, it can lead people, who are highly capable of rational thought, to behave in deeply irrational ways and, to some degree, we are all vulnerable to this.

Our Relationship with Reality

To help picture our relationship with reality, I have created a simple illustration. It is not designed to be quantifiable.

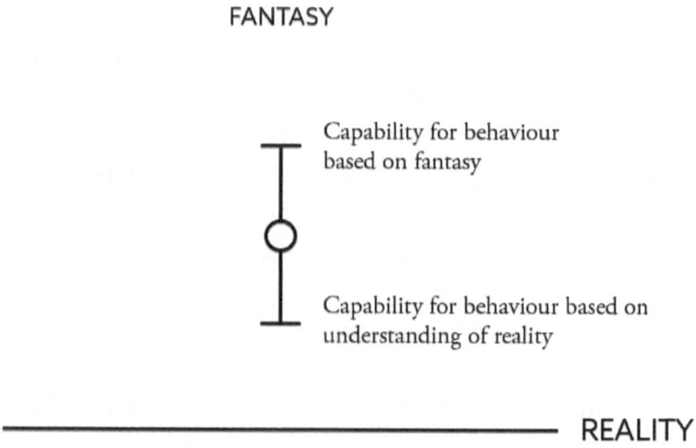

We both have a maximum understanding of reality and a limit to the fantasy-based thinking on which we base our behaviour.

In this illustration, the individual 'O' behaves within their behavioural range 'I.' Reality is the baseline and, above it, there is no limit to behaviour based on fantasy. Here I use the word 'fantasy' to cover both ignorance and the belief in fictional narratives or ideas. An individual's behavioural range depends on the limits of their *capability* to base behaviours *on reality,* and their *capacity* to base behaviours *on fantasy.*

We all have a general limit to our *irrational* fantasy-based behaviour (the top of the 'I') beyond which we would consider our behaviour *irrational.* The reality-end of our behavioural range is defined by our understanding of reality, which has a limit because we cannot base our behaviour on understandings we do not possess.

To develop the previous illustration, let's imagine three different individuals with different abilities to behave based on reality and fantasy.

Holding fantasy-based ideologies increases our capacity for poor behaviour-reality interaction and is therefore detrimental to our lives. Conversely, a better understanding of reality increases our ability to behave successfully. As fully understanding reality is impossible, we can only strive toward *better understanding* and the more we do this, the better the outcome of our behaviour.

If I hold a fantasy-based idea that I can survive an unaided fifty-foot fall onto concrete, acting on it is unlikely to have a successful outcome. If we mistakenly believe that *everyone* at work thinks homophobic jokes are funny, then our jokes may harm our careers. If a business invests heavily in a product that no one needs, the business may go bust. If a jealous partner of a faithful person acts on paranoia, they may destroy the relationship they wish to protect.

The better we understand reality the more able we are to make good decisions. This is why governments use vast resources to gather intelligence, why businesses invest in market research, and why our ability to communicate with our partners increases the quality of our relationships (and why the plotlines of almost all romantic dramas rely on poor communication). The better we can understand the reality of ourselves, the better we can make decisions that result in a satisfying life.

A Basis of Fact

To have any hope of having a grounding in reality, we must first understand what counts as a *basis of fact*. That is, how we determine *what* a fact is, *how* we discover facts, and, when so much information comes from other people, *who* is trustworthy and *why*.

Some of this is common sense. Journalists with decades of experience, solid reputations for detailed analysis and speaking truth to power, should be trusted more than those with a reputation for espousing vacuous opinions or disinformation for their gain. Scientists who have spent careers dedicated to uncovering facts, and who perform well under peer review, should generally be trusted more than politicians who use flagrant lies to gain power.

Reality is apolitical and neither side of the political spectrum bases all their thinking, or policy, on the best available understandings. Instead, they base decisions on the version of reality that best suits their agenda and, invariably, their agenda is to gain (or retain) power.

Reality is subject to manipulation but that doesn't mean all interpretations are equal. We've been refining our understanding of the world for thousands of years and, today, millions of scientists working in innumerable fields continue this work and seek to share their knowledge. We can use this information to shape our behaviour and in so doing contribute to the long history of *human progress.*

Ignorance & Understanding

The fact that we can never fully understand reality means that we exist in a state of eternal ignorance.

We're not stupid; it's just that there's a lot more that we don't grasp than that we do. Ancient Buddhist scholars recognised this and made the concept of ignorance central to their belief system. In their view, *ignorance* is an innate flaw, or a primordial force, that afflicts us all, and *wisdom* is the antidote.

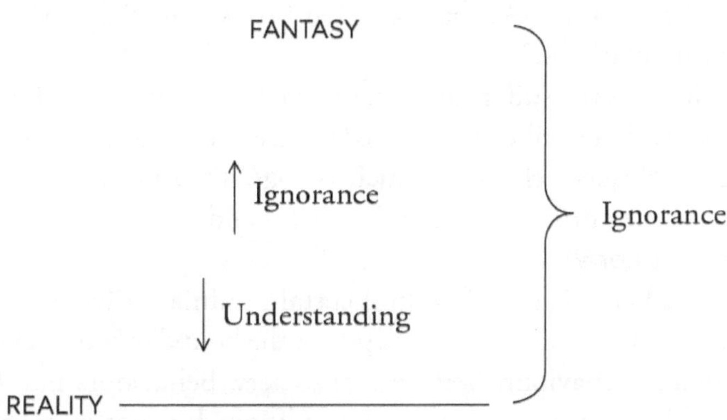

Ignorance comes in many forms, though.

Natural ignorance might be the innocent ignorance of a child or that which results from the limits of human knowledge.

Cultural ignorance is a product of the denigration of certain knowledge, the discouragement of curiosity, or the punishment of thinking differently. Such dogmatic ignorance, especially when combined with force, can be very harmful.

Wilful ignorance is what results when we choose not to know something because it makes us uncomfortable. Both culture and cognitive dissonance can drive wilful ignorance.

Forced ignorance is caused by the dissemination of propaganda, disinformation, and other false narratives. Forced ignorance enables a shift toward fantasy-based ideas and can cause people to be blinded to the suffering of others or reject the evidence of their own experience. We can see this in the propagation of fascist myths, constant political lying, and restricted information environments.

Collective Behavioural Range

Imagine someone beating their dog to death in a park in central Paris. Horrible, right? *How could they do such a thing?* Now imagine a living lobster being tossed into a pot at the restaurant around the corner. At the most, hard to watch, right? Maybe even unremarkable?

Why does the suffering of one animal sicken us when that of another is almost taken for granted? There's no rational reason, of course. Lobsters feel pain as much as dogs, it's just that inflicting pain on one animal is *socially acceptable* and inflicting pain on another is not.[141]

So in Paris, it is OK to boil certain animals alive but not dogs or cats—boiling pets is outside of the boundaries of socially acceptable behaviour. Within any society, behaviours may be tolerated or accepted in certain conditions but not in others. What is considered *socially acceptable* is driven by ideas. Some ideas are *fantasy-based* (for example that lobsters, crabs and octopuses don't feel pain) and some are more *reality-based* (that dogs and cats do).

In this, Socially Accepted Behaviour Boundaries (SABBs) are not based on reason. Indeed, being rational can even be a cause for social ostracization.

The 19th Century atheist Charles Bradlaugh faced discrimination for his reality-based views. In many countries, homosexual people who act on the reality of their biology are persecuted by those with fantasy-based beliefs who deem their rational behaviour unacceptable. Vegans endure social derision because people struggle with the cognitive dissonance that arises from eating animals while simultaneously being opposed to their suffering. Those who have rallied reason to demand rights for women, the abolition of slavery, reduction of inequality, and the protection of the environment, have all faced discrimination, legal prosecution, and social sanction for pushing back against socially accepted behaviours. Because challenging cultural norms means holding beliefs that sit outside of them, this too, can be viewed as socially unacceptable behaviour—regardless of how noble the cause.

Socially Accepted Behaviour Boundaries (SABBs) are defined by the *collective ability* to understand reality and use this understanding to define ideas of morality, identity, law, and social convention.

We might imagine that the process looks something like the image below, where every black figure represents a person and the range depicted by the shape represents the extent to which their values are based in fantasy or reality.

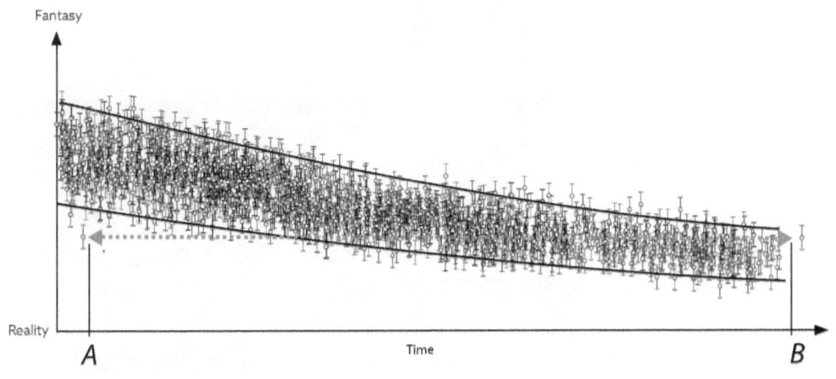

Collectively, ideally, we are advancing toward a society with behaviours that better reflect reality.

Like the hypothetical society illustrated above, with luck, humanity's macro trend is that of moving steadily toward behaving according to a greater understanding of reality. Someone in Time-A who thinks women should be able to vote, or who is an atheist, would be considered socially unacceptable; while in Time-B, the same person's *other* beliefs; say that women should stay in the home, or ideas of race, would be considered socially unacceptable and out of touch with newer SABBs that have formed thanks to an increased social understanding of reality.

At an inter-societal level, the risk of conflict increases when there is a significant distance between the behavioural range of one group and another. Imagine, for instance, a fantasy-leaning Society A. An embodiment of a practical-but-impossible reality like those discussed at the start of this book. Maybe a theocracy. And now imagine a Society B that bases its behaviour on a much more realistic understanding of the world.

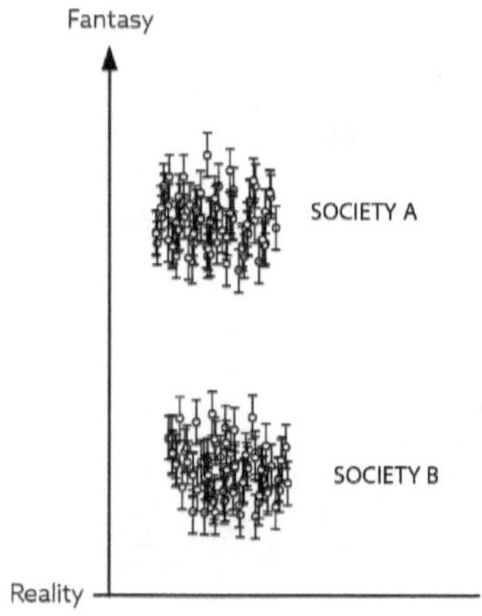

Two such societies will have trouble cooperating because the successful existence of Society B intrinsically threatens the ideas valued by Society A.

Correspondingly, if *two* fantasy-leaning societies hold divergent views (say another theocracy), the likelihood of conflict further increases because the fantasy-basis of both societies is threatened by competing fantasy-based ideas.

Regimes that justify their power using myths bind themselves to ideological fragility because *reality* contradicts them and therefore the truth poses a constant existential threat. The more regimes lean on myth, the less common ground they can hold with reality-based societies (or even other fantasy-based regimes) and cooperation thus becomes harder to maintain. In general, the further a *social reality* diverges from actual *reality*, the harder life will be and the more vulnerable the society will be to negative forces or events.

Two different *reality-based* societies, on the other hand, will, by nature, hold greater common ground and thus have an easier time cooperating. In this scenario, ideological differences come down to interpretation, not dogma and so it becomes easier for members of each group to see themselves in the *others*.

It's hard to imagine present-day Sweden and Norway or Germany and Denmark going to war. These advanced societies, with a free press, good education, and systems generally based on a scientific understanding of reality, simply have too much common ground to seek each other's destruction.

Correspondingly, all wars of aggression depend on myth and fantasy. False claims of weapons of mass destruction justified the invasion of Iraq by the US and the UK (although the psychopathic nature of Saddam Hussein's regime may have justified some form of intervention). The scarecrow of a "Nazified Ukraine" was used to justify the Russian invasion in 2022. Myths of racial superiority we rallied in support of Europe's numerous colonial wars. False accusations and exaggerated claims justified American interference in Vietnam in the 1950s. Social Darwinist ideas behind National Socialism led to World War II. Osama Bin Laden's interpretations of the Quran—and the belief that America held Islam's most holy sites in their "grip" due to their presence in Saudi Arabia and their support for Israel—led to 9/11 and the conflict that followed. Myths of Russian aggression was, in part, used by Germany to justify the start of World War I.

Human beings have started countless wars and every single time it's been because one or both parties believed (or manufactured a belief) in a corrupt version of reality.

Common Ground

The same illustration helps us picture common ground.

Not everyone in a society shares ideological common ground with everyone else. Nevertheless, all can coexist so long as they operate within the boundaries of socially acceptable behaviour.

Common ground is both metaphorical and material. Your friend might be a bit of a conspiracy theorist, and I may hold little common ground with her, but because *you* share common ground with your friend, I am likely to accept them *by extension* and vice versa. Broad social ideas, for example, national identity or cultural tradition, also help create common ground amongst those who hold differing beliefs.*

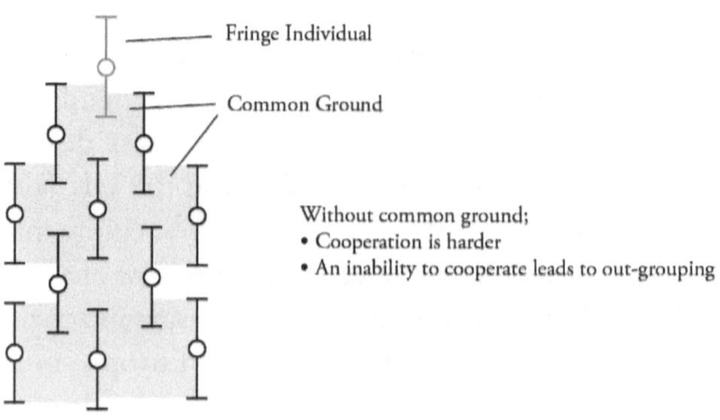

---

* This concept of overlapping common ground illustrates the most insidious aspect of racism: that no level of behavioural conformity can ever be enough because the possibility of *common ground* is denied because of the pigmentation of someone's skin, ethnicity, or some other unchangeable characteristic. For the Nazis, no matter how much a Jew may have contributed to society, common ground was denied thus the possibility of social cooperation was negated.

Existing outside of the behavioural range of your society makes life harder. Thinking a little differently is generally tolerated, thinking too differently is not.

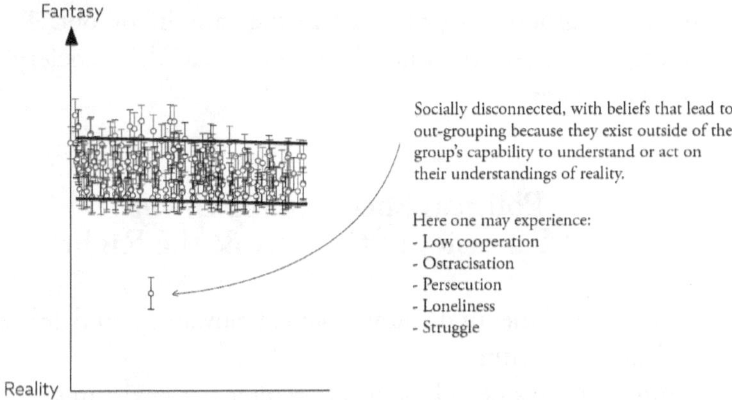

The further a person diverges from their social reality, the harder their life will be. This is why activists are more effective when they adhere to superficial norms like fashion. You're more likely to take a woman seriously if she's wearing a suit, as ridiculous as that may be. If you wish to change *idea-A* then it may be beneficial to conform to less important ideas *B, C* and *D*.

George William Domhoff, Distinguished Professor Emeritus and research professor of psychology and sociology at the University of California, Santa Cruz, observes:

> *First, social-psychological studies of small groups show that "moral exemplars"—those who stand outside the general consensus and at first are labelled as "extremists"—can often be very effective, but with one important qualification: they can't be too extreme or else they will be ignored. Thus, the trick for any social change agent is to be just extreme enough to be an "effective extremist."*

If our behaviour is too outlandish (and I use that word on purpose) we start to lose the benefits of being in-group—access to fairness, care, and cooperation. Justice may be lacking, our suffering can be ignored, and we might face prejudice that constrains our ability to participate.

It is, however, not just behaviour that determines who is in-group or out-group or to what extent they are 'in' or 'out.' Far more important, are the underlying ideas that drive society's *definition of group*.

The Political Spectrum of *Group* and the Fantasies of the Left & the Right

Group boundaries underlie all political movements and define the political spectrum.

Humans have a deep biological preference to exist in social groups and to share resources within them.[142–150] This *group preference* has been evolutionary selective. Thanks to these evolutionary forces, we struggle to exist outside of a social group and find social isolation destabilising for both body and mind.[151–156]

As the existence of a social group *means* the existence of group-boundaries and, as group boundaries define the properties that make someone ingroup or outgroup, social groups are inherently discriminatory.

Outside that of our kin, or those in our immediate community, our group-boundary definitions are primarily ideological (say that of nation, culture, tradition, borders, or religion). In-group members benefit from care, cooperation, and fairness while outsiders receive few or none of these social benefits.[157–165]

When it comes to defining who is in-group and who is out-group, *rightist* thought generally uses narratives or ideas to constrict boundaries and exclude people. This may include using ideas of race, place of birth, sexuality, religion, or ancestral heritage, to infer fundamental differences that justify social exclusion.[50,166] *Leftist* thought tends to see such group boundary definitions as discriminatory and aims to expand them to include more people. The logical conclusion of the leftist ideal of moral equality is the complete elimination of group boundaries, which, of course, stands in opposition to *group preference*. There's a limit to left-wing thinking, past which implies the impossible idea that you can dissolve group boundaries without eroding constituency.

If we examine the political spectrum from a perspective of *group boundary definition* it can help us understand other aspects of political expression. Thanks to the tendency of both the extreme right and the extreme left to gravitate toward authoritarianism, it's often thought that the two are somehow close together. French philosopher Jean-Pierre Faye articulates this idea in his 'horseshoe' theory of the political spectrum. Today political theorists consider this to be largely incorrect and, in terms of policy, there is no reliable political spectrum even if some broad tendencies can be discovered.

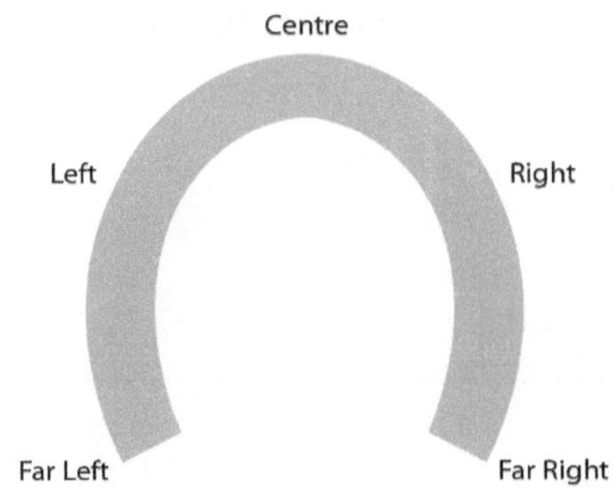

The horseshoe theory of the political spectrum currently has little support [167,168]

The similarities between the far-left and the far-right are better explained as a spectrum not of politics but of *group boundary preference* ranging from constricted group boundaries (exclusive) to open group boundaries (inclusive). At the heart of the matter, this, more than policy, is what splits the left and the right.

The figure below illustrates the political spectrum as an expression of *group boundary preference*.

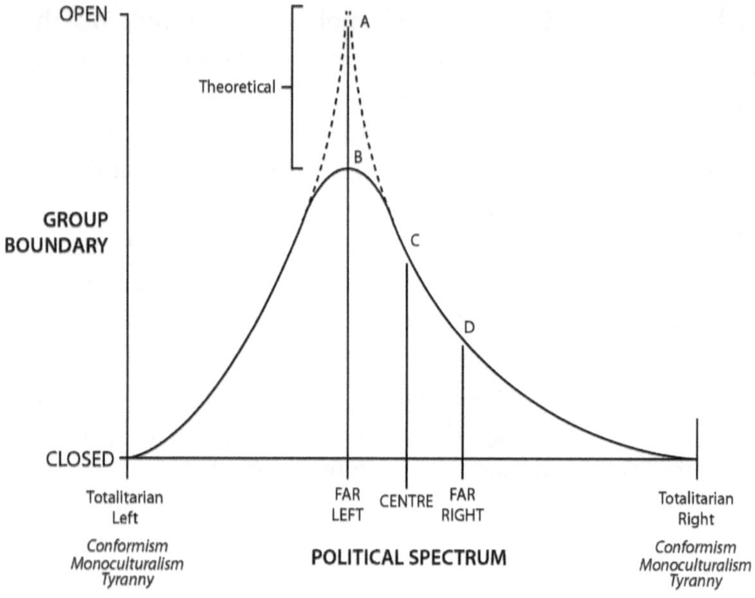

Political Spectrum & Group Boundary Openness

Point A

The fantasy of the left.

The far-left imagines a group without boundaries. Logically, this is where the concept of moral equality leads; where society should extend its benefits to anyone who desires to receive them and any form of discrimination is morally wrong.

Noble as this is, to have a group, boundaries must exist and, as people tend to react negatively to an eroded sense of identity or belonging, the destruction of group boundaries leads to the erosion of constituency.[169–171] Working to eradicate group boundaries is to work against the reality of human nature and, in the long term, never works.

Even if the opening of group boundaries has little or no real-world impact, right-wing politicians easily leverage group-prejudice to gain electoral support.[172] Studies from Germany, Sweden, and France show that although migration does not necessarily *generate* anti-immigration attitudes or fears, it triggers and strengthens existing ones.[173]

In line with this, Alexander Gauland, a leading member of AfD, the far-right German party, described the Syrian immigration crisis as a "gift."[174] To try and stem the loss of constituency, governments in both Germany and Sweden have instituted more restrictive policies on immigration and immigrant rights both validating and delivering right-wing preference.[169] Although those in the centre or the right may agree on principles of care, in general, they see the dissolution of all group boundaries as a threat to society, which if taken to extremes, it may well be.

Point A is theoretical because the total elimination of group discrimination also requires the dissolving of a wide array of hierarchical groups, be they social, religious, or economic, and doing so requires the use of force. At the same time, such governments require force to protect their regime of total equality from dissent—to "save the revolution," if you will.

Applying such force requires a bureaucratic concentration of power. To efficiently apply force at scale requires the concentration of power into hierarchical and bureaucratic systems. The resulting 'unfairness to protect fairness' is the practical expression of far-left desires of total equality and has led to the authoritarianism that has followed all successful far-left movements. [175–180]

Although both the far-right and the far-left end up with oppressive regimes, the fundamental difference between them is that the far-right makes no pretence of inclusivity. Their thesis is predicated on its opposite: exclusivity and exclusion.

Point B
The point of maximal possible openness, while retaining sufficient group boundary definition to maintain a *distinct group*. This position is far short of the left's ideal. However, anything beyond this point is likely to push group members toward leaders who are more willing to define group boundaries.

Point C

The natural position of the group. People want to identify with a group and therefore expect some boundaries. Where *the group* means shared benefits, identity, and cooperative existence, expanding to include those who have traditionally been outsiders may come at a cost, real, imagined, or emotional, to those already established within the group.

The natural concept of *group* does not comply with concepts of equality *(classically, equality before the law, and equality of opportunity)* with the well-accepted base-line proposition that all are considered of equal moral value.[181-183] Taking this at face value no one should be seen as less or more deserving of common group benefits however, to access equality under law, or equality of opportunity, one must first have the properties that allow them to be considered *in-group* and therefore subject to those laws and protections.

Equality is not the right goal for human societies because humans have an innate preference for fairness, not sameness.[184] Here, fairness is expressed in its abstract; *equality*—everyone has a right to the same benefits—effectively paving over the complex, context-based reality of fairness and compassionate group order.

Unfortunately, from a leftist perspective, there is probably no 'good' answer to the question of group-boundary definition. However, acknowledging that groups must have *some boundaries*, and therefore must exclude *some people*, is a useful starting point for leftist thinkers.

Point D

The fantasy of the right.

People with right-leaning tendencies tend to fear the destruction of the group and see those on the left as trying to achieve just that.

In reality, as there are few intrinsic differences in the nature of in or out-group people and, as group boundaries are primarily ideological, rightists must use fictional narratives to institute and enforce tighter group boundaries. Given their aims, rightist myths are by nature discriminatory, and when taken to their end conclusions lead to the authoritarianism that has followed all successful far-right movements.

Understanding Understanding

If there is one thing that precipitates a political change that aligns with our innate pretence for fairness, cooperation, and care, it is gaining a better understanding of reality. To do this, we need to understand *how* to understand.

Reality can be broken down into three categories: physical, social, and personal.

Physical reality refers to that thin slice of the world we experience first-hand and which is best understood through science.

Scientists share their methods and conditions and other scientists repeat the experiments and see if the results can be verified. Consensus takes time, sure, but this is the only decent framework we have for reliably improving our understanding of reality.

Social reality describes the complex geography of our social group. We cannot make good decisions for society without good information. Some people are better than others at providing this information because their life's work is based on discovering truths. Where social scientists work to understand the complex reality of our social environment, journalists work on exposing the truth in relation to power. The findings of these broad fields inform us of how things are, how they could be better, and who is standing in the way.

When it comes to journalism, a big question in the 21st Century is *who should we believe?* Although bias is always present, it is also true that some people have better intent and better methods, when it comes to describing reality. Quality journalism has multiple credible sources, verification, checks on bias, balance, documentation, context, and fairness.

Journalism that consistently aims to mislead can be considered *propaganda*. Distinguishing *journalism* from *propaganda* can be tricky but results speak loudly. *Journalism* tends to lead to understanding, empathetic responses, and an awareness of nuance. *Propaganda* tends to simplify, and make us anxious, angry, or hateful, toward a certain group of people.

Personal reality is the world of our inner thoughts and feelings. Many of us live lives that do not fit who we are or, as we change with time, do not fit who we become. As adults, at some point, we must take responsibility for the values we hold and the behaviours that they drive. To assume this responsibility, we first need to figure out what our values *actually* are.

Behaviour communicates values and so the first step is observing how we behave. What do we seek? What do we work for? How do we go about it? How do we treat our friends? What do we do in our leisure time? Who do we trust and why? What sort of person do we befriend? What do we eat? What do we buy? What media do we consume? The answers to these questions communicate values.

I occasionally eat eggs, which means that I believe it is OK for unwanted male chicks to be killed en masse. I occasionally buy cheap clothes when I can afford alternatives suggesting that I believe that the labour practices involved are justifiable. I occasionally fly without it being *strictly* necessary suggesting that I am not unwilling to fuel the climate catastrophe. These are not the beliefs I would *say* I hold, or would advocate for, but my behaviour betrays the murky reality of my values.

These are all easy-to-reach examples of things that I could do better. Only a behavioural change would suggest a change in my values because *liking values*—or merely identifying with them—is not the same as holding them.

A trickier thing I could do better is work on my self-awareness. This may require the support of psychoanalysts or other trained practitioners who can help me unearth the subconscious biases that guide my behaviour.

Lastly, I can accept that I am ignorant and can never fully understand reality. With this, I give myself space to be wrong, to accept when I am, and allow myself to change. Accepting ignorance allows us to remain open-minded to new information and learn to make better decisions.

CHAPTER 15

THE GAP BETWEEN LAW AND REALITY

Matching the undertones of the society I grew up in, as an adolescent I held sexist, xenophobic, racist, and homophobic feelings. None of these were based on personal experience nor from parental guidance, and despite intellectually rejecting discriminatory ideas, on occasion, visceral emotions could still arise from within. Looking back at the culture of the 1980s, where sexism, racism, and homophobia were normalised, and where discriminatory language was pervasive across media and public conversation, it's no surprise that my developing mind was impacted.[185]

It's hard to challenge norms as a child especially if you're never exposed to conversations that call them into question. Although I very rarely feel these ideas now, some do still exist in deep recesses and can be raked up from time to time. These days, they are never homophobic, rarely racist, are on occasion xenophobic, and sometimes, sexist or commoditising of women. Once implanted, *ideas-felt* are hard to shake.

Had I been born in the UK today, it's possible that I would not have inherited many of these ideas. Had I been born fifty years before, I may have promoted these ideas, or worse, acted on them, making them much harder to relinquish.

Most people hold unsavoury or discriminatory ideas of some kind at some level. Acknowledging their existence and recognising that these ideas are not *you*, or even necessarily *of you*, is a good starting point for dealing with them. Likewise, understanding how common such feelings are, can help us have empathy for ourselves and realise that *we're* not bad, but simply burdened by an inheritance of bad ideas.

This understanding can also enable us to have more empathy for those brought up in more ignorant environments and who, as a result, are imbued with discriminatory concepts that lead to poor intuitive judgements. Socially, moral emphasis is placed on behaviour—*believe what you like but don't act on it*—because it's action that leads to harm. This in turn directs our collective focus toward the *suppression of feelings* rather than considering how to improve the felt-ideas that drive them.

The Fast-Changing world

Things have moved faster in the last century than ever before, and this has left many people feeling left behind. The German sociologist, Hartmut Rosa identifies three categories in the acceleration of modern life: technological acceleration, the acceleration of processes of social change, and the acceleration of the pace of life.

The acceleration of the pace of life relates to the "*compression of actions and experiences in everyday life*," something that seems to happen despite the belief that technological advances should increase our free time.[186] Where transport doubles in speed, freeing up time, we quadruple the distance we travel; where the internet increases our access to information it also increases the amount of information we access; where emails save time by delivering a letter instantly, we spend more time writing more letters to more people.

This drives what Harmut Rosa calls "*the paradoxical phenomenon of simultaneous technological acceleration and increasing time scarcity.*" People flick through TV channels, watch ever shorter media, skip from task to task, or attempt to do multiple things simultaneously, spending ever-increasing time in *the abstract* and away from the present moment.

Social acceleration is where *"attitudes and values as well as fashions and lifestyles, social relations and obligations as well as groups, classes, or milieus, social languages as well as forms of practice and habits are said to change at ever increasing rates."* [186] In this, Rosa provides an example of acceleration in our professional lives; where a job was once handed from father to son through generations, we now skip through multiple careers in a single life.

This is all part of an increasingly abstracted life, as discussed in Chapter 12. *Abstract* components of life can be sped up, made more efficient, distilled, manufactured, and sold, while our important *emotional* processes cannot. Relationships take time to build, and spending time with your children, caring for others, and looking after yourself are not processes that can be accelerated. In *the emotional,* there is little efficiency that can be gained without diminishing the quality of experience.

The German Philosopher Hermann Lübbe claims that Western societies experience a *"contraction of the present"* as a consequence of accelerating cultural and social innovation. [187] For Lübbe, socially, the past is what *is no longer valid* and the future is *what is not yet valid*; therefore, *the present* is the period where there is the stability to process the past and make decisions on the future. Only in these periods is there the certainty required to orientate, evaluate, and set expectations.

In such an accelerated social environment, *beliefs* change rapidly and are forced to coexist with competing beliefs that might be radically different. Social expectations are constantly evolving, and this has a severe emotional impact.

When feelings you've long held now mark you as a bad person it's natural to think that *things have gone too far*. When your feelings become *outlawed*, now, that is something else.

The Legal Social-Reality Gap

Laws serve to enable high levels of social cooperation. This involves establishing standards, maintaining order, and resolving disputes. Laws outline what behaviours are wrong and how they should be punished and, thus, they play a big part in determining what we deem socially acceptable.

Changes in the law can cover significant ideological and behavioural ground and thus can change far faster than ideas, especially those melded to our subconscious. Laws can be passed by one government and repealed by the next, and so exist in a state of flux and can be highly unstable. In contrast, socially held ideas, as discussed in Chapter 11, change slowly and with less volatility.

Accordingly, two types of behavioural boundaries exist.

Socially Accepted Behavioural Boundaries (SABBs) are those we addressed in the last chapter, and Legal Behavioural Boundaries (LBBs) are determined by laws and protected by the threat of social sanction.

In an ideal world, these would be one and the same, but in reality, one changes slowly and the other with the stroke of a legislator's pen. SABBs and LBBs interact with and influence one another. Problems arise, however, when large numbers of people find their erstwhile acceptable feelings, or behaviours, designated illegal.

Gender discrimination is a great example.

In the following illustration, a hypothetical Legal Behavioural Boundary leaps from a sexist position to a less sexist position, while the SABB slowly trends downwards but has a long way to go before catching up.

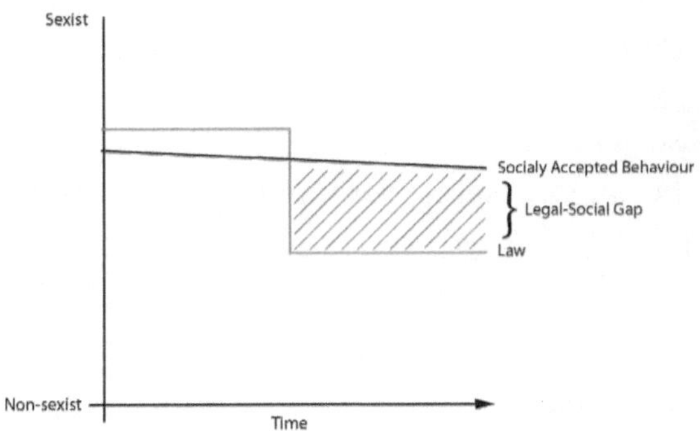

Such leaps have (thankfully) happened, but they've caught many people out.

Imagine you are a sixty-year-old man named Gary who grew up in a society saturated with widespread gender-based discrimination. For most of your life, this was perfectly normal, and the social reality that resulted gave credibility to the ideas that lay behind the prejudice. The normalisation of the behaviours blinded you to the damage they inflicted. What's more, discriminatory ideas about women shaped your views on masculinity, affecting the ideas that underpin your self-concept and self-worth, making undoing them especially hard.

You, Gary, like a lot of men of your generation, were used to having a bikini calendar in the workshop, and topless teenagers in your daily paper—why not? You find sexist jokes funny, and, sure, who can resist flirting with a beautiful woman, even if she's a colleague? For you, it's just *harmless fun*. And so, you're floored when you are disciplined for a "funny" email you sent to a few colleagues.

Your anger peaks when it turns out you'll lose your job if you do it again. You have worked there for nearly thirty years! At that moment, you want to burn it all down, but you remember the mortgage, and the pension, so you have little choice but to *comply*. The emotional damage is done, though.

You used to feel integral and now you feel like an awkward outsider. You must walk on eggshells, be careful of what you say, never quite knowing what is considered *wrong* today, and consciously censor yourself when you express your feelings, thoughts, and humour. These days, you only find *full acceptance* in a narrowing group of friends, and because of this—despite holding the same economic position in society—you no longer feel like you *fully belong.*

You, Gary, have lost something of great material value: the security of feeling fully in-group.

I Am Oppressed!

When the law explicitly tells us that long-held feelings are wrong, and that we must not act according to them, *suppression* can quickly come to feel an awful lot like *oppression.* Just as a fascist leader makes expressing *anti-regime ideas* illegal, we may feel that the law has been weaponized against us.

In this situation, we cannot *be how we feel we are*, and we cannot say *what* we *feel to be true*, or perhaps worse, we cannot even argue our point of view without risking social sanction.

This is not oppression in the true meaning of the word, but it does not matter what you call it. How a person *feels* is *their* reality. This is likely why Donald Trump presents himself as a victim. He feels like the world is against him because, in some ways, it is. It is harder to explicitly be *who he is* these days, and he hates it. The days of walking into a dressing room while teenage girls are changing are over, as are the days of boasting about assaulting women, but it's still how he wants to express himself and *other people* are stopping him.[188,189]

Of course, change is possible, but it is not cost-free. Changing our minds is effortful and, as Dr Lisa Feldman Barrett, points out, *"triggering neural plasticity can sometimes be an unpleasant experience even if the thing we are learning is something we want to engage in."*[190]

Taking a new moral position comes at a cost, and the

longer we have behaved with prior moral positions, the higher this cost is likely to be. We must admit being wrong for long periods of our lives, and this may challenge our self-concept of being a 'good' person. We may have to explain ourselves to friends who have no intention of changing, and who see it as an act of surrender. We may need to reconsider how we see our loved ones. Ultimately, we may not be able, or willing, to pay the price.

Because of this, there is a *real* emotional and neurological resistance to change, and understandably it can be far more comfortable to hold on to our views, despite their growing unpopularity, and the social pressure this creates.

Meanwhile, for the young, new moral positions are cheap. With little or no prior behaviour based on the *old ideas,* they can easily imagine themselves heroic, riding a moral high horse. It would be wise, however, to maintain humility, one day, they too will feel the burning judgment of others for the attitudes of their time.

The Risks of Fast Social Change

In her book *Recollections of My Nonexistence* (2020), Rebecca Solnit describes the feeling of being out of place in the modern world:

> *"As you grow older you become an immigrant from a vanished country, a country some of your peers may remember but the young may find unimaginable or incomprehensible. You could call it the land of before; before some great change, before we did things this way, before we decided that was unacceptable, before we shed new light on an old problem. I was shaped by a world that no longer quite exists, so I can't imagine myself at, say, 18 in the present moment, because to do so is to imagine someone utterly different. She does not exist, and I — as we*

all do – exist as the cumulative effect of my experiences, opportunities or lack thereof, and ideals."[191]

It doesn't take long to feel left behind.

Computerisation, automation, robotics, the internet, email, outsourced manufacturing, outsourced services, social media, and the accelerated globalisation of markets, have reinvented work, life, and communication.

Changes in the workplace are generally accepted. People might dislike them, they might even find them financially punishing, but they understand that businesses must compete. Changes to culture or identity, however, are harder to swallow, especially if they coincide with a worsening economic situation.

The emotional experience of cultural change is powerful. It is frustrating to exist in *the gap* and accelerated social change, combined with longer lives, means that more people exist there than ever before. This creates a broad audience vulnerable to exploitation by populist politicians who focus on grievances and identity politics, who attack change and promise to bring back yesterday—*when they felt like insiders*—when things were, well, *great*.

In today's accelerated world, this is a growing problem.

How People in the Gap React

If you find yourself caught in the gap between what you've always considered socially acceptable and what legislation—or social mores—now does not, you have three choices: work to change yourself and your ideas, begrudgingly comply but retain your old beliefs, or reject change and live in deviance.

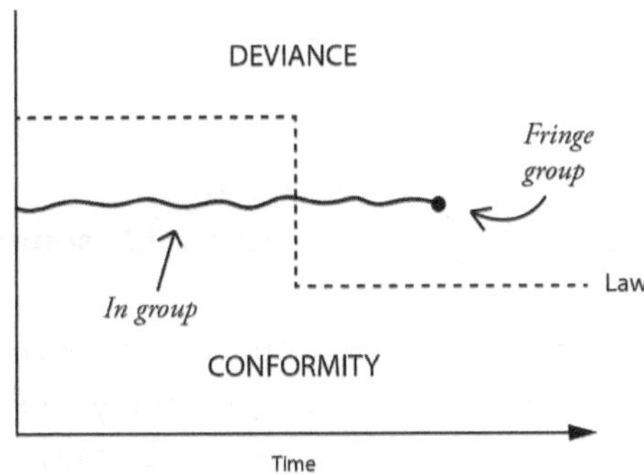

I Will Do What I Want!
Secure People & Cognitive Deviance

Those with a lot of power and agency are the least likely to *need* to comply with change and are most able to live in *cognitive deviance*, especially if they retain the support of their peers. They are not vulnerable and so even though they know their behaviour is 'wrong,' they expect to get away with it.

This attitude of resistance to change frequently drives acts of sexual abuse. The paedophile scandals of the church, where crimes were covered up by institutions and offenders were moved to other churches, often to repeat their behaviours, are a good example of cognitive deviance at a personal and organisational level.

Harvey Weinstein, Jeffery Epstein, and their ilk knew full well that what they were doing was illegal; that their behaviour violated Legal Behavioural Boundaries, but they did it anyway. Their view on what was socially acceptable (for their circles, at least) sat far outside the law and their public takedown exposed how common this is.

Beliefs take a long time to change. A law can be passed but this means little if it's not enforced or taken seriously by the judiciary. The tell-tale signs of such a gap include ignored complaints, low prosecution rates, slap-on-the-wrist punishments, pay-offs, hush-ups, the closing of ranks, organisational cover-ups, victim blaming, and victim persecution.

It's All Stupid!
Insecure People & Cognitive Dissonance

People unprotected by wealth and power are *rightly afraid* of falling foul of the law. For most people, losing a job could result in the repossession of a home or the loss of healthcare coverage, both of which they cannot afford to lose. *Not conforming* might be ruinous.

The insecure who find themselves in *the gap* are more likely to turn toward cognitive dissonance. In this, if they *do* adapt their behaviours, they may modify or 'edit' their past to eliminate the gap between the new values and prior behaviour.

If they do not conform, they may see the new rules as *nonsense* and seek information that invalidates new moral judgements—regardless of how fair they are. This could include 'facts' from dubious sources, the misrepresentation of scientific studies, or the use of conspiracy theories to support their beliefs.

For example, an insecure person with visceral feelings against gay people may lean into cognitive dissidence and think, "*It's a biblical fact that homosexuality is immoral*," or "*gay people are not persecuted anyway—it's all nonsense*," or "*the gays (and other political scapegoats) are manipulating and controlling society.*"

They Don't Want You to Know This But…
Conspiracy Theories

Conspiracies exist, but they're never driven by a global ring of politicians and celebrities with aims to control the world. As Karen Douglass, a Professor of Social Psychology at the University of Kent, explains "*it is political economy, not conspiracy theory, that explains what is fundamentally wrong with society*," and yet it's easy to get sucked into the idea that there's some big nefarious explanation when the world seems like it's gone crazy.[192]

Real conspiracies tend to fail because it is extremely difficult to carry out conspiratorial plans and keep everyone quiet—even when relatively small numbers of people are involved. Hidden conspiracies that involve hundreds of people are extremely unlikely. Conspiracies where, for example, "doctors" or "scientists" conspire against *us*, and it's all kept secret for years, is in the realm of the impossible.

Douglass and her co-authors, write that conspiracy theories stem from a desire for understanding and subjective certainty, a desire for control and security, or the desire to maintain a positive self or group image.[193] Corresponding with these desires, it has been found that low-status social groups are more likely to hold conspiracy beliefs than those in high-status groups.[194–197]

If you exist well inside your society's Socially Accepted Behaviour Boundaries, or are generally secure, playing free and loose with reality may have few consequences. If you exist on the fringes of society, the loss of common ground may lead to social ostracization and all its attendant consequences. Unfortunately, existing on the fringes of society causes us to be worse at reading reality and thus increasingly vulnerable.[198]

When we share common ground with very few people, it increases our tendency resort to para-social connections like online communities and celebrities that further narrow our ideological frame of reference and reduce our exposure to counter-conspiracy ideas.[198]

Conspiracy theories untether us from a more rational basis

of reality, and instead grounds us in alternate realities, based on fictional stories, not facts. As stories can be easily manipulated, so can their believers.*

It should be no surprise then that extremist movements are characterised by holding excessive conspiracy beliefs. Conspiracy theories contribute to the process of radicalisation but also justify the sort of violence that often characterises these groups.[199] Such theories have played integral roles in a wide array of mass prejudice, terrorism, and genocide.[200]

In "The Power of Unreason" Jamie Bartlett and Carl Miller explain that conspiracy theories work as a "radicalisation multiplier" in that they demonise the other, delegitimise voices of dissent or moderation (the sheeple), and label naysayers as a part of the conspiracy.[201]

> *When people lose confidence in their core beliefs, they become literally "dis-illusioned" because they lack a functional blueprint of reality. Without such a map, there is no basis for determining what behaviors are appropriate or desirable, leaving no way to plot a course to self-esteem.*

Sheldon Solomon, et al., *The Worm at the Core* (2015).

---

* As conspiracy theories provide an over-arching explanation with little or dubious evidence, people popularly imagine them to be similar to religion, but conspiracy theories have some fundamental differences.

Where conspiracy theories explain why people are downtrodden, excluded, victims, failures, or why they can't do better—religions tend to explain why people are great, chosen, righteous and can do better. In this sense, conspiracy theories and religions serve opposite ends, regardless of what they have in common. If conspiracy theorism is to be considered 'religion-like' then it can only be as a *religion of the damned*.

Thus, when religion and conspiracies mix, the impact is potent. People see themselves as both *victims* and *chosen* and religious fanaticism arrives as justified by grievance. It is no surprise, then, that conspiracy theories are prevalent within Christian and Islamic terrorist organisations.[201–203]

CHAPTER 16

WHAT CAN WE DO?

Most of this book is about understanding *why we are* and *how we can be.*

This work has helped me to better understand our relationship between *the abstract* and *the emotional* and how too much focus on the former comes at a cost to the latter—which holds importance when it comes to finding life satisfaction. I have gained a better understanding of our relationship to ideas and how they shape how we are and who we become.

The fact that has become most evident is that, for better or worse, *ideas rule our lives* and that without taking a hard look at what these ideas are, we are doomed to live within their confines.

In this chapter, I will try to sum-up how to make use of the information contained in this book. I have found that these have helped me simplify my life and provide a structure for determining how to live it, and how to think about it.

Who Am I?

The 'I' itself is an ideological construct and there is no permanence in 'you' or 'yourself.' This may sound disorientating, but it is instead *freeing.* We are constantly changing and accepting this allows our ideas about ourselves to constantly change too.

This flexibility allows our self-concept to be more in tune with reality, enabling a more harmonious existence between who we become and how we feel about it.

To attempt to fix our self-concept to a certain point in time is to act against reality, which necessitates the use of force—be it emotional suppression, self-deception, or leaning into fiction—and neither is beneficial in the long run.

It is hard to define who we are, other than the likelihood that we are innately decent, in this, it is easier to say what we are not. We are not fixed in any of our attributes, we are not permanently 'like' anything. I know of people who have gone from shy to gregarious, from pessimistic to joyful, from hateful to accepting, from overweight to athletic, from bitter to kind, from broke to rich and from rich to broke, from weak to strong, healthy to unhealthy, sick to well, passionless to finding direction, unloved to loved, angry to calm. If we must give the self a permanent attribute, it is one of malleability and constant change.

We are not a construct of consumerist culture. We are not the clothes we wear, the car we drive, the house we own, the beauty of our partner, or the money we have—and to *feel* like this is the case, is a form of poverty that leads us to feel inherently insecure. When trying to determine our net worth, first and foremost we should look at our contribution, direct and indirect, to our society. Humans only exist in groups, and it is only *through* others that we find value.

Allow Yourself to Change

It's easy to get stuck being a certain type of person and this is increasingly true with age. To help disconnect from the idea of having fixed attributes, it can be helpful to communicate changes to our friends and avoid creating the trap of 'being like' one thing or another. Tell people how you were wrong yesterday and that you are probably wrong about a whole load of other things today. Openly accepting our likely ignorance frees us from constraints of perceived certainty or knowing. We can be kind to ourselves, reality is impossible to understand, and therefore, in our attempts to base our decisions on *reality,* we can only hope to be less wrong.

We lean more conservative as we get older. We engage less with complexity and rely more on experience, but as our experience is increasingly based on a world that no longer exists, so it becomes less useful over time. If we don't keep learning, the common ground we share shrinks and we get written out of the scene.

"Strong opinions, weakly held" is an approach developed by Stanford Professor Paul Saffo that describes the idea of holding confident and well-defined points of view but being open to change if new evidence and perspectives emerge. This approach encourages intellectual humility, open-mindedness, and a willingness to challenge our assumptions in the face of new information.

Understand reality, remain creative.

Examine The Ideas That Rule Us

We know *how* to ride a bike but we do not need to understand the complex neurology and biomechanics that explain *why* we can ride a bike. Likewise, most people are not philosophers, but all people hold a philosophy. Whether we understand them or not, as we engage in this business of living, we use a set of ideas as a guide.

Our philosophy might not be strongly defined, be riddled with hypocrisy, or be totally incoherent, but nevertheless, it still constitutes a philosophy—a set of ideas that we use to live our lives.

These ideas are typically inherited from older generations. Perhaps they are adapted to better fit modern times, or even reacted against, but either way, the ideas we are born into tend to define the scope of ideas, that we end up living to.

Weak philosophies lead to insecurity, second guessing, a lack of commitment, or to fear following paths that may be better for us. Likewise, if the ideas that make up our self-concept are poorly thought through, then ourselves *as-a-concept* also feels insecure. This leads to defensive behaviour where challenges to our ideas, or simply people living in different ways, can feel like a subtle attack on our person.

Without scrutinising the ideas we live by, taking stock of the options, and choosing for ourselves, we are unable to develop a more cohesive philosophy that allows us to be more confident in our actions.

Beyond a preference for fairness, empathy, and cooperation, all of our ideas about how to live are largely superficial. Many of them have been passed around for a long time but that doesn't make them any less made up.

Understand Important Realities
Wealth, Health & Happiness

Within society there are various realities that have a significant impact on your long-term ability to live a happy and healthy life.

We all live in a highly financialised society and therefore it is imperative to become financially literate and understand how budgeting, saving, debt, interest and investments will affect your life, and your ability to reach financial independence, in the long run. You should understand the best ways to save money in the country in which you live because these are hard, but relatively easy-to-understand, realities that will almost certainly impact your life for better or worse.

Build a reality-based view on health and the outcomes based on differing behaviour. Ask, do we want to live a long healthy life, or one in which we suffer decades of chronic disease or disability? The average *healthy* lifespan in Europe is 65 years, meaning that many will have a health condition that seriously affects their life many years before and many others will live healthily for a lot longer. The better information you have about lifestyle choices and their impacts on your later life the better you can base decisions on reality which will give you the best chances of a healthier life. Do not underestimate the value of good health, it's worth more than any wealth we could ever hope to attain.

Understand yourself better. This takes time and effort and, as we also change, it is a lifelong process. Spend time introspecting, build a philosophy of life, and discuss it with others. Try and figure out what you *actually* like, what you *actually* enjoy. What things contribute to your well-being? What work motivates you? What really impacts you in a positive or negative way? Let science and our communal understanding of reality guide your experiments.

Try to determine exactly what situation you want in life. Use this understanding to work toward a life that is in line with who you are and adapt it as your body and mind change over time. If you can better understand reality, and use that knowledge to guide your life, you will be wealthier (in the ways that matter) and happier.

It won't work if you understand reality but stick your head in the sand and carry on as you were, though. The saying "*hard decisions, easy life*" (and its flip side "easy decisions, hard life") is worth bearing in mind when looking at options, decisions, and lifestyle.

What leads to a well-lived, happy, satisfying life?
  - *How do we convert theory into practice?*
What is important in life and why?
  - *Does our behaviour communicate these values?*
Are the ideas that make up our world-view rooted in fantasy or reality?
  - *How do we tell the difference between fact and fiction?*
Is my behaviour leading me in the direction that I want to go?
  - *If I behaved like this forever, where do I arrive?*

Behaviour Communicates Values

We are persuaded by words, words tug at emotions, and when we dearly want to believe the words, they can offset ghastly behaviours. This can create a great deal of confusion both politically and in personal relationships.

A partner, politician, or friend, may care for us according to their words, but their actions can betray a different perspective. By using behaviour as a guide, we can cut through this manipulation.

Try this. On one side of a bit of paper, write down what they say. On the other, write down how they behave—what they actually do.

What values do their behaviours communicate? How do these compare to the words?

Likewise, spend time thinking about what values your behaviours communicate.

What do you spend your money on?
Where do you find your information?
Where do you draw group boundaries?

Avoid the Calcification of the Abstract

How do we stay psychologically youthful?

We can find answers in the things that stand in opposition to an abstracted life and help protect us from its effects. This might be achieved through creativity, play, the study of the new, the detail, the intricacy of change, and cultivating openness. We might try to reduce pre-judgement in a way that prevents *experience*.

When *knowing* takes from us the ability to appreciate the new that is in front of us every day, then how do we reinvoke our capacity for wonder? The key is to notice change and engage with changing things. That is, plants, people, children, nature—the living world—and allow ourselves to see with new eyes. Take new paths, go to the unknown, and experience vast natural wonders that inspire feelings of awe.

We can beat creeping functionalism by creating *without purpose*. Creativity is a human trait but *purely* creative pursuits are often side lined in favour of productive endeavours. This is practical but being productive and creative can coexist. It might help to see pure creativity as having no certain outcome, no certain form, no definite plan, no expectation of profit, and perhaps no functionality other than the act of creation itself. Although effective art is powerful in how it communicates values, art does not have to be effective, or great, to deliver tangible emotional value to its creator.

Leverage Innate Values

Examine how you can improve your life by ensuring fair, caring, and cooperative conditions for all of those around you. Doing so will make your life better as well as theirs.

If you are in a position of relative power, you have two choices: create a fair and caring environment or spend your life-energy delivering force to ensure cooperation. Doing the latter is a choice that leads you to be on the receiving end of resentment, disdain, or even hatred. Living in this way is stressful, bad for our health, and breeds a cynicism that can rot your opinion of all humanity, and ultimately it can make you lonely.

When we oppress another, we oppress ourselves.

Support Change

Play the game. Be an active player. Speak up when things are not fair or empathetic and give material support to things that are.

You do not have to be radical to attend a protest against environmental destruction or to ask the police to stop shooting unarmed minorities. These are reasonable causes relating to fairness and care, and they're worth walking through the streets to support.

Every social change that has been achieved has been achieved by regular people like you. It is true, individuals with great clarity and high motivation tend to lead movements, but without others providing common ground with broader society their visionary ideas would struggle to connect.

Forgive the Past

Recognise that your ability to change *how you think* is a testament to other people's ability to do the same.

Forgive those who once held 'wrong' ideologies and give them space to be right *right now*.

In Hannah Arendt's words:

> *Trespassing is an everyday occurrence which is in the very nature of action's constant establishment of new relationships within a web of relations, and it needs forgiving, dismissing in order to go on by constantly releasing men from what they have done unknowingly.*

Those who promote progress will meet less resistance if they promote forgiveness for their behaviours based on the ideas of yesterday at the same time as they campaign to change them. Humiliating the opposing group is not useful.

Allow people to be reborn into the new ideological world.

Realpolitik

The goal of social change is not to force bad actors out. The powerful will never cooperate if your ultimate end-goal is to outgroup them. Behavioural change cannot present an existential threat.

People hold destructive ideas, and consequences are important, but we can't lose sight of our shared humanity. Many bad behaviours are a product of socialisation, and the same person would likely have acted differently had they been born in a different time and place.

Instead of portraying those who have behaved upon poor ideas as *bad people* it is more productive to allow them to be considered decent people driven by poor ideas. Such a view enables the sharing of responsibility between the individual and the society that made them.

Pay it Forward

Pay it forward. Your grandchildren will thank you. Remember the reality of how long social change takes when it comes to the *actual* changing of minds.

Of course, changing a law makes a huge difference right now, but it might take 2-3 generations to see your project through to completion. Such change is a multi-generational process and that itself is beautiful.

The reality of the time required to deliver complete social change might be daunting but, if your behaviour is to be based on reality, you must be more strategic, more patient, and build the stamina required for the long haul.

Politics

Be aware of the fundamental basis of group that underlies right- and left-wing politics and the failings inherent in both.

Notice the use of force in society, starting from the humble lie, and recognise that the majority of force is only required to ensure cooperation in unfair and uncaring situations.

My Journey and Future

The work involved in writing this book has not been entirely fun (read exhausting and expensive) but it has been valuable.

I'm better at talking than writing but organising my ideas has helped me understand them and, thus, myself. I have a sense of why I live the way I do and how I want to move forward. Finding this has been liberating and worth the effort.

I am interested in figuring out the realities that I live within and have taken responsibility for practical things I once put off. My finances are in order. I have saved toward a decent pension and, based on the likely financial realities, I'll be able to support myself as I age.

I continue to work within normal systems but not as much as I used to. I am freer than I was, and I spend more time doing the things I love. I have communicated and shared ideas with millions of people. And I am trying to make a difference.

I have changed the structure of my business to have more of a personal impact on people's lives. I do my best to organise my relationships in line with innate human concepts of fairness and care that support effective cooperation.

I try not to be a hypocrite and I am more aware of my failings.

I have developed systems that enable me to avoid focusing on making money and allow me to spend time on projects that I find meaningful.

I am more flexible and can challenge old ideas of myself without challenging my identity because I know, and feel, that these ideas do not define me.

Searching for facts has simplified how I think and how I form opinions. I accept that our understanding is not absolute, and our grasp of reality is constantly improving. I change my mind in response to new evidence. I take a cost-benefit analysis of proposed understandings and try to choose the better option.

In short, writing this book has created more freedom in how I approach and move through the world. Understanding the failures of both rightist and leftist thinking, I do not feel the need to be strongly attached to a specific ideology or political stance.

"There is no right or wrong way to live" is untrue.

Making decisions based on fantasy has material consequences for our social well-being and this has a cascading impact on our emotional health. An abstracted life is miserable, lonely, and stressful, and that's no way to live.

Thank you for reading. I hope you have found this book interesting, and with luck, valuable.

One last thing!

Thank you for reading this book. Honestly, it was a monster of a project which took (at a rough estimate) seven thousand hours to research, think, write, draft, and rewrite (several times over). On top of this, editing, academic scrutiny, and production costs, have come in at over fifteen thousand dollars.

Based on the reality of modern publishing, I am unlikely to see that money again, but if this book helps a bunch of people see the world differently—or to live a better life—then I can accept such a loss with a sort of pleasure. Thanks to the nature of *contributionism*—there is a good chance that what does not come back in financial terms will instead be returned in other emotionally rewarding ways.

One way you can help this process is to leave a review and recommend this book to your friends. *Word of mouth* is the best way for any book to find another reader and *leaving a review* is the best way to help an author out. Sure, monolithic tech platforms and their algorithms need to be fed, but more importantly, authors (at least this one) like to hear what readers, like you, think of their ideas.

A review not only helps, but it completes the circle and makes us both feel good.

I read every review, so I look forward to hearing your thoughts about this book.

Thank you in advance,

Nathan

Don't forget you can get access to more thinking, tools, book recommendations, and references using the following URL (for free):

njmurphy.com/getmore

BIBLIOGRAPHY PART 1

1. Eagleton, T. *Ideology*. (Routledge, 2013).

2. Gabora, L. The Power of 'Then': The Uniquely Human Capacity to Imagine Beyond the Present. *Psychology Today* (2010).

3. Mcbrearty, S. & Brooks, A. S. The revolution that wasn't: a new interpretation of the origin of modern human behavior. *Journal of Human Evolution* 39, 453–563 (2000).

4. Mellars, P. *Rethinking the Human Revolution: New Behavioural and Biological Perspectives on the Origin and Dispersal of Modern Humans*. (2007).

5. Marean, C. W. *et al.* Early human use of marine resources and pigment in South Africa during the Middle Pleistocene. *Nature* 449, 905–908 (2007).

6. Tylén, K. *et al.* The evolution of early symbolic behavior in *Homo sapiens*. *Proceedings of the National Academy of Sciences* 117, 4578–4584 (2020).

7. Sopher, P. Where the Five-Day Workweek Came From. *The Atlantic* (2014).

8. Beaven, B. History of the two-day weekend provides lessons for a four-day working week. *The Independent* (2020).

9. Drover, M. Fashion Crimes: The Rabbit Hole of Criminalized Cross-Dressing in US History: Drover '19 at Boston MFA in Boston, MA. *Antioch College* (2017).

10. Maglaty, J. When Did Girls Start Wearing Pink? *Smithsonian* (2011).

11. Narang, D. The Psychological Factors that Affect Makeup Usage and the Perception of Makeup in Different Situations. (2013).

12. Grigg, T. Health & Hygiene in Nineteenth Century England in Museums Victoria Collections. (2008).

13. Haggett, A. Looking Back: Masculinity and mental health - the long view. *The British Psychological Society* (2014).

14. van Eerde, W. & Azar, S. Too Late? What Do You Mean? Cultural Norms Regarding Lateness for Meetings and Appointments. *Cross-Cultural Research* 54, 111–129 (2020).

15. Joy, M. *Why We Love Dogs, Eat Pigs, and Wear Cows: An Introduction to Carnism.* (2011).

16. Sharma, S. *et al.* Maturation of the adolescent brain. *Neuropsychiatric Disease and Treatment* 449 (2013).

17. Greene, M. F. 30 Years Ago, Romania Deprived Thousands of Babies of Human Contact. *The Atlantic* (2020).

18. Castano, D. Effects of institutionalization on Romanian adoptees. *Rowan University* (2021).

19. Driskell, J. E., Copper, C. & Moran, A. Does mental practice enhance performance? *Journal of Applied Psychology* 79, 481–492 (1994).

20. Ellen, M. & Taube, K. *The Gods and Symbols of Ancient Mexico and the Maya: An Illustrated Dictionary of Mesoamerican Religion.* (Thames and Hudson, London, 1993).

21. Victor Davis Hanson. *Carnage and Culture.* (Doubleday, NY, 2000).

22. Bereska, T. *Deviance, Conformity, and Social Control in Canada.* (Pearson, 2017).

23. de Graaf, J., Wann, D. & Naylor, T. *Affluenza: The All-Consuming Epidemic.* (Berrett-Koehler Publishers, 2005).

24. Primack, B. A. *et al.* Social Media Use and Perceived Social Isolation Among Young Adults in the U.S. *American Journal of Preventive Medicine* 53, 1–8 (2017).

25. Cacioppo, J. T. & Patrick, W. *Loneliness – Human Nature and the Need for Social Connection*. (W. W. Norton & Company, 2009).

26. Tang, A. M. China's Agricultural Legacy. *Economic Development and Cultural Change* 28, 1–22 (1979).

27. Lin, J. Y. The Needham Puzzle: Why the Industrial Revolution Did Not Originate in China. *Economic Development and Cultural Change* 43, 269–292 (1995).

28. Coccia, M. Socio-cultural origins of the patterns of technological innovation: What is the likely interaction among religious culture, religious plurality and innovation? Towards a theory of socio-cultural drivers of the patterns of technological innovation. *Technology in Society* 36, 13–25 (2014).

29. Robertson, J. M. & Bradlaugh Bonner, H. *The Life and Legacy of Charles Bradlaugh: Volume 1 & 2*. (T. Fisher Unwin, 1894).

30. Cavanagh, E. Infidels in English Legal Thought: Conquest, Commerce and Slavery in the Common Law from Coke to Mansfield, 1603–1793. *Modern Intellectual History* 16, 375–409 (2019).

31. Harriet Sherwood. Church of England weekly attendance falls below 1m for first time. *The Guardian* (2016).

32. Gregory A. Smith et al. *In U.S., Decline of Christianity Continues at Rapid Pace An Update on America's Changing Religious Landscape.*

33. Graeber, D. & Wengrow, D. *The Dawn of Everything - A New History of Humanity*. (Penguin, 2022).

34. Gert, B. & Gert, J. The Definition of Morality. *Stanford Encyclopedia of Philosophy*.

35. Heydari, A., Teymoori, A. & Trappes, R. Honor killing as a dark side of modernity: Prevalence, common discourses, and a critical view. *Social Science Information* 60, 86–106 (2021).

36. Nye, R. A. *Masculinity and Male Codes of Honor in Modern France.* (University Press of California, 1998).

37. Gray, K., Schein, C. & Ward, A. F. The myth of harmless wrongs in moral cognition: Automatic dyadic completion from sin to suffering. *Journal of Experimental Psychology: General* 143, 1600–1615 (2014).

38. Flack, J. C. & de Waal, F. B. M. Any animal whatever. Darwinian building blocks of morality in monkeys and apes. *Journal of Consciousness Studies* 7, 1–29 (2000).

39. Trivers, R. L. The Evolution of Reciprocal Altruism. *The Quarterly Review of Biology* 46, 35–57 (1971).

40. de Waal, F. *Primates and Philosophers: How Morality Evolved.* (Princeton Science Library, 2006).

41. Anacker, C., O'Donnell, K. J. & Meaney, M. J. Early life adversity and the epigenetic programming of hypothalamic-pituitary-adrenal function. *Dialogues in Clinical Neuroscience* 16, 321–333 (2014).

42. Sapolsky, R. *Behave. The Biology of Humans at Our Best and Worst.* (2018).

43. Anda, R. F., Butchart, A., Felitti, V. J. & Brown, D. W. Building a Framework for Global Surveillance of the Public Health Implications of Adverse Childhood Experiences. *American Journal of Preventive Medicine* 39, 93–98 (2010).

44. Anda, R. F. *et al.* The enduring effects of abuse and related adverse experiences in childhood. *European Archives of Psychiatry and Clinical Neuroscience* 256, 174–186 (2006).

45. Fergusson, D. M., Boden, J. M., Horwood, L. J., Miller, A. L. & Kennedy, M. A. MAOA, abuse exposure and antisocial behaviour: 30-year longitudinal study. *British Journal of Psychiatry* 198, 457–463 (2011).

46. Lango Allen, H. *et al.* Hundreds of variants clustered in genomic loci and biological pathways affect human height. *Nature* 467, 832–838 (2010).

47. Rietveld, C. A. *et al.* GWAS of 126,559 Individuals Identifies Genetic Variants Associated with Educational Attainment. *Science* 340, 1467–1471 (2013).

48. Lapp, H. E. & Hunter, R. G. Early life exposures, neurodevelopmental disorders, and transposable elements. *Neurobiology of Stress* 11, 100174 (2019).

49. Allen, T. A., Von Kaenel, S., Goodrich, J. A. & Kugel, J. F. The SINE-encoded mouse B2 RNA represses mRNA transcription in response to heat shock. *Nature Structural & Molecular Biology* 11, 816–821 (2004).

50. Lapp, H. E. & Hunter, R. G. Early life exposures, neurodevelopmental disorders, and transposable elements. *Neurobiology of Stress* 11, 100174 (2019).

51. Ponomarev, I., Wang, S., Zhang, L., Harris, R. A. & Mayfield, R. D. Gene Coexpression Networks in Human Brain Identify Epigenetic Modifications in Alcohol Dependence. *The Journal of Neuroscience* 32, 1884–1897 (2012).

52. Maze, I. *et al.* Cocaine dynamically regulates heterochromatin and repetitive element unsilencing in nucleus accumbens. *Proceedings of the National Academy of Sciences* 108, 3035–3040 (2011).

53. Ponomarev, I., Wang, S., Zhang, L., Harris, R. A. & Mayfield, R. D. Gene Coexpression Networks in Human Brain Identify Epigenetic Modifications in Alcohol Dependence. *The Journal of Neuroscience* 32, 1884–1897 (2012).

54. Donohue, J. J. & Levitt, S. The Impact of Legalized Abortion on Crime over the Last Two Decades. *American Law and Economics Review* 22, 241–302 (2020).

55. Fumagalli, M. & Priori, A. Functional and clinical neuroanatomy of morality. *Brain* 135, 2006–2021 (2012).

56. Gogolla, N. The insular cortex. *Current Biology* 27, R580–R586 (2017).

57. Herz, R. S. Verbal priming and taste sensitivity make moral transgressions gross. *Behavioral Neuroscience* 128, 20–28 (2014).

58. Gray, K., Schein, C. & Ward, A. F. The myth of harmless wrongs in moral cognition: Automatic dyadic completion from sin to suffering. *Journal of Experimental Psychology: General* 143, 1600–1615 (2014).

59. Jones, A. & Fitness, J. Moral hypervigilance: The influence of disgust sensitivity in the moral domain. *Emotion* 8, 613–627 (2008).

60. Chan, E. Y. & Septianto, F. Disgust predicts charitable giving: The role of empathy. *Journal of Business Research* 142, 946–956 (2022).

61. Sherman, G. D. & Haidt, J. Cuteness and Disgust: The Humanizing and Dehumanizing Effects of Emotion. *Emotion Review* 3, 245–251 (2011).

62. Mazur, L. B. & Gormsen, E. Disgust Sensitivity and Support for Organ Donation: Time to Take Disgust Seriously. *Journal of General Internal Medicine* 35, 2347–2351 (2020).

63. Tanaka, G., Hou, X., Ma, X., Edgecombe, G. D. & Strausfeld, N. J. Chelicerate neural ground pattern in a Cambrian great appendage arthropod. *Nature* 502, 364–367 (2013).

64. Sousa, A. M. M., Meyer, K. A., Santpere, G., Gulden, F. O. & Sestan, N. Evolution of the Human Nervous System Function, Structure, and Development. *Cell* 170, 226–247 (2017).

65. Haidt, J., Rozin, P., Mccauley, C. & Imada, S. Body,

Psyche, and Culture: The Relationship between Disgust and Morality. *Psychology and Developing Societies* 9, 107–131 (1997).

66. Harris, L. T. & Fiske, S. T. Dehumanizing the Lowest of the Low. *Psychological Science* 17, 847–853 (2006).

67. Fiske, S. T. Stereotype Content: Warmth and Competence Endure. *Current Directions in Psychological Science* 27, 67–73 (2018).

68. Freeman, J. B., Rule, N. O., Adams Jr., R. B. & Ambady, N. Culture shapes a mesolimbic response to signals of dominance and subordination that associates with behavior. *NeuroImage* 47, 353–359 (2009).

69. Telzer, E. H., Masten, C. L., Berkman, E. T., Lieberman, M. D. & Fuligni, A. J. Gaining while giving: An fMRI study of the rewards of family assistance among White and Latino youth. *Social Neuroscience* 5, 508–518 (2010).

70. Hardway, C. & Fuligni, A. J. Dimensions of family connectedness among adolescents with mexican, chinese, and european backgrounds. *Developmental Psychology* 42, 1246–1258 (2006).

71. Kraus, M. W., Piff, P. K. & Keltner, D. Social class, sense of control, and social explanation. *Journal of Personality and Social Psychology* 97, 992–1004 (2009).

72. Conway, M. A., Wang, Q., Hanyu, K. & Haque, S. A Cross-Cultural Investigation of Autobiographical Memory. *Journal of Cross-Cultural Psychology* 36, 739–749 (2005).

73. Fredrickson, B. L. *et al.* A functional genomic perspective on human well-being. *Proceedings of the National Academy of Sciences* 110, 13684–13689 (2013).

74. Heisel, M. J. & Flett, G. L. Purpose in Life, Satisfaction with Life, and Suicide Ideation in a Clinical Sample. *Journal of Psychopathology and Behavioral Assessment* 26, 127–135 (2004).

75. Lew, B. *et al.* Meaning in life as a protective factor against suicidal tendencies in Chinese University students. *BMC*

Psychiatry 20, 73 (2020).

76. Wang, M.-C., Richard Lightsey, O., Pietruszka, T., Uruk, A. C. & Wells, A. G. Purpose in life and reasons for living as mediators of the relationship between stress, coping, and suicidal behavior. *The Journal of Positive Psychology* 2, 195–204 (2007).

77. Van Tongeren, D. R., Green, J. D., Davis, D. E., Hook, J. N. & Hulsey, T. L. Prosociality enhances meaning in life. *The Journal of Positive Psychology* 11, 225–236 (2016).

78. Dakin, B. C., Laham, S. M., Tan, N. P.-J. & Bastian, B. Searching for meaning is associated with costly prosociality. *PLOS ONE* 16, e0258769 (2021).

79. Routledge, C. & FioRito, T. A. Why Meaning in Life Matters for Societal Flourishing. *Frontiers in Psychology* 11, (2021).

80. Twenge, J. M., Catanese, K. R. & Baumeister, R. F. Social Exclusion and the Deconstructed State: Time Perception, Meaninglessness, Lethargy, Lack of Emotion, and Self-Awareness. *Journal of Personality and Social Psychology* 85, 409–423 (2003).

81. Stillman, T. F. et al. Alone and without purpose: Life loses meaning following social exclusion. *Journal of Experimental Social Psychology* 45, 686–694 (2009).

82. Vogel-Scibilia, S. Ostracism: The Power of Silence. *Psychiatric Services* 54, 114–114 (2003).

83. Ren, D., Wesselmann, E. D. & Williams, K. D. Hurt people hurt people: ostracism and aggression. *Current Opinion in Psychology* 19, 34–38 (2018).

84. Poon, K.-T. & Teng, F. Feeling unrestricted by rules: Ostracism promotes aggressive responses. *Aggressive Behavior* 43, 558–567 (2017).

85. Haidt, J. & Joseph, C. Intuitive ethics: how innately prepared intuitions generate culturally variable virtues. *Daedalus* 133,

55–66 (2004).

86. FitzPatrick, W. Morality and Evolutionary Biology. *plato. stanford.edu.*

87. Pinker, S. *The Language Instinct: How The Mind Creates Language (P.S.).* (HarperCollins, 2010).

88. University of California - Riverside. Researchers Show How The Brain Turns On Innate Behavior. *ScienceDaily* (2006).

89. Machery, E. A Plea for Human Nature. *Philosophical Psychology* 21, 321–329 (2008).

90. Lee, C. R., Chen, A. & Tye, K. M. The neural circuitry of social homeostasis: Consequences of acute versus chronic social isolation. *Cell* 184, 1500–1516 (2021).

91. Xia, N. & Li, H. Loneliness, Social Isolation, and Cardiovascular Health. *Antioxidants & Redox Signaling* 28, 837–851 (2018).

92. Hawkley, L. C. & Cacioppo, J. T. Loneliness Matters: A Theoretical and Empirical Review of Consequences and Mechanisms. *Annals of Behavioral Medicine* 40, 218–227 (2010).

93. Cole, S. W. *et al.* Myeloid differentiation architecture of leukocyte transcriptome dynamics in perceived social isolation. *Proceedings of the National Academy of Sciences* 112, 15142–15147 (2015).

94. Litt, E., Zhao, S., Kraut, R. & Burke, M. What Are Meaningful Social Interactions in Today's Media Landscape? A Cross-Cultural Survey. *Social Media + Society* 6, 205630512094288 (2020).

95. Umberson, D. & Karas Montez, J. Social Relationships and Health: A Flashpoint for Health Policy. *Journal of Health and Social Behavior* 51, S54–S66 (2010).

96. Joshua, The Bible (World English). *wikisource.org.*

97. Taijfel, H. Experiments in intergroup discrimination.

Scientific American 223, 96–102 (1970).

98. Yang, X. & Dunham, Y. Minimal but meaningful: Probing the limits of randomly assigned social identities. *Journal of Experimental Child Psychology* 185, 19–34 (2019).

99. Wang, Y. *et al.* Born for fairness: evidence of genetic contribution to a neural basis of fairness intuition. *Social Cognitive and Affective Neuroscience* 14, 539–548 (2019).

100. Henrich, J. *et al.* Markets, Religion, Community Size, and the Evolution of Fairness and Punishment. *Science* 327, 1480–1484 (2010).

101. Warneken, F. & Tomasello, M. Altruistic Helping in Human Infants and Young Chimpanzees. *Science* 311, 1301–1303 (2006).

102. Li, J., Wang, W., Yu, J. & Zhu, L. Young Children's Development of Fairness Preference. *Frontiers in Psychology* 7, (2016).

103. Tabibnia, G., Satpute, A. B. & Lieberman, M. D. The Sunny Side of Fairness. *Psychological Science* 19, 339–347 (2008).

104. Wang, Y. et al. Born for fairness: evidence of genetic contribution to a neural basis of fairness intuition. *Social Cognitive and Affective Neuroscience* 14, 539–548 (2019).

105. L. Sun. *The Fairness Instinct: The Robin Hood Mentality and Our Biological Nature.* (2013).

106. Hauser, M., McAuliffe, K. & Blake, P. R. Evolving the ingredients for reciprocity and spite. *Philosophical Transactions of the Royal Society B: Biological Sciences* 364, 3255–3266 (2009).

107. Wrangham, R. W. Two types of aggression in human evolution. *Proceedings of the National Academy of Sciences* 115, 245–253 (2018).

108. Coie, J. D. & Dodge, K. A. Aggression and antisocial behavior. in *Handbook of child psychology: Social, emotional, and personality development* 779–862 (John Wiley & Sons,

Inc, 1998).

109. Lagerspetz, K. M. J. & Lagerspetz, K. Y. H. Changes in the Aggressiveness of Mice Resulting from Selective Breeding, Learning and Social Isolation. *Scandinavian Journal of Psychology* 12, 241–248 (1971).

110. Huesmann, L. R., Dubow, E. F. & Boxer, P. Continuity of aggression from childhood to early adulthood as a predictor of life outcomes: implications for the adolescent-limited and life-course-persistent models. *Aggressive Behavior* 35, 136–149 (2009).

111. Tellegen, A. *et al.* Personality similarity in twins reared apart and together. *Journal of Personality and Social Psychology* 54, 1031–1039 (1988).

112. Greene, J. D. The secret joke of Kant's soul. in *Moral psychology, Vol. 3. The neuroscience of morality: Emotion, brain disorders, and development* 35–80 (Boston Review, 2008).

113. McEllistrem, J. E. Affective and predatory violence: A bimodal classification system of human aggression and violence. *Aggression and Violent Behavior* 10, 1–30 (2004).

114. Dambacher, F. *et al.* Out of control: Evidence for anterior insula involvement in motor impulsivity and reactive aggression. *Social Cognitive and Affective Neuroscience* 10, 508–516 (2015).

115. Wrangham, R. W. Two types of aggression in human evolution. *Proceedings of the National Academy of Sciences* 115, 245–253 (2018).

116. Tulogdi, A. *et al.* Brain mechanisms involved in predatory aggression are activated in a laboratory model of violent intra-specific aggression. *European Journal of Neuroscience* 32, 1744–1753 (2010).

117. Tulogdi, A. *et al.* Neural mechanisms of predatory aggression in rats—Implications for abnormal intraspecific aggression.

Behavioural Brain Research 283, 108–115 (2015).

118. Dambacher, F. *et al.* Reducing proactive aggression through non-invasive brain stimulation. *Social Cognitive and Affective Neuroscience* 10, 1303–1309 (2015).

119. Dambacher, F. *et al.* Out of control: Evidence for anterior insula involvement in motor impulsivity and reactive aggression. *Social Cognitive and Affective Neuroscience* 10, 508–516 (2015).

120. Siegel, A. & Victoroff, J. Understanding human aggression: New insights from neuroscience. *International Journal of Law and Psychiatry* 32, 209–215 (2009).

121. Craig, I. W. & Halton, K. E. Genetics of human aggressive behaviour. *Human Genetics* 126, 101–113 (2009).

122. Weinshenker, N. J. & Siegel, A. Bimodal classification of aggression: affective defense and predatory attack. *Aggression and Violent Behavior* 7, 237–250 (2002).

123. Crick, N. R. & Dodge, K. A. Social Information-Processing Mechanisms in Reactive and Proactive Aggression. *Child Development* 67, 993 (1996).

124. Babcock, J. C., Tharp, A. L. T., Sharp, C., Heppner, W. & Stanford, M. S. Similarities and differences in impulsive/premeditated and reactive/proactive bimodal classifications of aggression. *Aggression and Violent Behavior* 19, 251–262 (2014).

125. Hare, B., Melis, A. P., Woods, V., Hastings, S. & Wrangham, R. Tolerance Allows Bonobos to Outperform Chimpanzees on a Cooperative Task. *Current Biology* 17, 619–623 (2007).

126. Wrangham, R. W. Hypotheses for the Evolution of Reduced Reactive Aggression in the Context of Human Self-Domestication. *Frontiers in Psychology* 10, (2019).

127. Ganna, A. *et al.* Large-scale GWAS reveals insights into the genetic architecture of same-sex sexual behavior. *Science* 365, (2019).

128. Långström, N., Rahman, Q., Carlström, E. & Lichtenstein,

P. Genetic and Environmental Effects on Same-sex Sexual Behavior: A Population Study of Twins in Sweden. *Archives of Sexual Behavior* 39, 75–80 (2010).

129. Barron, A. Homosexuality may have evolved for social, not sexual reasons. *The Conversation* (2020).

130. Gómez, J. M., Gónzalez-Megías, A. & Verdú, M. The evolution of same-sex sexual behaviour in mammals. *Nature Communications* 14, 5719 (2023).

131. LeDoux, J. E. As soon as there was life, there was danger: the deep history of survival behaviours and the shallower history of consciousness. *Philosophical Transactions of the Royal Society B: Biological Sciences* 377, (2022).

132. LeDoux, J. E., Moscarello, J., Sears, R. & Campese, V. The birth, death and resurrection of avoidance: a reconceptualization of a troubled paradigm. *Molecular Psychiatry* 22, 24–36 (2017).

133. Baron-Cohen, S. & Wheelwright, S. The Empathy Quotient: An Investigation of Adults with Asperger Syndrome or High Functioning Autism, and Normal Sex Differences. *Journal of Autism and Developmental Disorders* 34, 163–175 (2004).

134. Warrier, V. *et al.* Genome-wide analyses of self-reported empathy: correlations with autism, schizophrenia, and anorexia nervosa. *Translational Psychiatry* 8, 35 (2018).

135. Melchers, M., Montag, C., Reuter, M., Spinath, F. M. & Hahn, E. How heritable is empathy? Differential effects of measurement and subcomponents. *Motivation and Emotion* 40, 720–730 (2016).

136. Nitschke, J. B. *et al.* Orbitofrontal cortex tracks positive mood in mothers viewing pictures of their newborn infants. *NeuroImage* 21, 583–592 (2004).

137. Greene, J. D., Sommerville, R. B., Nystrom, L. E., Darley, J. M. & Cohen, J. D. An fMRI Investigation of Emotional Engagement in Moral Judgment. *Science* 293, 2105–2108

(2001).

138. Rilling, J. K. *et al.* A Neural Basis for Social Cooperation. *Neuron* 35, 395–405 (2002).

139. Dossey, L. The Helper's High. *Explore* 14, 393–399 (2018).

140. Bloom, P. Empathy and Its Discontents. *Trends in Cognitive Sciences* 21, 24–31 (2017).

141. Bloom, P. *Against Empathy: The Case for Rational Compassion.* (Vintage Digital, 2017).

142. Meyer, M. L. *et al.* Empathy for the social suffering of friends and strangers recruits distinct patterns of brain activation. *Social Cognitive and Affective Neuroscience* 8, 446–454 (2013).

143. Arceneaux, K. Anxiety Reduces Empathy Toward Outgroup Members But Not Ingroup Members. *Journal of Experimental Political Science* 4, 68–80 (2017).

144. Jamison, L. What Empathy Is Made Of. *Boston Review* (2014).

145. Berent, I., Platt, M. & Sandoboe, G. M. People's Intuitions About Innateness. *Open Mind* 3, 101–114 (2019).

146. Redhead, D. & Power, E. A. Social hierarchies and social networks in humans. *Philosophical Transactions of the Royal Society B: Biological Sciences* 377, (2022).

147. Curry, O. S. Morality as Cooperation: A Problem-Centred Approach. in 27–51 (Springer International Publishing, 2016).

BIBLIOGRAPHY PART 2

1. Chowdhury, M. A. Why Infanticide Happens Almost Exclusively to Girls and Not Boys. *E-IR*.

2. Roberts, D. *Human Insecurity: Global Structures of Violence.* (Zed Books, 2008).

3. Saslow, E. The White Flight of Derek Black. *The Washington Post* (2016).

4. Crocq, M.-A. & Crocq, L. From shell shock and war neurosis to posttraumatic stress disorder: a history of psychotraumatology. *Dialogues in Clinical Neuroscience* 2, 47–55 (2000).

5. Dursa, E. K., Reinhard, M. J., Barth, S. K. & Schneiderman, A. I. Prevalence of a Positive Screen for PTSD Among OEF/OIF and OEF/OIF-Era Veterans in a Large Population-Based Cohort. *Journal of Traumatic Stress* **27**, 542–549 (2014).

6. Dohrenwend, B. Why Some Soldiers Develop PTSD While Others Don't. *Association for Psychological Science (APS)* (2013).

7. Meagher, R. E. *Killing from the Inside Out: Moral Injury and Just War.* (Cascade Books, 2014).

8. Bunce, F. *An Encyclopaedia of Buddhist Deities, Demigods, Godlings, Saints, and Demons with Special Focus on Iconographic Attributes.* (D.K. Print World Ltd, 1994).

9. Lurker, M. *A Dictionary of Gods and Goddesses, Devils and Demons.* (Routledge, 2015).

10. Jordan, M. Encyclopedia of gods: over 2,500 deities of the world. *Choice Reviews Online* 31, (1993).

11. Puckett, K. 'I just feel the whole system is rather stupid' — One man's 14-year battle with the planning laws. *Building. co.uk*.

12. Altman, T. When Were Credit Scores Invented? A Brief Look At History. *OppU* (2023).

13. Fourcade, M. & Healy, K. Classification situations: Life-chances in the neoliberal era. *Accounting, Organizations and Society* 38, 559–572 (2013).

14. Brown, K. J. The hyper-regulation of public space: the use and abuse of Public Spaces Protection Orders in England and Wales. *Legal Studies* 37, 543–568 (2017).

15. Waugh, B. London council bans 'standing in pairs' in town centre – unless you're at a bus stop. *Metro* (2016).

16. Appleton, J. PSPOS — Blank-Cheque Powers. *Manifesto Club* (2016).

17. Brighouse, R. Challenging public spaces protection orders. *Legal Action Group* (2018).

18. Greater Manchester Law Centre. Public Space Protection Orders: 'outright ridiculous to deeply unjust'. *Greater Manchester Law Centre* (2019).

19. Dahl, R. *The Concept of Power.* (Bobbs-Merrill, 1957).

20. Hubbard, B. *MBS The Rise to Power of Mohammed Bin Salman.* (Penguin Random House, 2021).

21. Labour Report. *Saudi Ministry of Labor* (2012).

22. House of Saud. *Wikipedia*.

23. Editorial. Mohammed bin Salman: Saudi Arabia's great young reformer may struggle to control the forces he has unleashed. *The Independent* (2018).

24. Office of the Director of National Intelligence. *Assessing the Saudi Government's Role in the Killing of Jamal Khashoggi.*

25. Kirchgaessner, S. Saudi woman given 34-year prison sentence

for using Twitter. *The Guardian* (2022).

26. HRW. Saudi Arabia: Religious Thinker on Trial for His Life. *Human Rights Watch* (2019).

27. RSF. Seven more journalists, writers and bloggers arrested in Saudi Arabia. *Reporters Without Borders* (2019).

28. Knipp, K. Blogger Raif Badawi was sentenced to 10 years in prison and 1,000 lashings by a Saudi court. His crime: using free access to the Internet to 'insult Islam.' *DW* (2014).

29. Alvaredo, F., Chancel, L., Piketty, T., Saez, E. & Zucman, G. *World Inequality Report 2018*.

30. Prokop, A. Campaign Finance: 40 charts that explain money in politics. *VOX* (2014).

31. Douglas, E. Texas abortion law a "radical expansion" of who can sue whom, and an about-face for Republicans on civil lawsuits. *The Texas Tribune* (2021).

32. Shwayder, M. Voting rights in the US a hot issue. *DW* (2018).

33. Growth in Mass Incarceration. *The Sentencing Project* (2023).

34. The Washington Post. In four years, President Trump made 30,573 false or misleading claims. *The Washington Post* (2021).

35. Chancel, L., Piketty. Thomas, Saez, E. & Zucman, G. *World Inequality Report 2022*.

36. Helliwell, J. F. *et al. World Happiness Report 2023*.

37. List of countries by incarceration rate. *Wikipedia*.

38. Killings by law enforcement. Rates and counts by country. *Wikipedia*.

39. Henry, M., Watt, R., Mahathey, A., Ouellette, J. & Sitler, A. *The 2019 Annual Homeless Assessment Report (AHAR) to Congress*.

40. Ausmaß und Struktur von Wohnungslosigkeit. *Bundesministeriums für Arbeit und Soziales* (2022).

41. Rule of Law Index. *World Justice Project* (2023).

42. Best Healthcare in the World. *WiseVoter.com* (2023).

43. Rosenberg, L. U.S. Political Finance: Americans spend more on elections, but they lead from behind. *Sunlight Foundation* (2014).

44. Loubser, R. & Steenekamp, C. Democracy, well-being, and happiness: A 10-nation study. *Journal of Public Affairs* 17, e1646 (2017).

45. Besley, T. & Kudamatsu, M. Health and Democracy. *American Economic Review* 96, 313–318 (2006).

46. Houle, C. Inequality and Democracy: Why Inequality Harms Consolidation but Does Not Affect Democratization. *World Politics* 61, 589–622 (2009).

47. Graeber, D. & Wengrow, D. *The Dawn of Everything - A New History of Humanity*. (Penguin, 2022).

48. Williams, Z. David Cameron volunteering at a food bank? He's got some nerve. *The Guardian* (2022).

49. Zacka, B. Why Bureaucrats Don't Seem to Care - A researcher's reflection on eight months of observing workers at an anti-poverty agency. *The Atlantic* (2017).

50. Arendt, H. *The Origins of Totalitarianism*. (1973).

51. Frakt, A. Putting a Dollar Value on Life? Governments Already Do. *New York Times* (2020).

52. Montgomerie, J. & Tepe-Belfrage, D. Caring for Debts: How the Household Economy Exposes the Limits of Financialisation. *Critical Sociology* 43, 653–668 (2017).

53. Lai, K. *Financialization of Everyday Life*. vol. 1 (Oxford University Press, 2018).

54. Piff, P. K. Wealth and the Inflated Self. *Personality and Social Psychology Bulletin* 40, 34–43 (2014).

55. Black, S. E., Devereux, P. J., Lundborg, P. & Majlesi, K.

Poor Little Rich Kids? The Role of Nature versus Nurture in Wealth and Other Economic Outcomes and Behaviours. *The Review of Economic Studies* 87, 1683–1725 (2020).

56. Luthar, S. S. & Latendresse, S. J. Children of the Affluent. *Current Directions in Psychological Science* 14, 49–53 (2005).

57. Luthar, S. S. The Problem With Rich Kids. *Psychology Today* (2013).

58. Saner, E. Poor little rich kids – the perils of inheriting vast wealth. *The Guardian* (2016).

59. D. Brown, C. China's Great Leap Forward. *Education About Asia, Association for Asian Studies* Volume 17:3, (2012).

60. Petty, T. *Capital in the Twenty-First Century* . (Harvard University Press, 2014).

61. Guyton, J., Langetieg, P., Reck, D., Risch, M. & Zucman, G. Tax Evasion at the Top of the Income Distribution: Theory and Evidence. *NBER Working Paper No. w28542* (2021).

62. Alstadsæter, A., Johannesen, N., Le Guern Herry, S. & Zucman, G. Tax evasion and tax avoidance. *Journal of Public Economics* 206, 104587 (2022).

63. Akinci, M. Inequality and economic growth: Trickle-down effect revisited. *Development Policy Review* 36, O1–O24 (2018).

64. Papageorge, N. W. & Thom, K. Genes, Education, and Labor Market Outcomes: Evidence from the Health and Retirement Study. *Journal of the European Economic Association* **18**, 1351–1399 (2020).

65. Levy, N. *Hard Luck: How Luck Undermines Free Will and Moral Responsibility.* (Oxford University Press UK, Oxford, UK, 2011).

66. European Commission. Euromyths. *EU Commission Blog.*

67. Freeden, M. *Ideology: A Very Short Introduction.* (Oxford University Press, 2003).

68. Sweeny, K., Melnyk, D., Miller, W. & Shepperd, J. A. Information Avoidance: Who, What, When, and Why. *Review of General Psychology* 14, 340–353 (2010).

69. Nyhan, B., Reifler, J. & Ubel, P. A. The Hazards of Correcting Myths About Health Care Reform. *Medical Care* 51, 127–132 (2013).

70. Nyhan, B., Reifler, J. & Ubel, P. A. The Hazards of Correcting Myths About Health Care Reform. *Medical Care* 51, 127–132 (2013).

71. Tyng, C. M., Amin, H. U., Saad, M. N. M. & Malik, A. S. The Influences of Emotion on Learning and Memory. *Frontiers in Psychology* 8, (2017).

72. Smith, D. *et al.* Cooperation and the evolution of hunter-gatherer storytelling. *Nature Communications* 8, 1853 (2017).

73. Berns, G. S., Blaine, K., Prietula, M. J. & Pye, B. E. Short- and Long-Term Effects of a Novel on Connectivity in the Brain. *Brain Connectivity* 3, 590–600 (2013).

74. Mahmoodi, A., Nili, H., Bang, D., Mehring, C. & Bahrami, B. Distinct neurocomputational mechanisms support informational and socially normative conformity. *PLOS Biology* 20, e3001565 (2022).

75. Krysan, M. & Moberg, S. Trends in racial attitudes. *University of Illinois Institute of Government and Public Affairs* (2016).

76. Britton, J. *Fifty Years since Smoking and Health Progress, Lessons and Priorities for a Smoke-Free UK.*

77. Adult smoking habits in the UK: 2019 . *Statistical Bulletin* (2020).

78. Voigtländer, N. & Voth, H.-J. Persecution Perpetuated: The Medieval Origins of Anti-Semitic Violence in Nazi Germany*. *The Quarterly Journal of Economics* 127, 1339–1392 (2012).

79. Huchet-Bodet, A., Albakri, M. & Smith, N. *Attitudes to Equalities: The British Social Attitudes Survey 2017.*

80. Crockett, A. & Voas, D. Generations of Decline: Religious Change in 20th-Century Britain. *Journal for the Scientific Study of Religion* 45, 567–584 (2006).

81. Clark, D. *Average Weekly Attendance for the Church of England from 2009 to 2021.*

82. Dennis, R. *English Industrial Cities 19C: A Social Geography: 4* . (Cambridge University Press, 2008).

83. Conrad, N. G. *Marginalization of Atheism in Victorian Britain the Trials of Annie Besant and Charles Bradlaugh.* (Washington State University, 2009).

84. Matousek, R. *How Does the UK Feel towards the LGBTQ+ Community?*

85. Sherwood, H. Sex is for married heterosexual couples only, says Church of England. *The Guardian* (2020).

86. Parveen, N. Justin Welby under fire over C of E's zero-hours contracts. *The Guardian* (2018).

87. Kettell, S. On the Public Discourse of Religion: An Analysis of Christianity in the United Kingdom. *Politics and Religion* 2, 420–443 (2009).

88. Jawad, R. *Religion and Faith-Based Welfare - From Wellbeing to Ways of Being.* (Bristol University Press, 2012).

89. Curtice, J., Clery, E., Perry, J., Phillips, M. & Rahim, N. *Religion Identity, Behaviour and Belief over Two Decades (British Social Attitudes 36).*

90. Paine, T. *The Rights of Man.* (1792).

91. Stanley, J. *How Fascism Works: The Politics of Us and Them.* (Random House, 2018).

92. Boyle. Matthew. *First-Time Buyer Statistics: Average Age to Buy a House in the UK.*

93. Pickert, R. Young Homebuyers Are Vanishing From the U.S. *Bloomberg* (2019).

94. Borrett, A. How UK house prices have soared ahead of average wages. *The New Statesman* (2021).

95. Henretty, N. *Housing Affordability in England and Wales: 2016.*

96. Delgado, M. U.S. House Prices Are Rising Exponentially Faster Than Income (2021 Data). *Real Estate Witch.*

97. Wiles, C. Golf and gaff. *Inside Housing.*

98. Goodrich, S., Cowdock, B., Fleischer, J. & Marks, T. *Permission Accomplished: Assessing Corruption Risks in Local Government Planning.*

99. Hammond, G. Foreign ownership of homes in England and Wales triples. *Financial Times* (2021).

100. Trusilina, E. Continuous investment growth: top 5 countries where Chinese nationals are buying property. *Tranio.*

101. Smith, C. *Housing Affordability in England and Wales: 2021.*

102. Khan, M. Revealed: The £3bn cost of London's housing crisis. *The Telegraph* (2015).

103. *Generation Pause: 60% of under 45s Left behind by Housing Crisis.*

104. Clark, W. A. V. Do women delay family formation in expensive housing markets? *Demographic Research* 27, 1–24 (2012).

105. Ghebreyesus, T. A. *Global Status Report on Alcohol and Health 2018.*

106. Hosford, P. Sober Ireland: What's it like to not drink in Ireland? *The Journal* (2014).

107. The costs of alcohol to society. *Institute of Alcohol Studies* (2020).

108. Mongan, D. & Hope, A. *Social Consequences of Harmful Use of Alcohol in Ireland.*

109. Trocki, C. *Opium, Empire and the Global Political Economy A Study of the Asian Opium Trade 1750-1950*. (Routledge, 1999).

110. Park, W. H. *Opinions of Over 100 Physicians on the Use of Opium in China* . (American Presbyterian Mission Press, 1899).

111. Courtwright, D. T. *Dark Paradise - A History of Opiate Addiction in America*. (Harvard University Press, 2021).

112. International Opium Convention: Chapter VI. Narcotic Drugs and Psychotropic Substances . *The Hauge* (1912).

113. Baum, D. Legalize It All - How to win the war on drugs. *Harper's* (2016).

114. Timothy L. Tyler. *Wikipedia*.

115. Lopez, G. Purdue Pharma admits to crimes for its OxyContin marketing. But no one is going to prison. *Vox* (2020).

116. Pollan, M. *Caffeine: How Caffeine Created The Modern World*. (2020).

117. Lovering, R. On Moral Arguments Against Recreational Drug Use. *Philosophy Now* (2015).

118. Lopez, G. The war on drugs, explained. *Vox* (2016).

119. Rolles, S. *Cannabis Policy in the Netherlands: Moving Forwards Not Backwards*.

120. Tran, M. Government drug adviser David Nutt sacked. *The Guardian* (2009).

121. Hooijer, A. & Vernimmen, R. Global LiDAR land elevation data reveal greatest sea-level rise vulnerability in the tropics. *Nature Communications* 12, 3592 (2021).

122. Most Important Problem. *Gallup Poll* (2023).

123. Americans' views of the problems facing the nation. *Pew Research Center* (2021).

124. McKie, D. & Galloway, C. Climate change after denial: Global reach, global responsibilities, and public relations. *Public Relations Review* 33, 368–376 (2007).

125. McCright, A. M. & Dunlap, R. E. Cool dudes: The denial of climate change among conservative white males in the United States. *Global Environmental Change* 21, 1163–1172 (2011).

126. Dunlap, R. E. Climate Change Skepticism and Denial. *American Behavioral Scientist* 57, 691–698 (2013).

127. McKie, D. & Galloway, C. Climate change after denial: Global reach, global responsibilities, and public relations. *Public Relations Review* 33, 368–376 (2007).

128. Mendl, M. & Paul, E. S. Do animals live in the present? *Applied Animal Behaviour Science* 113, 357–382 (2008).

129. Killingsworth, M. A. & Gilbert, D. T. A Wandering Mind Is an Unhappy Mind. *Science* 330, 932–932 (2010).

130. Perlovsky, L. & Ilin, R. Brain. Conscious and Unconscious Mechanisms of Cognition, Emotions, and Language. *Brain Sciences* 2, 790–834 (2012).

131. Bradt, S. Wandering mind not a happy mind. *The Harvard Gazette* (2010).

132. Steptoe, A. Happiness and Health. *Annual Review of Public Health* 40, 339–359 (2019).

133. Veenhoven, R. Social conditions for human happiness: A review of research. *International Journal of Psychology* 50, 379–391 (2015).

134. COVID-19 pandemic triggers 25% increase in prevalence of anxiety and depression worldwide. *World Health Organisation* (2022).

135. Šrol, J., Čavojová, V. & Ballová Mikušková, E. Finding Someone to Blame: The Link Between COVID-19 Conspiracy Beliefs, Prejudice, Support for Violence, and Other Negative Social Outcomes. *Frontiers in Psychology* 12, (2022).

136. Aksoy, C. G., Eichengreen, B. & Saka, O. *The Political Scar of Epidemics.*

137. Rideout, V. & Robb, M. B. *Social Media, Social Life: Teens Reveal Their Experiences.*

138. Rosin, H. The Overprotected Kid. *The Atlantic* (2014).

139. Tremblay, A. & Bellisle, F. Nutrients, satiety, and control of energy intake. *Applied Physiology, Nutrition, and Metabolism* 40, 971–979 (2015).

140. Breuning, L. G. The War in Your Brain Between Healthy and Unhealthy Habits. *Psychology Today* (2014).

141. Conte, F. *et al.* Humane Slaughter of Edible Decapod Crustaceans. *Animals* 11, 1089 (2021).

142. Crespi, B. J., Flinn, M. v. & Summers, K. Runaway Social Selection in Human Evolution. *Frontiers in Ecology and Evolution* 10, (2022).

143. Bergstrom, T. C. Evolution of Social Behavior: Individual and Group Selection. *Journal of Economic Perspectives* 16, 67–88 (2002).

144. Wilson, D. S. & Sober, E. Reintroducing group selection to the human behavioral sciences. *Behavioral and Brain Sciences* 17, 585–608 (1994).

145. Hill, K. R. *et al.* Co-Residence Patterns in Hunter-Gatherer Societies Show Unique Human Social Structure. *Science* 331, 1286–1289 (2011).

146. Dunbar, R., Harcourt, A. H. & de Waal, F. B. M. Coalitions and Alliances in Humans and Other Animals. *Man* 28, 370 (1993).

147. Caporael, L. R. The Evolution of Truly Social Cognition: The Core Configurations Model. *Personality and Social Psychology Review* 1, 276–298 (1997).

148. Bissonnette, A. *et al.* Coalitions in theory and reality: a review of pertinent variables and processes. *Behaviour* 152, 1–56 (2015).

149. Taijfel, H. Experiments in intergroup discrimination. *Scientific American* 223, 96–102 (1970).

150. Yang, X. & Dunham, Y. Minimal but meaningful: Probing the limits of randomly assigned social identities. *Journal of Experimental Child Psychology* 185, 19–34 (2019).

151. Cole, S. W. *et al.* Myeloid differentiation architecture of leukocyte transcriptome dynamics in perceived social isolation. *Proceedings of the National Academy of Sciences* 112, 15142–15147 (2015).

152. Hawkley, L. C. & Cacioppo, J. T. Loneliness Matters: A Theoretical and Empirical Review of Consequences and Mechanisms. *Annals of Behavioral Medicine* 40, 218–227 (2010).

153. Xia, N. & Li, H. Loneliness, Social Isolation, and Cardiovascular Health. *Antioxidants & Redox Signaling* 28, 837–851 (2018).

154. Haslam, S. A. *et al.* Social identity makes group-based social connection possible: Implications for loneliness and mental health. *Current Opinion in Psychology* 43, 161–165 (2022).

155. Correll, J. & Park, B. A Model of the Ingroup as a Social Resource. *Personality and Social Psychology Review* 9, 341–359 (2005).

156. Lee, C. R., Chen, A. & Tye, K. M. The neural circuitry of social homeostasis: Consequences of acute versus chronic social isolation. *Cell* 184, 1500–1516 (2021).

157. L. Sun. *The Fairness Instinct: The Robin Hood Mentality and Our Biological Nature.* (2013).

158. Tabibnia, G., Satpute, A. B. & Lieberman, M. D. The Sunny Side of Fairness. *Psychological Science* 19, 339–347 (2008).

159. Warneken, F. & Tomasello, M. Altruistic Helping in Human Infants and Young Chimpanzees. *Science* 311, 1301–1303 (2006).

160. McAuliffe, K., Blake, P. R., Steinbeis, N. & Warneken, F. The developmental foundations of human fairness. *Nature Human Behaviour* 1, 0042 (2017).

161. Li, J., Wang, W., Yu, J. & Zhu, L. Young Children's Development of Fairness Preference. *Frontiers in Psychology* 7, (2016).

162. Henrich, J. *et al.* Markets, Religion, Community Size, and the Evolution of Fairness and Punishment. *Science* 327, 1480–1484 (2010).

163. Wang, Y. *et al.* Born for fairness: evidence of genetic contribution to a neural basis of fairness intuition. *Social Cognitive and Affective Neuroscience* 14, 539–548 (2019).

164. Henrich, J. *The WEIRDest People in the World How the West Became Psychologically Peculiar and Particularly Prosperous.* . (Macmillan Publishers, 2020).

165. Tomasello, M. *A Natural History of Human Morality.* (Harvard University Press, 2016).

166. Stanley, J. *How Fascism Works: The Politics of Us and Them.* (2020).

167. Berlatsky, N. Let's Put an End to 'Horseshoe Theory' Once and for All. *Pacific Standard* (2018).

168. Choat, S. Horseshoe theory' is nonsense -the far right and far left have little in common. *The Conversation, Volume 12* (2017).

169. Secen, S. Electoral competition dynamics and Syrian refugee discourses and policies in Germany and France. *European Politics and Society* 1–25 (2022).

170. Lin, Y. & Xi, T. Trade shock, refugee, and the rise of right-wing populism: Evidence from European Parliament elections. *China Economic Quarterly International* 2, 124–137 (2022).

171. Steinmayr, A. Did the refugee crisis contribute to the recent rise of far-right parties in Europe? *Econstor* 24–27 (2017).

172. Kaufmann, E. *Whiteshift: Populism, Immigration and the Future of White Majorities.* (Abrams Press, 2018).

173. Dennison, J. & Geddes, A. A Rising Tide? The Salience of Immigration and the Rise of Anti-Immigration Political Parties in Western Europe. *The Political Quarterly* 90, 107–116 (2019).

174. Hermsmeier, L. Germany Has a Problem. *New York Times* (2023).

175. Arendt, H. *The Origins of Totalitarianism* . (The World Publishing Company, 1962).

176. Pearce, B. *1903—Second Congress of the Russian Social-Democratic Labour Party.* (New Park Publications, 1978).

177. World Report 2020: Vietnam. *Human Rights Watch* (2020).

178. Pike, D. The Pol Pot Regime; Race, Power, and Genocide in Cambodia under the Khmer Rouge, 1975-79. *Political Science Quarterly* 112, 349–350 (1997).

179. Aguirre, B. E. Social Control in Cuba. *Latin American Politics and Society* 44, 67–98 (2002).

180. Bergmann, T. Diktatur des Proletariats. *Historisch-kritisches Wörterbuch des Marxismus, vol. 2 Bank bis Dummheit in der Musik* (2021).

181. Steinhoff, U. *Do All Persons Have Equal Moral Worth?* (Oxford University Press, 2014).

182. Carter, I. Respect and the Basis of Equality. *Ethics* 121, 538–571 (2011).

183. Kymlicka, W. *Contemporary Political Philosophy.* (Oxford: Clarendon Press., 1990).

184. Hauser, M., McAuliffe, K. & Blake, P. R. Evolving the ingredients for reciprocity and spite. *Philosophical Transactions of the Royal Society B: Biological Sciences* 364, 3255–3266 (2009).

185. Ours, J. C. van & Chen, S. *In Sickness and in Health: The Mental Health Effects of Same-Sex Marriage Legalisation.*

186. Rosa, H. *Social Acceleration: A New Theory of Modernity.* (Columbia University Press, 2015).

187. Backhaus, K. *Die Beschleunigungsfalle Oder Der Triumph Der Schildkröte.* (Schäffer-Poeschel Verlag, 1998).

188. Taggart, K., Garrison, J. & Testa, J. Teen Beauty Queens Say Trump Walked In On Them Changing. *Buzzfeed News* (2016).

189. *In Shocking Tape Trump Boasts of Sexually Assaulting Women: 'When You're a Star…You Can Do Anything'.* (Democracy Now (YouTube), 2016).

190. Huberman, A. *The Science of Emotions & Relationships.* (Huberman Lab Podcast, 2021).

191. Solnit, R. Rebecca Solnit: 'Younger feminists have shifted my understanding'. *The Guardian* (2020).

192. Douglas, K. M. *et al.* Understanding Conspiracy Theories. *Political Psychology* 40, 3–35 (2019).

193. Douglas, K. M., Sutton, R. M. & Cichocka, A. The Psychology of Conspiracy Theories. *Current Directions in Psychological Science* 26, 538–542 (2017).

194. Abalakina-Paap, M., Stephan, W. G., Craig, T. & Gregory, W. L. Beliefs in Conspiracies. *Political Psychology* 20, 637–647 (1999).

195. Crocker, J., Luhtanen, R., Broadnax, S. & Blaine, B. E. Belief in U.S. Government Conspiracies Against Blacks among Black and White College Students: Powerlessness or System Blame? *Personality and Social Psychology Bulletin* 25, 941–953 (1999).

196. Goertzel, T. Belief in Conspiracy Theories. *Political Psychology* 15, 731 (1994).

197. Uscinski, J. E. & Parent, J. M. *American Conspiracy Theories.* (Oxford University Press, 2014).

198. Cacioppo, J. T. & Patrick, W. *Loneliness – Human Nature and the Need for Social Connection.* (W. W. Norton & Company, 2009).

199. van Prooijen, J. & Douglas, K. M. Belief in conspiracy theories: Basic principles of an emerging research domain. *European Journal of Social Psychology* 48, 897–908 (2018).

200.Douglas, K. M. *et al.* Understanding Conspiracy Theories. *Political Psychology* 40, 3–35 (2019).

201. Bartlett, J. & Miller, C. *The Power of Unreason Conspiracy Theories, Extremism and Counter-Terrorism.*

202.Newkirk, P. Conspiracy theories, fake news, racism fueling KKK's rise — in the 1920s. *The Washington Post* (2017).

203.Daskin, E. Justification of violence by terrorist organisations: Comparing ISIS and PKK. *Journal of Intelligence and Terrorism Studies* 1, 1–14 (2016).